JOSEPH CONRAD

JOSEPH CONRAD

JOSEPH CONRAD

by

J. I. M. STEWART

DODD, MEAD & COMPANY
NEW YORK

Library of Congress Catalog Card Number: 68-15412

Printed in the United States of America
by The Cornwall Press, Inc., Cornwall, N. Y.

Acknowledgments

For the materials of my first chapter, a sketch of Conrad's career, I am much indebted to G. Jean-Aubry's pioneer *Joseph Conrad: Life and Letters*, Jocelyn Baines's authoritative biography, Zdzisław Najder's *Conrad's Polish Background* with its illuminating introduction, and Norman Sherry's *Conrad's Eastern World*, an outstanding instance of timely research carried out not in great libraries but "on location."

J.I.M.S.

Contents

Contents

JOSEPH CONRAD

References to Conrad's fiction, as given within parentheses in the text, are to the collected edition published in Great Britain by Dent. The collected edition published in America by Doubleday follows the same pagination.

CHAPTER

I

Conrad's Life and Literary Career

Joseph Conrad was born on 3 December 1857 at Berdyczów in Podolia, a part of the Ukraine which had belonged to Poland until the Partition of 1793. The great majority of the inhabitants were Ukranians, but most of the land was owned by a Polish upper class. Conrad's parents both belonged to this class, which was rather numerous in proportion to the total population. It was essentially what in England would be called a landed gentry, but in a substantial sense it was a nobility as well, since no higher rank of society existed. Moreover, it was very fully an aristocracy. Its values were soldierly, chivalric, and traditional; every member of it was on his honour to strive, by one means or another, for the freeing of Poland as a nation from the tyranny of her conquerors; at the same time, in the virtual absence of a higher bourgeoisie, it was the sole repository of polite culture. Literature—and particularly, though not exclusively, patriotic literature—was held in high esteem.

Conrad's grandfather, Teodor Korzeniowski, a headlong patriot devoid of practical ability, wrote a five-act tragedy.

1

His father, Apollo, who was even more patriotic and even more incapable of managing estates or anything else, wrote a great deal, and may almost be said to have made literature his vocation. His mother, Ewa Bobrowska, was more highly educated than was customary among the Polish gentry. Her own people, the Bobrowskis, were cautious and prudent in political matters, but Ewa threw in her lot wholeheartedly with her husband, whose courageous if ill-conceived underground activities earned them both banishment at the hands of the Russian authorities when their son was only four years old. From the fatigues and privations of this sentence Ewa died three years later, and Conrad then spent a long and lonely childhood in the company of his father, whose temperament grew increasingly sombre. But if Conrad's early surroundings were gloomy, he at least lived amid a litter of books, and although his formal studies remained irregular and unsatisfactory, it is clear that he became widely read, and even that he began to cherish literary ambitions of his own. His career becomes more explicable when we thus realize that from his earliest years he was steeped in the tradition of letters. His father did much translating from the French, and he himself (like most children of his class) had a good command of French from an early age. The influence of the French literary tradition upon him was to be considerable, although it has been exaggerated by some critics.

Apollo Korzeniowski died in 1869, when Conrad was eleven, and the orphan was taken charge of by a Bobrowski uncle, Tadeusz. It was not an easy relationship. Conrad was a difficult boy, for his earlier childhood had landed him with a good many of those behaviour problems from which are likely to stem the neurotic components in a mature personality. Tadeusz Bobrowski is abundantly on record, and it is evident that he was a good and sensible man, who became almost obsessively concerned with the welfare of his sister's son. Of the boy's father—although he had been fond of him—he had no very high opinion, judging him ineffectually quixotic and disastrously unpractical. There can be little doubt that Conrad had absorbed all his father's ideals, while at the same time being aware of numerous disasters, including his mother's death, which an obstinate fidelity to them had brought about. Now in his uncle Tadeusz he was up against a wholly different point of view. The doubt about the ultimate validity of ideal codes of conduct which was to haunt Conrad's mind for life may well have had its origin in this confrontation.

By the time that he was sixteen, Conrad was eager to get away from Poland. There was nothing surprising in this. Only in that part of the kingdom which was under Austrian rule could he look forward to living in any security. In Russian Poland, as the son of a convict, he was liable to twenty-five years of service as a private soldier in the Russian army, and this danger sharpened when his uncle failed to secure Austrian citizenship for him in 1872. His health—or nervous constitution—was not good, and in such cases Polish (and Russian) doctors were frequently disposed to recommend a period of residence abroad. Conrad's early reading had included the romances of Captain Marryat, so it was no doubt he himself who hit upon the plan of going to sea. Although his uncle for long opposed this, the doctors were again on the boy's side: an open-air life abroad would be best of all. The argument that it was the duty of all young Poles of good family to remain in Poland and fight for its liberation would not have impressed Tadeusz Bobrowski, and with Conrad himself we do not know that at this time it weighed at all. There was nothing strange in the idea even of permanent exile, since many of Poland's *élite* were constrained to live outside the country. In any case, it may have been in Bobrowski's mind that Conrad would simply have his adventure out and eventually come home in a more amenable frame of mind. Contacts were made in Marseilles with a view to his training in the French merchant service, and he left Poland in October 1874, shortly before his seventeenth birthday. He was not to return for fifteen years.

He carried out of Poland a hatred of Russia and all things Russian, including Tolstoy (to whom his sole reference appears to be by way of an aspersion cancelled in the manuscript of *Under Western Eyes* [1]) and Dostoevsky, with whom he has, in fact, some temperamental affinity. This was clearcut. But he also carried away a confused attitude towards revolutionary ardour and underground conspiracy; on the one hand there was his loyalty to his father's memory, on the other there was both his mother's death and the well-founded upper-class persuasion that revolutions sweep away such idealists as first promote them, and result only in fresh tyrannies in the end. It was to be the latter attitude that prevailed with him.

But he had another and more positive Polish heritage, which had been very well educed by Mr. Zdzisław Najder. The partition of Poland and the passing of the country under oppressive foreign dominions had imposed upon imaginative literature a large part of the task of expressing and propagating national aspirations. In the romantic writers of the mid-nineteenth century, notably Mickiewicz and Slowacki, the moral life was viewed as in close association with public responsibility. This meant, Mr. Najder writes, "that the moral problems of an individual were posed in terms of the social results of his actions; and ethical principles were based on the idea that an individual, however exceptional he might be, is always a member of a group, responsible for its welfare."[2] Thus the principal character in Mickiewicz's most significant work, *Pan Tadeusz*, fails as a young man when he permits himself to forget his public duty at the call of private feeling; for this he has to atone by many years of heroic service to his country. Another romantic writer whose work Conrad must have known intimately, Zygmunt Krasiński, presented in *The Un-Divine Comedy* a disillusioned picture both of the decaying feudal order and of the ruthlessly acquisitive and materialist society likely to succeed upon it. Much of all this must have become part of the texture of Conrad's mind. Mr. Najder suggests the possibility of one more specific influence which appears to be of considerable interest. A popular Polish literary form was the *gaweda*, a tale set in the mouth of a narrator who is himself clearly characterized, and whose point of view is a significant element in the whole.[3] Conrad's Marlow may owe something to this tradition. The important consideration is that Conrad left his native country well-seen in a rich and vigorous native literature. It is unlikely that he ever forgot it. He certainly did not forget his Polish. His wife was to complain that when in a fever he talked it all the time.

In Marseilles, which became his base for three and a half years, Conrad left boyhood behind him and passed through a young manhood of which not much is securely known. He was intelligent, well-bred, with a good knowledge of French, and in the enjoyment at least of the moderate degree of independence that goes along with a regular family allowance. Moreover, his uncle Tadeusz Bobrowski—who was his paymaster—was a comfortable thousand miles away, and had to exercise his guardianship only through the medium of long, affectionate, and often severely admonitory letters. Conrad was evidently undisciplined, inconsiderate, and as prone to losing all his possessions as to spending all his money. Bobrowski saw in this the sad working of laws of heredity:

> You always, my dear boy, made me impatient—and still make me impatient by your disorder and the easy way you take things —in which you remind me of the Korzeniowski family—spoiling and wasting everything—and not my dear Sister, your Mother. . . .
> You write me a long letter admitting your fault, but you do not say how much you need to repair your stupidities, when the plainest common sense would have made you connect one with the other, and not expose me to uncertainty and disquiet. Further, knowing how I detest telegrams and how much trouble and cost they entail (for I live 28 miles from the station) you telegraph for 700 fr. in June. Finally, having had a whole month in which to inform me of your need of 400 fr. more, you wait again and as late as the 4th July you telegraph again. To top everything, on your departure you tell me to pay a debt of 165 fr. this time, thank God, by letter! Where is here consideration, prudence, and reflection??? Where is here respect for others'—this time my own —peace of mind? [4]

There is a great deal more of this. And then, in February 1878, the comedy of Bobrowski's apprehensions was turned into intense alarm. He received a "detested telegram" which read: *Conrad blessé envoyez argent—arrivez.* When he reached Marseilles, it was to discover that his ward (who was already out of bed) had tried to commit suicide—or had at least sent a revolver bullet *"durch und durch* near the heart." [5]

We do not know exactly what converging distresses drove Conrad to this desperate demonstration. He had been involved in gun-running in the interest of the Carlist cause in Spain, and in this and other picturesquely clandestine activities he had lost much more than he gained. There is also the possibility of a disastrous love-affair. But such evidence as exists has to be drawn either from supposedly autobiographical elements in the weakest of his novels, *The Arrow of Gold,* written thirty years later, or from the reminiscent *The Mirror of the Sea.* There, in a chapter called "The 'Tremolino,'" we find an account of the gun-running venture and kindred matters in which we may suspect a good deal of artistic manipulation of authentic experience. But it is certain that Conrad's Marseilles period was not devoted wholly to escapades. He had begun to learn seamanship, accomplishing a number of voyages to the West Indies and elsewhere, in effect as an apprentice in the service of a respectable firm of French shipowners. Yet it was the uncertainty of his professional prospects that may have conduced most to his sense of insecurity at the time he made the attempt upon his life. For it had turned out that his liability to military service under a foreign power constituted a bar to his legal entry into the French mercantile marine. This must have been a shattering blow. However, he presently discovered that British merchant ships were not so particular. On 24 April 1878 (having made a remarkably expeditious recovery from his wound) he embarked on the *Mavis,* an English freighter engaged in the humdrum business of carrying coal to Constaninople. He was to declare in later life that, even before leaving Poland, he had resolved that it was as an English seaman that he would make a career, even although at the time he "did not know six words of English." In fact, it seems to have been largely by chance that he came under the Red Ensign—which he calls "the symbolic, protecting warm bit of bunting flung wide upon the seas, and destined for so many years to be the only roof over my head." [6]

Conrad and the *Mavis* did not keep company for long, as we learn in Bobrowski's words:

You were idling for nearly a whole year—you fell into debt, you deliberately shot yourself—and as a result of it all, at the worst time of the year, tired out and in spite of the most terrible rate of exchange—I hasten to you, pay, spend about 2,000 roubles, I increase your allowance to meet your needs! All this is apparently not enough for you. And when I make a fresh sacrifice to save you from idleness and to ensure that you could stay on the English ship that you fancied, you leave the ship. . . . I have no money for drones and I have no intention of working so that someone else may enjoy himself at my expense. . . .[7]

We should notice that Conrad was only twenty when he received this dressing-down. There were future occasions upon which his uncle felt expostulation to be necessary, but not with quite this severity. It is true that Conrad was never for long at a time to seem wholly stable in his attitude to a seaman's career. He was prone to quarrel with captains or owners and throw up berths. Although he was so austerely to denounce "material interests" and "scramble for loot" in the business world, he was perpetually producing hopeful commercial schemes and endeavouring to persuade his uncle and others to invest in them. It even appears that the writer who was to depict in the silver of the San Tomé mine a sinister power destroying alike the idealist Charles Gould and the man of action Nostromo, himself contrived to lose a small inheritance in a gold-mining venture in South Africa.

We may find it curious that one who is perhaps the greatest of all writers about the sea should have been without a settled vocation for it. Yet this is certainly true of Conrad. His biographer Mr. Jocelyn Baines points out that he was always inclined to exaggerate the element of purpose in his career as a sailor while correspondingly suggesting that mere chance made him a writer. His attitude, as we might expect, was not a simple one. He was irked, particularly in later life, by those who regarded him as a hardened old salt with a knack of spinning exciting yarns about the sea. It could not be otherwise with an artist who took himself as seriously as did Flaubert or James. At the same time, unhappily, the profession of letters in England presented a not wholly congenial spectacle to a Polish nobleman with a strong sense that one ought to belong to an order pledged to ideals of conduct in which duty, fidelity, and corporate purpose were paramount. And this the British mercantile marine did largely provide. At the same time, the men prosecuting successful careers at sea must have been for the most part temperamentally remote from him, and it was natural that he should seek the society and esteem of his fellow artists.

With a number of these he was, in fact, to establish cordial relations—the first of them being John Galsworthy, with whom chance brought him into contact in 1893, before either had published a book. Galsworthy was a good friend, but he never arrived at much understanding of Conrad's work, while Conrad's expressed admiration for Galsworthy's was perhaps more what he considered due to their personal relationship than to an actual high critical regard. Conrad was always a little too profuse in appreciation and compliment, a characteristic which may be attributed in part to early training in formal courtesy, and in part to the expatriate's sense of never quite managing to belong. Closer to him in feeling and social background was R. B. Cunninghame Graham, a Scot who possessed strains of Spanish and Italian blood and a strong instinct for the adventurous life. But although with these men and others he maintained a familiar relationship, and although he could even get along well with one as alien to him in outlook as H. G. Wells, we end up with the impression that he always remained something of an odd man out. His contact with English society in general appears to have been rather limited. The fact that the greater part of his working life was to be passed in near-poverty must have been a factor here. He often seems to have spent substantial periods virtually without encountering people of any cultivation at all.

What remains most remarkable about his seafaring career—to return to that—is the success he made of it. Stranded in England with very little English (and with his uncle's last-quoted denunciation still virtually in his pocket), he contrived in the autumn of 1878 to ship as an ordinary seaman on a wool clipper making the run to Sydney: an experience which was to entitle the narrator of *The Nigger of the 'Narcissus'* to tell his story from the fo'c'sle. Within a few months of returning to London at the beginning of 1880, he had passed his examination as Second Mate ("My dear boy and Officer!" his uncle was to write enthusiastically),[8] and within three months of this, again, he had secured a berth as an officer on another wool clipper, the *Loch Etive*. On the return of this vessel from Australia he was on land for some months, and in this period a final flicker of mere irresponsibility appears in him, since he is on record as extracting £10 from his uncle under what a magistrate would have to call false pretences: he claimed, quite untruly, to have lost all his kit on a ship which had foundered at sea.* But, hard upon this, he gained his first berth as second mate on the barque *Palestine,* bound for Bangkok. The *Palestine* is the *Judea* of "Youth." Her disastrous voyage is the first episode in Conrad's actual sea-going career to provide the substance of an important work of imagination.

On his return to Europe he spent a holiday with Bob-

---

* Jerry Allen, in *The Sea Years of Joseph Conrad* (1965), judges it possible to rebut this charge.

rowski at Marienbad: the second meeting of uncle and nephew since Conrad had left Poland. He then sailed as second mate on the *Riversdale* and the *Narcissus*; passed his First Mate's examination at the end of 1884; and early in the following year, still as second mate, sailed on the *Tilkhurst* for Singapore. A letter dated 27 September 1885 from that port is his earliest known piece of writing in English. He returned to London, and on 10 November 1886 he received his master's certificate. In the same year as this magnificent achievement—for it can be called nothing else—he made an amusingly modest first incursion into authorship in the form of a short story, "The Black Mate," which he submitted for a competition in a popular magazine called *Tit-Bits*. *Tit-Bits* was not impressed, and Conrad's sense of decorum later prompted him to conceal the fact of this injudicious bid for fame.

A master's certificate did not necessarily bring a command, and in February 1887 he sailed as first mate on the *Highland Forest* for Samarang under Captain McWhirr, whose name, and something of whose character, he was to use in "Typhoon." (Conrad's attitude to proper names in his fiction is peculiar. The real Captain McWhirr is given an imaginary ship, the *Nan-Shan*; the real *Palestine* becomes the imaginary *Judea,* but on board it are the *Palestine's* real Captain Beard and Mr. Mahon. The pilgrim-ship the strange fate of which suggested *Lord Jim* was actually the *Jeddah,* but in calling it the *Patna,* Conrad is employing the name of another vessel in fact in Eastern waters at the time. Almayer of *Almayer's Folly* probably preserves what Conrad believed to be the spelling of Olmeijer, the actual name of his original; and Captain Lingard in the same novel [and elsewhere] and Captain Ellis in *The Shadow Line* also preserve the true names of the persons upon whom they are based. Conrad appears

to have attached some mysterious significance to such links
with actuality.)

His service on the *Highland Forest* ended when he sustained an injury from a falling spar at Samarang. It seems not
improbable that the accident produced or exacerbated a
neurotic condition; he went into hospital for a time at Singapore; then, then instead of returning to England, he signed
on as mate with the *Vidar*, a small steam-vessel in Arab
ownership, which pottered unexactingly about the Malay
Archipelago. This brings us very close to the beginning of
Jim's history in *Lord Jim*—as also to that phase of Conrad's
experience upon which all his earliest writing was to be
based. But he left the *Vidar* abruptly at the beginning of
1888, and appears to have been hanging about Singapore in
the expectation of returning home when he was unexpectedly
appointed to his first, and sole, sea-going command. The captain of the barque *Otago* had died at sea, and Conrad was
sent to take charge of the vessel at Bangkok. The passage
back to Singapore was impeded by calms in the Gulf of Siam,
and many of the crew went down with fever: upon this he
was to base *The Shadow Line*, the most closely autobiographical of his fictional works. He remained with the *Otago* only
until early in 1889, when he gave up his command and returned to England. According to one account, he had been
disappointed in a marriage-suit in Mauritius and felt unable
to face the discomfort of returning there. This was the end
of Conrad's contact with the Far East. He was now thirty.
Within five years his sea-going career was to be over.

But one exotic experience of considerable importance was
still ahead of him. This was the consequence of his engagement by the Société Anonyme Belge pour le Commerce du
Haut-Congo to command a river-steamer plying between certain of its trading posts on the river. It is an index of Conrad's

continued restlessness that, even during a period without prospect of a berth at sea, he should have accepted such an employment.* Conceivably he was unconsciously seeking what in fact he found: confrontation with something which could be regarded as almost an ultimate among the dark places of the earth. More probably this is a romantic view; Africa was merely an exciting novelty, and the ruthless and ghastly exploitation of human misery he stumbled upon there was as unexpected as it was shattering. Whether or not he was determined to get out as quickly as he could, the whole episode was comprehended within the year 1890. His physical health suffered, and there is no reason to suppose that, psychologically, there was anything wholesomely cathartic about the experience. "Heart of Darkness" is its sombre— perhaps excessively sombre—monument. We know that the manuscript of his first novel, *Almayer's Folly*, accompanied him up the interminable reaches of the nightmarish river. What he has to tell of the misery of a decaying trading post in Borneo probably gains some of its force from his glimpse of similar conditions in Africa.

The Congo episode had one unexpected consequence, the significance of which for Conrad has been variously assessed. His uncle had put him in touch with a distant kinsman, Aleksander Poradowski, who was supposed to have influence with those running Congolese affairs. Poradowski, who was an exile from Poland since the insurrection of 1863, lived in

---

* Even so, it failed him. The *Florida*, which he was to have commanded, proved to be undergoing repair, and it was as mate on the *Roi des Belges* that he made his voyage up the Congo. Because of the illness of its captain, he was in charge on the return journey, but seems to have received no assurance of a command thereafter. That he should have wanted one—as appears to be the case—suggests that he was less utterly revolted by his experiences than he was to represent Marlow in "Heart of Darkness" as being.

Brussels, and Conrad proposed to call on him when himself making his first return to Poland since he had left it as a boy. It must have been a journey highly charged with emotion, and Conrad was likely to be a good deal affected by anything out of the way that happened in the course of it. Two days after his arrival in Brussels, Poradowski died. His widow, Marguerite Poradowska, who was ten years older than Conrad, proved to be a woman of talent who had begun to make some sort of name for herself as a writer of fiction. She was extremely beautiful as well. The two struck up a lively correspondence, and it is not surprising to find that, within the next couple of years, Bobrowski is cautioning his nephew against the seductions of the lady, whom he describes as likely to be a stone round Conrad's neck, and ungallantly refers to in a phrase variously translated as "a patched-up grannie" and "a worn-out female." [9] In fact, Conrad's letters to Mme. Poradowska regularly begin "Chère Tante" or "Très chère Tante," scarcely a propitious form of address had the writer been romantically inclined. Nor do the letters themselves—at this time, at least—suggest anything of the sort. Conrad's raptures are reserved for his correspondent's achievements in authorship, and we have to remember that he was still without any literary acquaintances at all. He continued corresponding for many years, and there were occasional meetings as well. But for a period of nearly five years before 1900 no letters have been preserved, or at least published; and it has been conjectured that Conrad's English marriage followed hard upon a rejection by Mme. Poradowska. But there is no real evidence to support this.

The marriage (which took place in 1896) ought not to perplex us, although it may seem to have its surprising side. Jessie George, fifteen years younger than Conrad, was the daughter of a warehouseman who may or may not have become a bookseller. That she was a typist in commercial employment appears in a letter written by Conrad to Karol Zagórski, a Polish kinsman:

I announce solemnly (as the occasion demands) to dear Aunt Gabrynia and to you both that I am getting married. No one can be more surprised at it than myself. However, I am not frightened at all, for as you know, I am accustomed to an adventurous life and to facing terrible dangers. Moreover, I have to avow that my betrothed does not give the impression of being at all dangerous. Jessie is her name; George her surname. She is a small, not at all striking-looking person (to tell the truth alas—rather plain!) who nevertheless is very dear to me. When I met her a year and a half ago she was earning her living in the City as a "Typewriter" in an American business office of the "Caligraph" company. Her father died three years ago. There are nine children in the family. The mother is a very decent woman (and I do not doubt very virtuous as well).[10]

The daughter proved to be virtuous too. Marriage to Joseph Conrad, indeed, must have called for the exercise of this quality in its ancient Roman sense. It is possible to see Jessie Conrad as merely placid—an impression perhaps enhanced by the fact that, after an accident in 1904 which left her badly crippled, she turned very notably stout. But placidity would not in itself have made the relationship tolerable, particularly as Jessie was without intellectual pretensions or even much education, so that her husband's genius was something she had to take largely on trust. She can have been in no doubt about his circumstances and temperament. Both were excessively difficult. Only in the last period of his career—and even then very uncertainly—did Conrad feel other than near to destitution. He was, indeed, to make shockingly little out of his writing. Even when we recall the different value of money at the beginning of the present century, the sums over which he agonizes in his correspondence seem startingly small. On the other hand, it appears not to have been the sort of poverty that brings in question the assurance of tomorrow's dinner, and while one is imagining the Conrads in the most strained circumstances, a casual reference to "the maids" will remind us of something taken for granted in those days by even the poorest professional family. Conrad appears to have been extravagant; when he entertained, it was rather lavishly; household budgets no doubt suffered as a consequence. Jessie is unlikely to have demurred, since she must have realized that these occasional convivialities were important in the life of a man of melancholic humour.

It is clear that Conrad had something more than a husband's fair share of being trying in endless small ways. He would often behave with inappropriate seignorial hauteur. When he journeyed by train, he would admit his family to the same (first-class) compartment, but endeavour to insist that they betray no sign of being connected with him. He continually lamented that his sons were not fond of reading, but if he came into the room and found one of them engaged with a book, he would fidget around until the book was put down, and then pick it up himself and make off with it. (The elder boy, Borys, an intelligent child, perfected a two-book technique to defeat this annoyance.) Although his own breeding was perfect, it is not clear that he was always adequately alert to vindicate his wife's dignity in the presence of people who, like Ford Madox Ford, themselves abounded less in breeding than in cultivation. Many of his totally unconscious assumptions, carried over from the life of a Polish landed gentry, must have been disconcerting to the English lower-middle-class Jessie George.

None of this was, perhaps, very important. But when Edward Garnett, Conrad's first literary mentor, wrote that his "ultra-nervous organisation appeared to make matrimony extremely hazardous," [11] he was going to the heart of the matter. It was, no doubt, "ultra-nervous organisation" that made Conrad a great writer. "I had never seen before," Garnett elsewhere wrote, "a man so masculinely keen yet so femininely sensitive." [12] So far, so good: it is almost the formula of the potent artist. But Conrad's "nerves" (*"Les nerfs, les nerfs!"* he would cry out in despair when *"absolument embourbé"* and seeing everything as *"noir noir noir"*) went far beyond this.[13] One cannot read his letters, or Mr. Baines's biography, without concluding that he passed a large part of his life in states of pathological depression. We do not know whether he took medical advice specifically about it. Nothing much could have been done for him, anyway, since the time when distresses such as his might be mitigated by the employment of drugs was still half-a-century off. Conrad also suffered from gout. Its attacks were commonly co-incident with periods of particular nervous distress.

That Jessie's burden under all this was considerable may be illustrated by a single anecdote, recounted by herself. It concerns Borys, now grown up and on active service in the Great War:

Once, when I had been away from the house for a few hours (on one of many visits to see a surgeon, in fact), I was greeted on my return by a weeping maid. My startled "What is it?" drew another burst of tears and a few whispered words I could not catch. To my question as to the whereabouts of my husband, the girl's answer struck me almost dumb. "Mr. Conrad is upstairs, Mum, in Mr. Borys's room. He's been there all day, ever since he told us. . . ." "Told you what?" "He says he knows Mr. Borys has been killed, but we haven't had any telegram."

I made my painful way up the stairs (for I am very lame) and found him sitting by the book-shelves, aimlessly glancing at books and replacing them on the shelves. He looked up at my entrance, and came eagerly forward to know what Sir Robert Jones had said. "What's the matter?" I forced my dry tongue to articulate, my voice sounding to my own ears miles away. "Nellie tells me you have had no news!"

"Can't I have a presentiment as well as you?" he answered impatiently, and he added in a whisper, "I know he has been killed!" I saw that he was in no condition to be reasoned with. I could only soothe him as I would have soothed a child. Presently he grew a little calmer, and after a time he consented to eat something; soon he was sleeping soundly.[14]

Mrs. Conrad prefaces this anecdote with a reference to her "maternal feeling" for Conrad, and she also uses the phrase elsewhere. "At such moments he was to me a son as well as a husband," she says of this much older man. What we are in contact with here is a sufficiently normal component of marriage presenting itself in somewhat exaggerated form. Jessie's attitude may have irritated Conrad's friends. But there can be no doubt whatever that she was a strong and courageous woman. Few things can be harder to get along with domestically than a state of chronic dejection, particularly if the chief variant upon it is hysterical despair. Yet a marriage which, like the Conrads', is successful amid such adverse circumstances is likely to be the creation of both its partners. Conrad was himself a man of high courage, and fidelity and tenacity were qualities he thought well of. His wife had these things to rely on, and upon their basis was able to create the stable background his long creative struggle required. In describing the fight for *Nostromo* (it was like "the everlasting sombre stress of the westward winter passage round Cape Horn") he was to speak of "the even flow of daily life, made easy and noiseless for me by a silent, watchful, tireless affection." [15] We may be amused by the suggestion of the Conrad family tiptoeing about the house. But we shall estimate Jessie Conrad's achievement rightly only when we realize how rootless Joseph Conrad's English condition was. One of his short stories is relevant here. Its eventual title was to be "Amy Foster," but while he worked on it Conrad thought of it as "A Husband" or "A Castaway." It tells of a young Polish peasant who alone survives from an emigrant vessel wrecked on the Kentish coast. The local people are frightened of him and treat him with shocking inhumanity, but Amy Foster, who is a plain, simple-minded and kind-hearted girl, falls in love with his good looks and marries him. They have a child. But Amy is progressively bewildered and alienated by what she considers her husband's strange ways, and when he falls ill and cries out for water in his own language, she snatches up the child and runs away in a panic. He pursues her in despair and misery, and dies of exposure. "Amy Foster" is not a very good story; indeed, it is little more than a morbid anecdote, variously padded out. And the young castaway is not at all like Conrad. "He did not know the name of his ship. Indeed, in the course of time we discovered he did not even know that ships had names—'like Christian people.' ") [16] Yet his loneliness and bewilderment in a strange country are powerfully realized. Conrad, we have noticed, spoke Polish to Jessie when in fever. There can be no doubt of the nightmare that "Amy Foster" represented to him.

Conrad's marriage took place in the same month that saw the publication of his second novel, *An Outcast of the Islands*. His first, *Almayer's Folly*, had appeared in the previous year, 1895. During his honeymoon, spent in Brittany, he worked upon what was to be his third, *The Rescuer*, and at the same time began experimenting with short stories for the

magazines. It is difficult to tell how he thought of himself
at this time. Both novels had been well received. The second,
nearly twice as long as the first, had been written rapidly and
with a marked advance in technical competence. In Edward
Garnett, who acted as reader for his publisher, Fisher Unwin,
he had a backer who was influential in the literary world.
But if at this point he had decided to become a professional
writer, there was presently a good deal to give him pause.
The novels showed no sign of bringing in much money, and
Unwin's proposed terms for a volume of short stories were
not encouraging. *The Rescuer*—about the early part of which
Garnett was enthusiastic—began to go badly. Presently Conrad was quite stuck with it—as he was regularly to be, whenever he got it out and tried to get on with it, for almost the
whole of the rest of his life. He had discovered that he was a
writer liable to go dry, to sit for days and weeks before a
blank page, unable to set down a single word.

Conrad's linguistic situation may have been a factor here,
but the point cannot be pronounced upon with confidence,
since it seems uncertain what that situation was. He was to
believe that in English idiom he was never at fault, but
numerous oddities can be dug out of his prose, and many of
them are gallicisms. In *Nostromo* there is the celebrated case
of the three horsemen "arrested" in the course of a journey,
where all that is intended is that they have come to a halt. In
Lord Jim we read that "Rajah Allang pretended to be the
only trader in his country"(252); in *The Secret Agent* a woman
has "no conscience of how little she had audibly said"(282)
and a composer is "in pass of becoming famous"(222); in
"Amy Foster" there is a room "taken upon the space of that
sort of coach-house." [17] French is the key to all these trivial
oddities. Conrad talked English to the end of his life with a
foreign accent the strength of which is quite variously re-

ported on. Garnett, for example, declared it to be slight—but
also recorded: "When he read aloud to me some new written
MS. pages of *An Outcast of the Islands* he mispronounced so
many words that I followed him with difficulty. I found then
that he had never once heard these English words spoken,
but had learned them all from books!" [18]

The significant question here, of course, is the extent to
which French *remained* Conrad's instinctive second language. His letters to English friends are bespattered with
French. But so, if to a lesser extent, are those of Henry James.
It was a polite affectation of the age. Yet one letter to Cunninghame Graham (whose own second language was presumably
Spanish) not only drops into French but stays there for nearly
a thousand words. Ford Madox Ford, who was to collaborate
closely with Conrad for a time, gives the impression that
Conrad had virtually to translate from French as he worked.
Ford, however, is not a very reliable witness, whether on this
or anything else. Conrad himself ridiculed the idea that he
had ever deliberately chosen between French and English as
a literary medium, and insisted that something like a mystical
affinity with English had declared itself in him since his
youngest manhood. But Conrad, although more reliable than
Ford, is not wholly reliable either. Mr. Baines has pointed to
the significant fact that when Conrad kept a private diary in
the Congo, it was in English that he wrote.* There can, of
course, be no doubt that, for all ordinary purposes, he came
to think fluently in English; it is the most commonplace of
accomplishments to command a foreign language to that extent. There is here an imponderable factor in Conrad's cre-

---

* This, too, contains an odd gallicism, as Richard Curle points out. A track
along which Conrad has to tramp is "very accidented." [19] *Accidenté*, it may
be added, can mean several things: "picturesque" as well as "broken" or
"hilly."

ative struggle, all the same. What does not admit of argument
is the substantial importance for him of the French literary
tradition. He was to pick up tricks of English eloquence in
odd places, including the pages of Jeremy Taylor. But he
does not give the impression of being widely read in English
literature, or of taking much interest in the work of his
English contemporaries.

Whether or not he had misgivings about turning professional writer, he certainly made, during the first two or three
years of his marriage, a number of attempts to return to sea.
His last voyages now lay some time back: in 1891-2 he had
been twice to Australia as first mate of the *Torrens*. The
Torrens was one of the most distinguished ships of its time,
famous for its fast passages to Adelaide, and with its accommodation much in demand by the South Australian squir-
archy. Its captain, moreover, was an acquaintance who had
come forward with an offer of the berth—which as a consequence Conrad had not felt himself too senior to fill. But he
must now have concluded, not unreasonably, that the man
who had commanded even the obscure *Otago* with credit
some years ago should again have a ship of his own. He was
a competent seaman, and if he was obviously a foreigner, he
was equally obviously a man of breeding. It is possible that
the breeding was a little too noticeable. Bertrand Russell,
although he rapidly came to a sense of deep intimacy with
Conrad, declares that his first impression on meeting him was
of surprise: "He spoke English with a very strong foreign
accent, and nothing in his demeanour in any way suggested
the sea. He was an aristocratic Polish gentleman to his finger-
tips." [20] Russell, an aristocratic English gentleman, was simply
recognizing somebody of his own kind. The ship-owners to
whom Conrad was recommended by Cunninghame Graham
(an aristocratic Scottish gentleman) and others may have

felt—particularly on being told that the fellow had been
writing books—that here was not quite their man, and that
only for the bridge of a crack Cunarder, conceivably, would
this odd and socially intimidating person be a promising
recruit. (Conrad said he was hoping for "some tramp or good
collier." [21]) So nothing came of these attempts. We do not
know whether Conrad reflected that, had his applications
been directed to a French mercantile marine at this time, his
books would conceivably have been quite other than disadvantageous to him. But at least he had at length to admit
that his seafaring days were over.

It was the more necessary, then, to consider his chances as
a writer, and his misgivings may have been enhanced when
he reflected on how he had stumbled upon the activity in the
first place. In *A Personal Record* he gives an account of the
occasion. *Almayer's Folly*, he declares, was begun in idleness,
as a sort of holiday task, during a long spell of leave on shore.
And its prompting was wholly mysterious. One morning he
had found himself getting up from breakfast with unusual
expedition, violently or at least resolutely ringing the bell
and ordering the table to be cleared forthwith. He had then
sat down and begun to write:

It was not the outcome of a need—the famous need of self-ex-
pression which artists find in their search for motives. The necessity which impelled me was a hidden, obscure necessity, a
completely masked and unaccountable phenomenon. Till I began
to write that novel I had written nothing but letters, and not
very many of these. I never made a note of a fact, of an impression or of an anecdote in my life. The conception of a planned
book was entirely outside my mental range when I sat down to
write. . . .[22]

There is a good deal more to the same effect. "The ambition of being an author" had never entered his head—and here suddenly he was, one day after breakfast, intently engaged upon the fabricating of fiction. It would be guileless to take all this as literally true. Yet the picture suggests something well-documented elsewhere: Conrad's strong sense of the autonomous and hence uncontrollable character of the creative imagination; the helplessness of the mere diurnal man before its vagaries. Sometimes he expresses this moderately, if despondingly:

I *never mean* to be slow. The stuff comes out at its own rate. I am always ready to put it down; nothing would induce me to lay down my pen if I *feel* a sentence—or even a word ready to my hand. The trouble is that too often—alas!—I've to wait for the sentence—for the word.

What wonder then that during the long blank hours the doubt creeps into the mind and I ask myself whether I am fitted for that work.[23]

At other times he is driven to a kind of extravagant wailing before his own situation. Or he will assert that what he *has* managed to write must be regarded as sacrosanct; it may be deleted but must not be altered, since this would be to tinker with something that is not in a personal sense his own.

Conrad knew very well, however, that if the visitings of the Muse are unpredictable, the conscious intelligence can make useful preparations for them when they occur. He became a student of the Novel, and always upon the assumption that it had matured—more certainly in France, perhaps, than in England—into one of the highest literary forms. He was not always to know when, in his own work, this study was bearing fruit; for example, he was to see the writing of *Nostromo* as a process of nightmarish improvisation, whereas it is apparent to us that so complex and fully integrated a composition could have been achieved only on the basis of an intellectual appreciation of the most developed techniques of fiction.

In this early period of apprenticeship to professional writing, however, he appears to have felt that his special circumstances presented him with specific and quite humble needs. *Almayer's Folly* had been written piecemeal while sailing about the globe, and had taken four or five years to finish; even so, its English had required "editing" by friends before it could be offered for publication. To an extent which he cannot himself have been sure of, his difficulty in writing must have been, residually at least, linguistic; and it may have seemed likely that a more professional facility could be acquired by working hard at a level upon which it was unnecessary to suppose that the Muse was very desperately needed. Again, although he was from the first accepted by people of standing in literature as a significant writer, he had only a slight acquaintance among them; and in the mysterious fields of book and magazine publication, in particular, he badly needed closer contacts with people "in the know." In these circumstances lies the origin of his curious collaboration during these years with Ford Madox Ford.

Ford was to be described by H. G. Wells as "a great system of assumed personas and dramatised selves," [24] and the mere history of his name might seem to support this. He began as Ford Hermann Hueffer, his father having been an expatriate German musicologist and his mother—Catherine Madox Brown—a daughter of the Pre-Raphaelite painter Ford Madox Brown; he then became successively Ford Hueffer, Ford Madox Hueffer, and Ford Madox Ford. At the time of his first meeting with Conrad (who rented a house from him), he was a young man of twenty-four with several precocious books to his credit, two manuscript novels which were failing to find publishers, and a great air of having been bred to, and living in, the highest literary and artistic circles. His life, although variously hapless, was to be dignified by a passionate devotion to literature, and more particularly to the craft of fiction. His own novels are not really good (the best of them, *The Good Soldier*, reads like a synthetic major novel, brilliantly contrived), but he was one of the most notable discoverers and fosterers of talent in his time. Like Conrad, he had a high admiration for Flaubert, Maupassant, and Turgenev; and it was this community of taste that doubtless suggested to the two men the possibility of joint authorship. One might suppose, indeed, that such an admiration would preclude the notion that a work of any artistic significance could be composed in such a fashion. Certainly neither *The Inheritors* nor *Romance* (Ford had the larger hand in each) is a novel of any merit. But if it was Conrad's inward proposal that the whole project should be simply an exercise in facility and fluency, without any serious designs upon literary excellence, things did not after all work out quite that way. Both writers had an instinct for perfection, and they gave at least sporadic scope to it as they went along. In *Mightier than the Sword* Ford offers a lively account of arguing for three whole days with Conrad over the punctuation of the last sentence of "Heart of Darkness" (which is not, of course, a collaborated work). And in *Romance* (which is a novel almost as long as *Nostromo*) they agreed there was a single "immortal line"—a "famous sentence," Conrad records, "at which we both exclaimed: 'This is Genius!' " [25] A peasant is being questioned by a Spanish judge in Havana:

> "Where do you come from?"
> "The town of Rio Medio, excellency."
> "Of what occupation?"
> "Excellency—a few goats. . . ." [26]

It was this last sentence (certainly an extremely good one) that was judged alone to be immortal by the collaborators in *Romance*. And Ford is declared to be the creator of it.

Conrad's basic struggle at this period (apart from the struggle for mere livelihood) was to extend his range. His second novel, *An Outcast of the Islands*, stood in an unusual, and perhaps ominous, relationship to his first, *Almayer's Folly*. It was a kind of sequal in reverse—since the same setting and some of the same people were displayed at an earlier point in their history. He must then have taken alarm at the prospect of being typed as an exotic novelist, since from this time dates a 10,000-word fragment, *The Sisters*, the opening of which is set in Paris and the proposed theme of which appears to be a tragic love-affair. Conrad's difficulty in making sexual relationships a centre of interest is notorious— although it would have been rash, on a first observation of this trait, to assert that he would not come to write about sex very well. However this may be, it is plain that with *The Sisters* he had trespassed upon ground wholly uncongenial at the time, and the project foundered. He then embarked upon *The Rescuer*, and found himself in simultaneous trouble on two fronts. The novel stands in the same chronological and geographical relationship to *An Outcast of the Islands* as does *An Outcast of the Islands* to *Almayer's Folly*; once more, that is to say, we are taken farther back in time, and hear of old names in new but familiar-seeming situations. And then, barring the story's progress in a curiously literal sense, we have a stranded vessel, and on board her a lady who patently requires to be made love to. The situation may quite fairly be said to have brought Conrad absurdly to a standstill for more than thirty years. *The Rescue: a Romance of the Shallows* was to be published in 1920.

From these shallows of the Malay Archipelago Conrad escaped, appropriately enough, by way of blue water. He had made this escape before the collaboration with Ford (who disapproved of the manner of it) had begun, since it may be dated from the completing of *The Nigger of the "Narcissus"* in January 1897. Six months earlier, and four months after his marriage, he had completed a short story called "An Outpost of Progress," which he sent to his publisher with the observation that "there is no love interest in it and no woman." The same holds true, of course, of his first masterpiece. At the same time, *The Nigger of the "Narcissus"* is much more than the narrative of a heroic struggle against the elements. It is about human nature and human relationships as these reveal themselves in an isolated society under stress, and the man who could create it had nothing to fear from any specific circumscription of his imaginative sympathies in dealing with such a topic as romantic love. Conrad understood its importance, and on 10 January 1897 wrote to Garnett:

Nigger died on the 7th at 6 P.M.; but the ship is not home yet. Expected to arrive tonight and be paid off tomorrow. And the end! I can't eat—I dream—nightmares—and scare my wife. I wish it was over! But I think it will do! It will do!—Mind I only think—not sure. But if I didn't think so I would jump overboard.[27]

And a few months later he made in a preface to the book his most important avowal of his aims as an artist.[28] A great many setbacks and bafflements lay ahead of him, and to a man of his temperament they were to be a heavy burden. But with *The Nigger of the "Narcissus"* his artistic maturity had been attained. He was forty.

Conrad's uncle Tadeusz had died at the beginning of 1894.

He had been able to hail his nephew enthusiastically as "Master in the British Merchant Service";[29] he was spared the uneasiness of seeing him take to writing, a common Korzeniowski proclivity which Bobrowskis deprecated. Conrad's elder son was born in 1898, and was christened Alfred Borys Konrad Korzeniowski—his father having rejected, as too difficult for foreigners, such promising names as Władysław, Bogusław, Wienczysław, and Bohdan. His younger son was born eight years later, and christened John Alexander Conrad Korzeniowski. These events make up almost all that was significant in the outward course of Conrad's later life, which was lived out, for the most part, quietly in modest country dwellings. Although depressive, he seems not to have been by nature reclusive; he enjoyed the company of his fellow-writers and appreciated visitors. But his means were so narrow that he had on several occasions to rely upon grants from the Royal Literary Fund or some similar source; Jessie's crippled condition made travelling expensive and produced big doctors' bills as well; these circumstances conduced to isolation. Virginia Woolf, when she had reviewed *The Rescue* upon its eventually limping into print, found that her perfectly just dealing with the book left her with a bad conscience, and with this she endeavoured to cope, not altogether graciously, in the privacy of her diary:

I was struggling, at this time, to say honestly that I don't think Conrad's last book a good one. I have said it. It is painful (a little) to find fault there, where almost solely, one respects. I can't help suspecting the truth to be that he never sees anyone who knows good writing from bad, and then being a foreigner, talking broken English, married to a lump of a wife, he withdraws more and more into what he once did well, only piles it on higher and higher, until what can one call it but stiff melodrama. I would not like to find *The Rescue* signed Virginia Woolf.[30]

Mrs. Woolf was not a lump of a wife. In temperament she was rather like Conrad himself, and like Conrad she was sometimes surprisingly poor. She had not the additional strain of being the sole support of a household with children. Conrad, incidentally, had a substantial sense of what was owing to his boys. Because he had greatly admired the sort of nautical education given to gentlemen's sons on the *Conway* and similar training-ships, he sent Borys to *H.M.S. Worcester*, and on the very eve of the Great War found satisfaction in taking him to Poland to imbibe some sense of his ancestry. John, as soon as the family means permitted of it, was sent to a public school.

Financial circumstances are always likely to condition what, and how much, an author writes; and in Conrad they are a factor to be reckoned with throughout his career. Henry James has an amusing short story or fantasy, "The Next Time," in which Ray Limbert, an eminent writer with family responsibilities not unlike Conrad's, tries harder and harder to write in a popular manner, only to find that every "next time" has produced something more hopelessly distinguished than the time before. Conrad may occasionally come within hail of this paradox. Usually, indeed, he knew what he was about. Thus, immediately after finishing *The Nigger of the "Narcissus,"* he wrote a short story, "Karain," which returns to Malaya for the purposes of a sentimental concoction he described to Cunninghame Graham, very truly, as "Magazine-ish;"[31] and he had already produced in "The Lagoon" a similar pot-boiler which he had referred to contemptuously to Garnett as "very much Malay indeed." [32] We have to remember that, up to the period of the Great War (and to some extent beyond it) magazine publication was important to writers in a way that no longer obtains in Great Britain today. This is the reason why so many novels of the period, including Conrad's *Lord Jim, Nostromo, The Secret Agent,* and *Victory,* grew from the proposal to write a short story. There was a great deal of advantage in this situation. It made experiment possible without the danger of too disastrous a waste of working time.

Conrad's first stand-by here was *Blackwood's,* which specialized in good quality entertainment with a "real life" slant to it. Both "Youth" and "Heart of Darkness," which immediately followed upon "Karain" although they are of totally different merit, first appeared in *Blackwood's.* In both stories there is a narrator, Marlow, who is to be immensely significant for Conrad's art. But Marlow has every appearance of having been created for a magazine public on what may be called straight Ray Limbert principles. Here is the opening of "Youth":

This could have occurred nowhere but in England, where men and sea interpenetrate, so to speak—the sea entering into the life of most men, and the men knowing something or everything about the sea, in the way of amusement, of travel, or of bread-winning.

This, if we pause on it, is amazing nonsense. But we continue:

We were sitting round a mahogany table that reflected the bottle, the claret-glasses, and our faces as we leaned on our elbows. There was a director of companies, an accountant, a lawyer, Marlow, and myself. The director had been a *Conway* boy, the accountant had served four years at sea, the lawyer—a fine crusted Tory, High Churchman, the best of old fellows, the soul of honour—had been chief officer in the P. & O. service in the good old days when mail-boats were square-rigged at least on two masts. . . .

This induction, with its echo of Kipling's world—picked men yarning about their experiences here and there round the globe—proves to be quite inconsequent, but at least it has got *Blackwood's* readers turning the page. "Heart of Darkness" begins in precisely the same way. The Director of Companies (he has been promoted to these capital letters) is host on a cruising yawl in the estuary of the Thames, and his guests are the Lawyer, the Accountant, Marlow, and—as before—the anonymous "I" who is the chronicler of Marlow's narration. Only this time, as we shall see later, the setting is superbly integrated with the story. One might almost have concluded from the final paragraph of "Heart of Darkness" alone that the imagination of its author would soon outrun the popular magazine reader's scope.

This is just what happened in Conrad's next work. First hopefully thought of as "Jim, a Sketch," it started serialization in *Blackwood's* as *Lord Jim: A Tale* in October 1899. Nothing at the outset could have appeared more suitable for the magazine; here was a straight-out story of action and personal honour, in an exotic setting and upon a wholly masculine note (indeed, as what was projected was only the first part of the novel as we know it, the last page might have been reached without a woman heaving up on the horizon). But as the narrative began to turn upon itself and turn upon itself again, and as the problematical interior worlds of Jim and of Marlow himself were revealed as the true focus of their creator's interest, William Blackwood's misgivings must have deepened month by month, the more particularly as Conrad was a very poor hand at keeping to a timetable. Blackwood's dealings with Conrad were a model of probity and sympathy. But his ideal contributor was Anthony Trollope, who—he rather wistfully told his unreliable Polish gentleman—"went to a desk as a shoemaker goes to his last." [33]

Conrad's association with *Blackwood's* became tenuous, and although his books were never to fail of serial publication, it was not always in the most remunerative journals that they appeared. (*The Secret Agent* first came out in *Ridgway's, a Militant Weekly for God and Country*.) It was not until the *New York Herald* serialized *Chance* in 1912 that Conrad gained the substantial popularity into which it was Blackwood's laudable aim to nurse his writers.

Nearly all Conrad's finest work falls within a little more than a decade, for he finished *Lord Jim* in 1900 and *Under Western Eyes* in 1910. If *Chance* (1912) and *Victory* (June 1914) are as inferior as a number of critics hold, then the decline of his creative vitality must be viewed as a pre-war phenomenon. But the war certainly told on him heavily. Throughout its later course the life of his elder son was at risk, and from its first days (when he was actually in Poland with his family) it must have been clear that the fate of his native country hung upon its issue. It is not easy to assess the later course of Conrad's feelings here. According to one account, he was assailed upon this last visit to Poland by a ·sense of guilt which was by no means dissipated by the distinction with which he was received. Perhaps he was never quite without some feeling of this sort; we know that in 1899, when a debate was going on in Poland on the "Emigration of the Talents," he had been distressed upon being singled out by a popular novelist, Maria Orzenszkowa, as one who had failed in his duty to his country.[34] It is sometimes maintained that *Lord Jim* is the issue of a deep self-questioning in Conrad which this incident aroused, and in the light of the novel's crucial moment it is certainly startling to find him declaring in *A Personal Record* of his departure from Poland: "I verily believe mine was the only case of a boy of

my nationality and antecedents taking a, so to speak, standing jump out of his racial surroundings and associations." [35]
Indeed, the manner in which the oddly placed "so to speak"
is employed to hold up, and thus to emphasize, the image of
the "standing jump" goes far to convince one that Conrad is
deliberately seeking to evoke the association with Jim in his
readers' heads. We need not go so far as to persuade ourselves
(with Dr. Gustav Morf in his curious *The Polish Heritage of
Joseph Conrad*) that a sense of having betrayed Poland provides the concealed dynamic of all his most potent work. But
as he aged (and the ageing process set in early with him), he
may well have become a prey to doubts which as a young man
he had briskly repelled—and as a consequence have imposed
upon himself a yet further nervous burden. What does seem
to be clear about the inferiority of the work of his final phase
is that inferiority's involuntary and, as it were, unconscious
character. If his themes turn merely melodramatic, as Virginia Woolf believed, and if his vision grows dulled or sentimental, the explanation is not that—at least in any major
undertaking—he is deliberately making concessions to a larger
and less instructed public. It is rather, one comes to feel, a
matter of intellectual and emotional fatigue, of a protective
induration such as frequently accompanies premature senescence. Wordsworth's life affords another example. And just
as with the later Wordsworth wisdom comes to repose no
longer in childhood but in a near-dotage of solitaries and
pedlars, so in Conrad's last books—somebody has said—even
the young people are tired and apathetic and elderly.

In the spring of 1923, at the instance of his American
publisher, he paid a short visit to the United States. Since the
Titanic disaster in 1912 he had been grimly hostile to gigan-
tic liners—and had indeed produced two tremendous denun-

ciations of those commercial interests which he supposed to have been responsible for the greatest tragedy in the history of British seamanship. Now, on board the *Tuscania*, he wrote a milder depreciation of this "unpleasantly unsteady imitation of a Ritz Hotel." [36] ("The one statement that can safely be advanced about travelling at sea," he began, "is that it is not what it used to be.") Nevertheless, for the first time since he had come ashore from the *Otago*, he was able to feel him-himself the most important man on board; and he clearly enjoyed—at what was to be almost the end of his life—a first experience of eminence. In New York he was treated as a celebrity; he read a passage from *Victory* in the drawing-room of Mrs. Curtiss James, about whose social altitude he wrote home with a pleasing awe. He met the celebrated Colonel House, and also the most famous of all his living countrymen, Ignace Paderewski. He was similarly feted in Boston. He made a little tour of New England. And then, accompanied by Mr. and Mrs. Doubleday, he returned home on the *Majestic*. About the whole trip, which occupied six weeks, there hangs the suggestion of something out of character, and behind it one suspects a design on Doubleday's part to alleviate Conrad's deepening depression. Doubleday was a benevolent man. More than twenty years before, he had similarly made a special trip across the Atlantic in order to give his companionship to Rudyard Kipling and his wife when they were in very deep distress indeed.

Unfortunately, upon his return to England Jessie had to break the news that Borys had made a secret marriage. Whatever was the background of this romantic proceeding, Conrad appears to have been badly upset by it only for a short time, and Mrs. Borys was soon received in proper form by her parents-in-law. But his health and spirits were alike declining, and although he worked on a new novel, *Suspense*, and believed himself to be in possession of about six different lines of treatment which might be followed in it, it was to become plain when the unfinished book was posthumously published that his powers had departed from him. His worries about money and the future security of his family were now largely irrational. He would write letters about quite small sums—yet through his friend Richard Curle's somewhat diffuse account of the last days of his life there flit the figures of a secretary, a chauffeur and his wife, and a valet. Such people require the support of inferior servants, and of there one at least is on record: "Mama" Piper, the cook. But very real anxieties had lasted for too long, and although, only a few months before, *The Rover* had sold over 30,000 copies in a first impression, Conrad had forgotten that he need no longer be frightened to write out a cheque.

On 3 August 1924, after some premonitory attacks, he died of cardiac failure and was buried at Canterbury. His tombstone misspells his name, but carries, appropriately enough, the lines he had chosen from *The Faerie Queene* as epigraph for *The Rover*:

> Sleep after toyle, port after stormie seas,
> Ease after warre, death after life, does greatly please.

CHAPTER

II

"The Hallucination of the
Eastern Archipelago"

It is seldom difficult to enumerate literary influences which
may have been at work in the composition of a first novel,
and this holds of both the theme and the style of *Almayer's
Folly*. The central character, a commonplace person surrounded by commonplace persons, drifts to destruction while
immersed in dreams of improbable grandeur. This recalls
Flaubert's *Madame Bovary*, a novel which we know Conrad
to have been re-reading with attention some two years before
his own story was completed. "Je viens de relire *Madame
Bovary*," he wrote to Marguerite Poradowska in April 1892,
"avec une admiration pleine de respect." [1] And this French
orientation can be distinguished elsewhere. The naval officer
who called himself Pierre Loti (and who rose to the rank of
captain in 1906, fifteen years after being elected to the French
Academy) had published in 1883 *Mon frère Yves*, a novel
describing the world-wide wanderings of a sailor, and in
1886 *Pêcheur d'islande*, which is concerned with the life of

Breton fisher-folk; his technique of rendering exotic scenes in terms of impressionism, and his careful elaboration of style and cadence, bring him close to the early Conrad. Other relevant French writers are Daudet, to whom Conrad thought of sending a copy of his book; Balzac, from whom he was long afterwards to declare that "one can learn something"; [2] and Maupassant, for whose technique he early expressed unbounded admiration.[3]

Yet *Almayer's Folly* is not in the least like a book by any of these people, and it may be doubted whether it was composed with a very conscious sense of deliberate apprenticeship to great writers. In 1918 Conrad was to tell Hugh Walpole that he had read no Flaubert until *Almayer's Folly* was completed, and his memory could scarcely have been thus at fault had he been working with any clear notion of a relationship between Emma Bovary and his own protagonist. Nor is it necessary to suppose that he was affected only by French writers, and only by writers of eminence and literary sophistication. There is a good deal in *Almayer's Folly*—for example, the crudely unverisimilar character of much of the internal monologue, and the recourse to cliché in passages of romantic sentiment—which seems to echo the sort of ephemeral popular fiction that a sailor might pick up in port and pass the time with at sea. The specific influence of more considerable British writers is not easy to discern, although Conrad can scarcely have sat down to write an exotic novel without some thought of Stevenson, who died in the year before *Almayer's Folly* was published, and of Kipling, then in the first flush of his fame. Of earlier writers he had certainly read a good deal of Dickens. When, at the sombre close of the story, we read that "during a great flood the jetty of Lingard and Co. left the bank and floated down the river, probably in search of more cheerful surroundings"(203), the provenance of the small, out-of-key joke is clear enough. But when we turn back to the beginning and see, as it floats down the same muddy flood, a tree "raising upwards a long, denuded branch, like a hand lifted in mute appeal to heaven against the river's brutal and unnecessary violence"(4), we may find ourselves thinking of another of Dickens's characteristic powers. Conrad's own account of the genesis of *Almayer's Folly* says nothing of literary sources. When the book had to be laid aside for a time, it was not always because of some external interruption, but because he had ceased to command, or be commanded by, "the hallucination of the Eastern Archipelago." [4] Much of the best writing in the book is descriptive, but it is by no means to "pure" description in any mere picturesque interest that he is impelled. On the contrary, we feel from the start that the "hallucination" has demanded imaginative expression because of some inner significance which it carries for the writer. External nature as a sinister and alarming mystery constitutes—it is perhaps not too much to say—the central emotional focus of the novel. When Almayer, trapped for life as he is in Sambir, cries out in despair that it is an "infernal" place(142), we know that his creator agrees with him. And when Almayer's daughter, upon her first appearance before us, is seen with "her face turned towards the outer darkness"(16), we are being introduced to the Bornean jungle in two related aspects. In the first place it is a territory outside civilization, the haunt of tribes who seek "the gratification of their desires with the savage cunning and the unrestrained fierceness of natures as innocent of culture as their own immense and gloomy forests."(43) Hidden there is a life of "barbarous fights and savage feasting" in which only "ignorance" can imagine "a better side." Conrad is in fact immensely less tolerant than is the much-maligned Kipling of remote races and primitive cultures, and the degradation of "going native" is as vivid to him as it is to his hero. He views civilization, in fact, as a unique historical phenomenon, bounded alike in space and time, beyond the light of which (and it is a light uncertain in itself) lies only an absolute darkness of evil and misery.

In this first regard, then, the jungle is partly a fact and already partly a symbol. Upon a second level it is wholly symbolic—and it seems to be this in a manner which, in part at least, has eluded Conrad's conscious scrutiny. It is true that the jungle is more than once set over against the ocean in a symbolism that is wholly deliberate. When Dain Maroola is hoping to escape with Almayer's daughter, he reflects that "when the next day broke, they would be together on the great blue sea that was like life—away from the forests that were like death"(169)—although, even so, he is soon telling the girl that the sea is "cold and cruel, and full of the wisdom of destroyed life . . . like a woman's heart."(174) Chiefly it is the jungle, however, which, in key places in the book, speaks mysteriously of deeply buried dreads. The "hallucination," we may say, travelled about the world with Conrad because it demanded to be exorcized. It was still to be making this demand when he wrote "Heart of Darkness."

But there was something else that impelled Conrad to write in addition to his haunting sense of the "merciless" quality of tropical nature. This was the historical Almayer, actually William Charles Olmeijer, whom he encountered on his four short visits to Berau in Borneo when sailing as mate on the *Vidar*. *A Personal Record* contains an account of their first meeting—and the portrait of the man (down to his in-ability, like Coleridge in an equally neurotic condition, to open his letters) is vividly drawn.[5] Even so, it is difficult to account for the extent to which, according to Conrad's own statement of the case, this miserable trader subsequently haunted his imagination. "If I had not got to know Almayer pretty well it is almost certain there would never have been a line of mine in print." [6] Almayer, of course, has a brooding sense of living in exile, and it is this that finally overcomes and destroys him. He is, moreover, a man whose power to act effectively and with dignity has been paralyzed by some encroaching nervous malaise. In all this—as in the figure of Almayer's successor, Willems—Conrad may have seen some distorted shadow of his own fears. Nevertheless, *Almayer's Folly* is not a book in which we come to feel, as we read, that the writer has been fortunate enough to find his true inspiration at once.

There is already a certain deviousness in Conrad's way of telling his first story, although in outline it is clear enough.*

* Captain Tom Lingard, an adventurous trader in the Malay Archipelago, fights and destroys a band of Sulu pirates, carrying off from their prau a female child whom he subsequently adopts, causes to be educated in a convent, and is determined to marry to a white man before leaving her the large fortune he has built up. For this purpose he chooses Konrad Almayer, a young man of Dutch parentage who is in commercial employment in Macassar. Almayer is ashamed of marrying a native girl, and does so merely in hope of gain. Lingard then establishes him in Sambir, a lonely trading post in Borneo, some way up a river the entrance to which Lingard alone has the secret of reaching. There a child, Nina, is born, and sent to be educated, as her mother had been, among white people.

After some initial success, the trading post fails to prosper. This is partly because (in circumstances to be recounted in *An Outcast of the Islands*) Arab traders also discover the secret of the River Pantai, and partly because Almayer is a feeble and incompetent man, living on dreams of easy wealth to come. Lingard's fortunes also decline—and rapidly so when he becomes obsessed with the idea of finding gold and diamonds in great quantity in the centre of Borneo. Eventually Lingard goes to Europe to seek fresh capital and is never heard of again. Almayer's trade dwindles to nothing, and he is left stranded in Sambir with his native wife, who is repulsive to him and has reverted to savagery in all her ways.

Nina, when she has grown up to be a young woman of great beauty, returns home to Sambir, believing herself to have been scorned because of her Malay blood by the people who have been looking after her. Almayer is devoted to her in an unconsciously incestuous fashion, and his thoughts are

It begins, indeed, with a formal exposition of almost the whole theme of the book:

"KASPAR! Makan!"

The well-known shrill voice startled Almayer from his dream of splended future into the unpleasant realities of the present hour. An unpleasant voice too. He had heard it for many years, and with every year he liked it less. No matter; there would be an end to all this soon.

He shuffled uneasily, but took no further notice of the call. Leaning with both his elbows on the balustrade of the verandah, he went on looking fixedly at the great river that flowed—indifferent and hurried—before his eyes. He liked to look at it about the time of sunset; perhaps because at that time the sinking sun would spread a glowing gold tinge on the waters of the Pantai, and Almayer's thoughts were often busy with gold; gold he had failed to secure; gold the others had secured—dishonestly, of course—or gold he meant to secure yet, through his own honest exertions, for himself and Nina. He absorbed himself in his dream of wealth and power away from this coast where he had dwelt for so many years, forgetting the bitterness of toil and strife in the vision of a great and splendid reward. They would live in Europe, he and his daughter. They would be rich and respected. Nobody would think of her mixed blood in the presence of her great beauty and of his immense wealth.

---

all of gaining the money which will enable him to carry her off to a splendid life in Amsterdam. He has found a notebook of Lingard's which he believes to hold the secret of the gold and diamonds. When a new trader arrives in Sambir—Dain Maroola, the young and handsome son of the Rajah of Bali— he enters into an alliance with him to find the treasure. Dain and Nina fall passionately in love. Then, as once consequence of the intrigues and conflicting interests of various local factions which provide the background of the book, Dain's ship is destroyed by a Dutch naval vessel. He becomes a fugitive, although it is plain that, when he gets away, his father's great wealth will restore him to prosperity. Finally, to the horror and anguish of her father, Nina flees with him. Almayer thus sees his beloved daughter, equally with her hateful mother, turn back to the abyss of native life. What is left of his character disintegrates, and he takes to opium and dies.

Plenty of information has been packed in here, and a few following pages give, ostensibly as Almayer's retrospection, an equally succinct account of his early history, and of his mercenary marriage as arranged by the well-meaning Captain Lingard. Then we return to the present time of the first paragraphs; a young native called Dain appears in a canoe; he defers an interview which Almayer seems anxious about, and goes away after speaking about a brig in a gloomy tone of voice which Almayer fails to notice. Almayer turns back into his house, and encounters his daughter. It is now that Nina has her face turned towards the night, and we understand quite clearly that she is more interested in Dain than her father is aware of. She listens without interest as Almayer talks of some enterprise in which he and Dain are associated, and which is to bring in the riches that shall make departure from Sambir possible. Almayer goes to bed, and Nina, left to the contemplation of the nightly monsoon thunderstorm, stands "motionless, at each flash of lightning eagerly scanning the broad river with a steady and anxious gaze."(20)

In a sense we have had the whole story of *Almayer's Folly* in a single prodigal opening chapter, and it is unsurprising that in its remaining course the narrative is often evasive or devious. We have to wait more than fifty pages to learn why Dain Maroola spoke so gloomily about his brig, and much longer before considerable subsidiary complication—of the kind that reveals just who is smuggling gunpowder to whom —is at all clear to us. Here, in fact, right at the start, Conrad shows himself as not really wholeheartedly concerned with anything that could be called a gripping yarn. What he *is* so concerned with cannot readily be pinned down, since we are often aware of a conflict of interests. Conrad has taken great pains with the "natives," whether Malay or Arab, and they can at least be credited with their moments of coming alive.

Babalatchi, chief adviser to the local Rajah Lakamba, is pursued through the book with a solemn Gallic irony which turns upon describing the grotesque old savage by a variety of such periphrases as "the aged statesman of Sambir"; there is a wonderfully funny moment when he is constrained to soothe his sovereign by grinding the music of Verdi interminably out of a barrel organ; his primitive version of Machiavellian statecraft, and the ramshackle court in which it is exercised, are plausible and consistent, even if they are seldom without a hint of *opéra bouffe*. Yet we do not feel that Conrad's insight into native minds, or even his knowledge of native manners, is adequate to providing more than a picturesque background for something else.

We are thus thrown back on Almayer himself in seeking the main subject proposed in the book. But Almayer is not very satisfactory; indeed, he never becomes a particularly substantial or convincing presence. A full-length study of a weak and inadequate personality is never easy to sustain; dispassionateness is required, but sympathy and an empathic power are required as well; Almayer is so little entered into by his creator that we end up by wondering anew just where Conrad's interest in him came from. On the occasion of his marriage, we are told, he is "uneasy, a little disgusted, and greatly inclined to run away."(23) Over the page he is a man of "weak will" and "feebleness of purpose"; on the next page he is "cowed" by his wife's outbursts of savage nature; on the page after that he is simply a "poor wretch"; and at the beginning of the next chapter he is a "grey-headed and foolish dreamer."(35) When we learn, much later on, that he has always "prided himself upon his unflinching firmness" and believes in "the latent greatness of his nature,"(192) we have a sense that Conrad supposes himself to be contriving a more complex character-study than is in fact the case, and that *Almayer's Folly* is unsuccessful because obstinately inert at its purposed centre. In part the trouble lies, perhaps, in a technical inexpertness. Much of Almayer's speech, and nearly all his unspoken thought and reverie, are rendered in an idiom quite out of keeping with a man of his character, education, and environment.

There is one remaining major centre of interest, and here again Conrad seems to have succeeded ill with his conscious intentions. Nina Almayer, whose Malay blood is to carry the day with her, and Dain Maroola, the son of a rajah, pursue and consummate their love affair in what can only be called the jargon of English romantic fiction of the most popular and undistinguished cast. Dain, when he first sees Nina, is "dazzled by the unexpected vision . . . of so much loveliness met so suddenly in such an unlikely place."(55) He feels "the subtle breath of mutual understanding passing between their two savage natures."(63) Nina recognizes "with a thrill of delicious fear the mysterious consciousness of her identity with that being," and listens to "Dain's words giving up to her the whole treasure of love and passion his nature was capable of with all the unrestrained enthusiasm of a man totally untrammelled by any influence of civilized self-discipline."(64) Dain has a "quiet masterfulness it was her delight to obey"(65); he feels himself "carried away helpless by a great wave of supreme emotion, by a rush of joy, pride, and desire"(68)—and then again, as if Conrad were suddenly remembering that these people are coffee-coloured, he speaks "with all the rude eloquence of a savage nature giving itself up without restraint to an overmastering passion."(69) All this is a little more than mildly absurd. Conrad knows nothing whatever about the sexual life of savages, and is doing little more here than dip into the world of the European novelette. Yet it is with Nina and Dain, curiously enough, that we come nearest to the actual, yet concealed, dynamic both of *Almayer's Folly* and of the novel which was immediately to succeed it. Both books betray a powerful and troubled response to a submerged theme—"submerged" because never impressing us as part of the conscious intention of the writer. This theme has been succinctly defined by Mr. Thomas Moser as "the life of the forest producing death and equated with woman." [7]

"Forest" is Conrad's habitual word for external nature as it is viewed from such little enclaves of organized primitive society as Sambir. But although he uses "jungle" only infrequently, no doubt because it is a term primarily of Indian association, his forest is very much the jungle as it is known to the European imagination. It is a most threatening and sinister place. And into it Conrad regularly despatches his people to make love.

Dain and Nina arrive in this symbolical terrain in canoes—and as one might arrive in a trap the jaws of which have been cunningly disguised:

In a moment the two little nutshells with their occupants floated quietly side by side, reflected by the black water in the dim light struggling through a high canopy of dense foliage; while above, away up in the broad day, flamed immense red blossoms sending down on their heads a shower of great dew-sparkling petals that descended rotating slowly in a continuous and perfumed stream; and over them, under them, in the sleeping water; all around them in a ring of luxuriant vegetation bathed in the warm air charged with strong and harsh perfumes, the intense work of tropical nature went on: plants shooting upward, entwined, interlaced in inextricable confusion, climbing madly and brutally over each other in the terrible silence of a desperate struggle towards the life-giving sunshine above—as if struck with sudden horror at the seething mass of corruption below, at the death and decay from which they sprang.(71)

It is a gloomy epithalamium, and its tones are touched in again and again. Thus when we are told that Dain "feared not death, yet he desired ardently to live, for life to him was Nina," his persuasion is immediately followed by an ironic commentary using as its vehicle this dominant metaphor of the book:

As he skirted in his weary march the edge of the forest he glanced now and then into its dark shade, so enticing in its deceptive appearance of coolness, so repellent with its unrelieved gloom, where lay, entombed and rotting, countless generations of trees, and where their successors stood as if mourning, in dark green foliage, immense and helpless, awaiting their turn. Only the parasites seemed to live there in a sinuous rush upwards into the air and sunshine, feeding on the dead and the dying alike, and crowning their victims with pink and blue flowers that gleamed amongst the boughs, incongruous and cruel, like a strident and mocking note in the solemn harmony of the doomed trees.(166-7)

Despite the clutter of adjectives which is so characteristic of Conrad's elevated writing in its early phase, this vision of great columns, whether fallen or still upright, ceaselessly attacked by an ephemeral and deceptively beautiful lower vegetation, is impressive and alarming. It is unsurprising that Dain, despite the robustly sensual constitution attributed to him, makes an indecisive and almost reluctant lover, and that when he stands face to face with his mistress he is conscious only of "one of those long looks that are a woman's most terrible weapon; a look that is more stirring than the closest touch, and more dangerous than the thrust of a dagger."(171) As epilogue to their union, we are told that "a

sigh as of immense sorrow passed over the land."(173) When
we take leave of Almayer, who has lost Nina, we salute his
"young hopes, his foolish dream of splendid future, his
awakening, and his despair."(203) It scarcely seems suggested
that Dain, who has gained her, will have a different destiny.
An intense pessimism, obscurely implicated with some sexual
morbidity, can be the predominant impression we carry away
from *Almayer's Folly*.

An Outcast of the Islands is a simpler story.* Nevertheless,
it takes twice as long in the telling, and this is not to its
advantage. In several ways, Conrad has gained a facility which
we feel might prove dangerous to him. He has mastered the
craft of writing dialogue fluently, and is insufficiently aware
of when he has written enough, and also of when he is abus-
ing the novelist's necessary liberty to make his characters a
little more fluent, a little more resourceful in a "literary"
way, than they would naturally be. He has gained skill in the

* Peter Willems is a young Dutchman working in the same commercial
house in Macassar that had formerly employed Almayer. He has made the
same sort of marriage as Almayer, and from a similar motive; his wife is a
half-caste woman whom he despises, the daughter—unknown to him—of the
merchant Hudig upon whom he depends. Willems, although impeded and
embarrassed by his wife's numerous relatives, is a confident and self-satisfied
man, much pleased with the success and promise of his own petty career. He
behaves dishonestly and is disgraced. Like Almayer, he is a protégé of Captain
Lingard's; and now Lingard carries him off and quarters him on Almayer in
the still prosperous Sambir. The two men do not get on. Willems soon conceives an overwhelming sensual passion for a native woman, Aïssa, who becomes his mistress. The situation is exploited by Almayer's native rivals, who
constrain Willems to betray the secret of the navigation of the River Pantai
to the Arab trader Abdulla. This is the first step in the ruin of Almayer—
whose daughter Nina is still a small child—and indeed of Lingard himself.
Lingard punishes Willems by condemning him to live in isolation and destitution with Aïssa, whom Willems is by this time ready to loathe for having
lured him into the position of an outcast.

But Lingard, who is always full of good intentions, has brought Willems's
wife and child to join him in Sambir, and in a final jealous confrontation
Aïssa kills her lover.

handling of intrigue, and of conventions which make his Malays and Arabs psychologically plausible; Babalatchi is very active in this story—and still as "the careworn sage," "the barbarous politician," "the savage statesman," "the one-eyed puller of wires." Above all, Conrad has increased his already notable power to exploit landscape both as a vivid back-drop and as a state of the soul. "The mere scenery got a great hold on me as I went on," he was to record(ix)—and to this he was to add that the story itself was never very near his heart.

It is a story which, in some of its main features, curiously repeats that of *Almayer's Folly*. Peter Willems is contempt-ible rather than merely weak, and to this extent he differs from Kaspar Almayer. But in the first chapter we meet him "weaving the splendid web of his future"(11) just when he has been doing a little ineffective embezzling of his em-ployer's money. So when he is planted down in Sambir, we are at least certain that he is unlikely to sustain the white man's burden with any credit, and when he and Almayer are ironically described in a squabble as "two specimens of the superior race"(63) we accept the equation as entirely just. Almayer's wife is a full-blooded Malay and Willems's is a half-caste. Both men despise their women, and fear them or fear what they stand for. But Willems, at the beginning of his story, is in the greater state of self-delusion; he enjoys patron-izing Mrs. Willems's humble relations, and prides himself upon having "no colour-prejudices and no racial antipa-thies."(35) Yet we believe as imperfectly in his overwhelming and delirious sensual infatuation for Aïssa, the native woman he finds in Sambir, as we do in the extremity of his eventual revulsion when he discovers that his association with her has made him an outcast. This is partly because his passion ex-presses itself in the most improbable rhetoric: "I am jealous of the wind that fans her," he cries, "of the air she breathes, of the earth that receives the caress of her foot."(90) It is partly because a related absurdity attends much of what the narrative tells us of his emotions: "With that look she drew the man's soul away from him through his immobile pupils, and from Willems' features the spark of reason vanished."(140) But it is chieflly because Willems, whom we are invited to do nothing but despise, is altogether too feeble a character to stand at the centre of an action in which, once more, powerful unconscious forces appear to be at work beneath the surface of the fable.

The jungle is again the place for love:

Who was she? Where did she come from? Wonderingly he took his eyes off her face to look round at the serried trees of the forest that stood big and still and straight, as if watching him and her breathlessly. He had been baffled, repelled, almost frightened by the intensity of that tropical life which wants the sunshine but works in gloom; which seems to be all grace of colour and form, all brilliance, all smiles, but is only the blossoming of the dead; whose mystery holds the promise of joy and beauty, yet contains nothing but poison and decay.(70)

From the first Willems is revolted by what is happening to him. After an early meeting with Aïssa:

His face felt burning. He drank again, and shuddered with a depraved sense of pleasure at the after-taste of slime in the water.(72)

From the first, in fact, the relationship suggests to him his own destruction:

When the longed-for day came at last, when she sank on the grass by his side and with a quick gesture took his hand in hers, he sat up suddenly with the movement and look of a man awakened by the crash of his own falling house. All his blood, all his sensation, all his life seemed to rush into that hand leaving him without strength, in a cold shiver, in the sudden clamminess and collapse as of a deadly gun-shot wound.(77)

Of this, so excessive and so incongruous with the insensitive and assured Willems we have first known, there is a great deal. When he is again drawn into "the shapeless darkness of the forest" by his passion, its lethal associations drive him almost out of his mind:

He seemed to be surrendering to a wild creature the unstained purity of his life, of his race, of his civilization. He had a notion of being lost among shapeless things that were dangerous and ghastly. He struggled with the sense of certain defeat—lost his footing—fell back into the darkness. With a faint cry and an upward throw of his arms he gave up as a tired swimmer gives up: because the swamped craft is gone from under his feet; because the night is dark and the shore is far—because death is better than strife.(80)

In this and kindred confused passages there are two implications at play. The first is that Willems is overwhelmed by the horror and shame of going native, "by the flood of hate, disgust, and contempt of a white man for that blood which is not his blood, for that race which is not his race; for the brown skins; for the hearts false like the sea, blacker than night."(152) Eventually this consciousness reduces him to hysteria: "I am white! All white!"(271) The second implication is of an order in which white and brown become irrelevant; it concerns sexuality *per se,* and can be conveyed only by the jungle-imagery at its most violent, or by reducing Willems, as at the end, to simple physical impotence and macabre imagining:

It seemed to him that he was peering into a sombre hollow, into a deep black hole full of decay and of whitened bones; into

an immense and inevitable grave full of corruption where sooner
or later he must, unavoidably, fall.(339)

We are left with the same predominant vision as in *Almayer's
Folly*: "the darkness of the forests and of the heathen souls
of the savages"(128); the creepers destroying the trees; "the
pungent, acrid smell of rotting leaves, of flowers, of blossoms
and plants dying in that poisonous and cruel gloom."(324) At
the heart of "the hallucination of the Eastern Archipelago"
lurks the eminently Western and *fin de siècle* persuasion that
in its extremity sexual desire is a death-wish; that Eros and
Thanatos are one.

Conrad, unlike Almayer and Willems, eventually escaped
from Sambir. He appears to have had an instinctive feeling
that he ought to resist being taken for granted as an exotic
writer. That he realized how limited his art might become
were he to fail in this struggle is evident in the deliberate
concessions he made to the exotic image, both at this time
and later, in short stories produced frankly to make money.
Edward Garnett, so influential a literary mentor at the outset
of his career, had by long association acquired something of a
publisher's point of view, and he seems to have discouraged
the attempted break-away from a kind of writing which was
already achieving modest success. But as a critic also—and he
was a distinguished critic—Garnett had a strong case. "The
Return," written in 1897, is a long story of considerable
ambition which attempts, in a London setting, the psychological analysis of a radically deficient marriage. Garnett appears virtually to have forbidden Conrad ever to attempt
anything of the sort again, and he was assuredly perfectly
right. If one can conceive of such a theme treated by a D. H.
Lawrence in whose hands it is totally intractable one has

some notion of this desperate performance. Conrad finished
it in a state of distraction:

> The work is vile—or else good. I don't know. I can't know. . . .
> I have a physical horror of that story. I simply won't look at it
> any more. It has embittered five months of my life. I hate it.[8]

By the time this was written Conrad had already attempted
to break new ground in a full-scale novel, *The Sisters*, which,
as we have seen, he abandoned after writing some 10,000
words. Garnett thought poorly of it, and Conrad himself,
although speaking of it as a "cherished aspiration," appears
to have realized that the attempt was doomed to failure. The
principal characters are a young Russian of humble origins
and an orphaned Spanish girl; they are discovered as neighbours in Paris, where they are presumably heading for a
love-affair; in beginning to fabricate their story, Conrad is
supposed to have been consulting experiences of his own in
Marseilles. It is Mr. Moser who has distinguished the chief
curiosity of the story: Conrad, although so resolutely in re-
treat from his Archipelago, has in fact brought his Bornean
jungle with him and planted it down in Passy. The scene is
a courtyard between the dwellings of the potential lovers:

> Below in the damp and uniform gloom the grass sprang up,
> vigorous and conquering . . . covering the ground thickly with
> a prosperous, flourishing growth in a triumph of undistinguish-
> ably similar blades that pressed thick, low, full of life around
> the foot of soaring trunks of the trees; the grass unconquerable,
> content with the gloom, disputing sustenance with the roots,
> vanquishing the slender trees that strove courageously even there
> to keep their heads in the splendour of the sunshine.[9]

What is perhaps most significant about this queerly reminiscent passage is that it is not at all well done. Whether or not
it is some obscure sexual malaise that prevents Conrad from

getting ahead with his story, it is certain that the prose of *The Sisters* is curiously devitalized and flat. We have constantly to remember that, to the end of his life, his writing English at all remained something of a tour de force; it was only when his imagination was quickened that he was confidently at home with it; his uninspired writing is thus always liable to be, in a sense, doubly bad.   ,

Whatever inhibited the development of *The Sisters*, it was upon the Archipelago, after all, that Conrad next came to feel he must rely, if there was to be any full-scale successor to *An Outcast of the Islands*. His strange struggle with "The Rescuer" was the result. Here again it is easy to associate the breakdown with an idiosyncratic inability to do something the writer quite clearly *wants* to do: to contemplate with penetration and sympathy the development of a love relationship between a white man and a white woman. But other inhibiting factors may be at work. It may be that Conrad, unlike Lewis Carroll's Bellman, felt that what he said three times was *not* true, or at least was not likely to be very exciting. Fatigue, Garnett's advice, and a false start on *The Sisters* rendered the more alarming by money worries: these may have plunged him into a story about the early adventures of Captain Lingard. That he doggedly concluded these adventures after a fashion more than twenty years later may again have been partly a matter of money, and partly a matter of that determined frugality in the employment of materials which is surprisingly prominent in the practice of many artists even greater than Conrad. And although it is true that "The Rescuer" begins rather well, it is not merely the appearance of a lady on the scene that signals trouble. Pata Hassim, "nephew of one of the greatest chiefs of the Wajo," and his sister Immada, together with their follower Jaffir, are lifted from documentary sources, bob in and out of the action in a mute and more or less inconsequent way, and contribute to our general sense that the "hallucination" which had precipitated the two earlier novels has ceased to be compulsive and is now being conjured up merely by an act of the will. When "The Rescuer" finally ground to a halt, it would have been reasonable to feel that the Far East would never again inspire the imagination of the novelist. This was not, in fact, to be the case, since less than three years later Conrad was writing the second part of *Lord Jim*. But by then he was much surer of the boundaries of his art. And in *The Nigger of the "Narcissus"* he had produced what he knew to be a masterpiece.

III

The Nigger of the "Narcissus" and "Youth"

The Rescue opens upon Captain Lingard's ship, the *Lightning,* motionless in tropical waters:

> On the unruffled surface of the straits the brig floated tranquil and upright as if bolted solidly, keel to keel, with its own image reflected in the unframed and immense mirror of the sea. To the south and east the double islands watched silently the double ship that seemed fixed amongst them for ever, a hopeless captive of the calm, a helpless prisoner of the shallow sea.(5)

And presently we see a second vessel, the schooner-yacht *Hermit,* stranded on a mudflat, "heeling over, high and motionless upon the great expanse of glittering shallows."(53) The two craft themselves compose another double image, and it might almost be a metaphor for the immobilizing power against which Conrad had to struggle as he worked on the book. On the first page of *The Nigger of the "Narcissus,"* contrastingly, a ship is ready to go to sea: the decks swept, the windlass oiled, the last wedge driven in the main-hatch battens. At the end of the chapter the ship stirs at its moorings, bringing "a gleam of alert understanding"(26) to the features—until this moment "unthinking, reposeful and hopeless"—of the old seaman Singleton. On the next morning the *Narcissus* sails from Bombay, bound for London. Upon this voyage Conrad's genius comes into its own.

As a consequence of this enlargement of creative power, *The Nigger of the "Narcissus"* exhibits a larger thematic complexity than do the earlier novels, and thus becomes the first of Conrad's works to invite the sophisticated exegesis characteristic of much contemporary criticism. Yet we falsify the predominant effect if we make, as it were, a bee-line for some interpretation of this sort. Mr. Leo Gurko, for example, tells us that "the voyage of the *Narcissus*, from start to finish, is a penetration into the tensions, powers and mysteries of death," [1] and he digs out of the text—what is indeed easy enough—an astonishing profusion of mortuary imagery. But although the narrative has as its climax the death of the Nigger, James Wait, it is not, like Lawrence's great poem, a threnody: "Oh build your ship of death, oh build it . . ." Indeed Mr. Guerard, a subtler critic and one ready with an interpretation of his own, has no difficulty in exhibiting an equally crucial passage—the rescuing of Wait from the flooded deck-house—as the symbolical enactment of a birth.[2] Another commentator, Mr. Vernon Young (who believes that Wait is so named because he becomes a burden), is clear that there is a schematic relationship with "the subaqueous world of the underconsciousness," and reproves Conrad for playing down the arcane significances of his story.[3] It is perhaps true that, at a later date, Conrad approached disingenuousness in his insistence on the simplicity of moral stance his story was designed to enforce. In *Last Essays* he records with satisfaction how Stephen Crane appreciated his "effort to present a group of men held together by a common loyalty and a common perplexity in a struggle not with human enemies, but with the hostile conditions testing their faithfulness to the conditions of their own calling." [4] The least assuming criticism must find far more in *The Nigger of the "Narcissus"* than this reading of men and their work in Kipling's manner: "youthful faces, bearded faces, dark faces: faces serene, or faces moody, but all akin with the brotherhood of the sea; all with the same attentive expression of eyes, carefully watching the compass or the sails."(30) Nevertheless what Conrad here declares to be present *is* present—and is indeed far more immediately present than anything else. "There was no leisure for idle probing of hearts. Sails blew adrift. Things broke loose."(53) The service of the sea—"glorious and obscure," as it is called again and again—is a moral discipline in itself:

The men working about the decks were healthy and contented —as most seamen are, when once well out to sea. The true peace of God begins at any spot a thousand miles from the nearest land; and when He sends there the messengers of His might it is not in terrible wrath against crime, presumption, and folly, but paternally, to chasten simple hearts—ignorant hearts that know nothing of life, and beat undisturbed by envy or greed.

In the evening the cleared decks had a reposeful aspect, resembling the autumn of the earth . . .(31)

An appreciation of the book must begin from the forthrightness of its sentiment and the frankness of its eloquence. It is to these that other things are added.

Although Conrad did not agonize over this short novel as he was to do over much of his writing, it was the product of very great concentration, of an unflagging exercise of conscious art, and there is evidence that some passages were rewritten many times.[5] The narrative is constantly enriched with simile, and frequently with metaphor, to a point that

approaches saturation. The ship, "a high and lonely pyra-
mid,"(27) "a toy in the hand of a lunatic,"(53) "a great tired
bird speeding to its nest,"(161) pursues its varying fortune
over and beneath immensities: "the sea that stretching away
on all sides merged into the illimitable silence of all creation . . . immense and hazy, like the image of life, with a
glittering surface and lightless depths"(147, 155); the stars
that "remote in the eternal calm . . . glittered hard and cold
above the uproar of the earth . . . surrounded the vanquished
and tormented ship on all sides: more pitiless than the eyes
of a triumphant mob, and as unapproachable as the hearts of
men."(77) Yet this richness of effect is not at all indigestible
in a total impression, since it is varied and controlled by so
vigilant and patient an artistry. The long passage describing
the rescue of Wait during the storm has a grotesque quality
which is matched and furthered by the bizarre imagery: the
Finn, Wamibo, "all shining eyes, gleaming fangs, tumbled
hair; resembling an amazed and half-witted fiend gloating
over the extraordinary agitation of the dammed"(66); Wait
himself, screaming "piercingly, without drawing breath, like
a tortured woman"(67); the rescuers who, pressing round
him, "on the very brink of eternity . . . tottered all together
with concealing and absurd gestures, like a lot of drunken
men embarrassed with a stolen corpse"(71); the first mate
Mr. Baker, of whom it is recorded (in a related figure) that
"in the dark and on all fours he resembled some carnivorous
animal prowling amongst corpses."(78) But when we move
from this scene to the long paragraph at the end of Chapter
Three in which Conrad describes the righting of the ship
after the storm—one of the great places in his prose—we find
a use of figurative language which is both more sparing and
more restrained. The images are no longer reached out for
with conscious virtuosity; rather they gather, in their sugges-

tion, closer to the enacted scene itself. The foam is "as dazzling and white as a field of snow."(87) Water topples over the rail "with a rush of a river falling over a dam."(88) The vessel is "spouting thick streams of water through every opening of her wounded sides."(88) All the remaining images belong with this last one, emphasizing the ship's kinship to a sentient being—"enduring and valiant,"(49) as she has been called earlier. She goes off slowly, as though "weary and disheartened like the men she carried"(87); her torn canvas streams in the wind "like wisps of hair"(88); she runs "blindly, dishevelled and headlong, as if fleeing for her life."(88) But this sustained metaphor—the merit of which, in its place, is its centrality and obviousness—is balanced by a vivid particularity of concrete narration. In this there is just enough of nautical terminology to suggest the writer's authority without bringing any consciousness of perplexity to a reader without special knowledge of the sea. The whole description fuses suspense with momentum in a completely masterly way—finally to focus upon Singleton, thirty hours at the wheel, and to conclude with the short sentence upon which the whole book pivots: "He steered with care."(89)

The imagery might still be excessive were it not constantly borne forward on a strong, varied, and individual prose rhythm; through the instrumentality, that is, of the "unremitting never-discouraged care for the shape and ring of sentences"(ix) which Conrad speaks of in his Preface. It is this, too, that carries the audacities of sentiment, the unashamed and as it were antique magniloquence upon which a native English writer, more conscious of the hazards of boldly heightened prose, might not have ventured. This pitch sounds early in the book, in the great commemoration of a "devoured and forgotten generation" of men dedicated to the sea:

They had been strong, as those are strong who know neither doubts nor hopes. They had been impatient and enduring, turbulent and devoted, unruly and faithful. . . . Men hard to manage, but easy to inspire; voiceless men—but men enough to scorn in their hearts the sentimental voices that bewailed the hardness of their fate. It was a fate unique and their own; the capacity to bear it appeared to them the privilege of the chosen! Their generation lived inarticulate and indispensable, without knowing the sweetness of affections or the refuge of a home— and died free from the dark menace of a narrow grave. They were the everlasting children of the mysterious sea. Their successors are the grown-up children of a discontented earth.(25) [6]

The transition in the last sentence (with its accompanying lowering of the rhetorical pitch) may suggest a sense in which Conrad's own voice can be called "sentimental." The essential vision of *The Nigger of the "Narcissus"* is of the ship on its hazardous voyage as a microcosm both of man in nature and man in society. Her crew are a mixed lot. "On her lived timid truth and audacious lies; and, like the earth, she was unconscious, fair to see—and condemned by men to an ignoble fate."(30) But Conrad, however intermittent was his personal devotion to the sea, was emotionally and imaginatively committed to an exalted sense of the seaman's vocation. Here and elsewhere, therefore, he is inclined to set "sea" and "land" over against each other with an absoluteness which may strike us as facile and romantic. At the beginning of the novel we hear of the "infamy and filth . . . that comes down on all sides to the water's edge of the incorruptible ocean."(6) And at the close (after, indeed, a noble and elevated apostrophe to England: but this under the figure of "the great flagship of the race"), as the *Narcissus* comes up the Thames:

A low cloud hung before her—a great opalescent and tremulous cloud, that seemed to rise from the steaming brows of millions of men. Long drifts of smoky vapours soiled it with livid trails; it throbbed to the beat of millions of hearts, and from it came an immense and lamentable murmur—the murmur of millions of lips praying, cursing, sighing, jeering—the undying murmur of folly, regret, and hope exhaled by the crowds of the anxious earth. The *Narcissus* entered the cloud; the shadows deepened; on all sides there was the clang of iron, the sound of mighty blows, shrieks, yells. Black barges drifted stealthily on the murky stream. A mad jumble of begrimed walls loomed up vaguely in the smoke, bewildering and mournful, like a vision of disaster.(163-4)

Those who go down to the sea, and the ships in which they do so, are susceptible of varying evaluations. Dr. Johnson believed that "no man will be a sailor who has contrivance enough to get himself into a jail; for being in a ship is being in a jail, with the chance of being drowned." He added that "a man in jail has more room, better food, and commonly better company," and in his *Dictionary* took the prosaic view that a ship may be defined as "a large hollow building, made to pass over the sea with sails." We do not have to admit this degree of disenchantment to feel that Conrad a little too readily idealizes the sea at the expense of the land. In this some critics see the occasion of a sentimentality vitiating one of his major novels, *Chance*.

In its aspect as the celebration of a way of life, then, *The Nigger of the "Narcissus"* may be described as belonging (although the expression must seem an odd one) to the pastoral tradition in literature. A refined artistic medium is used to persuade us that it is precisely people without refinement— people rude, simple, and close to the elemental facts of nature —whom we ought most to admire in our society. We ought even to envy these seamen. Preserved by their calling and humble station from the pitfalls of a more sophisticated life ashore, they are innocent as we are not—and such innocence is the true happiness, however hard the toil by which it is maintained. And to this immemorial theme of Arcadia is added at least a hint of another: that of the Golden Age. Compared with our way of life, the seafaring life is good, yet it is not quite so good today as it was yesterday. Singleton, the "sixty-year-old child of the mysterious sea,"(26) cannot write his own name, and is judged "a disgusting old brute"(169) by the clerk in the shipping office. But by his fellows on the *Narcissus* he is respected as a survivor from an age sterner than their own, and one breeding better men.

But it is not by dwelling on these somewhat conventional facets of the story that we shall arrive at the essence of *The Nigger of the "Narcissus"*—any more than it is by treating the action and characters primarily as transparencies through which we can gaze at some overworld, or underworld, of archetypal images and cabalistic significances. ("Cabalistic" is Mr. Young's word for Conrad's "intent.") For the essence *is* the action—just such a single and completed action as classical criticism declares that every epic narrative ought ideally to be. But although what is really "there" is just what is placed concretely before us, the spectacle is yet in a high degree representative. The ship's complement is made up by chance; friends and strangers answer to their names as Mr. Baker calls the roll; personality reacts to personality in a manner that may be fateful for all. Scarcely a man who is given a face, a name, or a voice is other than a unique human being. But although each carries his own individuality, his own ultimate mystery, each is one in whom we recognize ourselves. And so with the voyage, the struggle to bring the *Narcissus* from India to England. It is a heightened struggle, and beyond anything that most of us have known. "In an unendurable and unending strain they worked like men driven by a merciless dream to toil in an atmosphere of ice and flame."(92) We acknowledge the image of the human condition, all the same. The voyage ends; it is a triumph; yet the heroes, as they take their wage and—innocent and estranged in the heart of London—make their bewildered way to pubs, brothels, families barely remembered: the heroes are also among those that in our hearts we still know.

It is in *The Nigger of the "Narcissus"* that Conrad, for the first time, brings central characters fully alive. Neither Almayer nor Willems has much real vitality, or even solidity; their creator's relationship to them is disadvantageous; they purport to be dispassionate studies in insufficiency and failure, and at the same time actually draw any dynamic they have from being unlikely *Doppelgänger* of a Joseph Conrad whose response to exile is not strong and positive, but negative and utterly feeble. They have only a kind of ectoplasmic life, as of spooks or bogies. But Wait and Donkin—the Nigger and his treacherous toady—are finely realized objective creations. They seem to have come alive on Conrad as he wrote, for neither begins very well. Wait is introduced to us as bearing "the tragic, the mysterious, the repulsive mask of a nigger's soul"(18)—and by the time we read this we already know "mysterious" to be a word Conrad overworks badly. A few pages earlier, Donkin has been introduced in a set description:

They all knew him! He was the man that cannot steer, that cannot splice, that dodges the work on dark nights; that, aloft, holds on frantically with both arms and legs, and swears at the wind, the sleet, the darkness; the man who curses the sea while others work. The man who is the last out and the first in when all hands are called. The man who can't do most things and won't do the rest. The pet of philanthropists and self-seeking land-lubbers. The sympathetic and deserving creature that knows all about his rights, but knows nothing of courage, of endurance, and of the unexpressed faith, of the unspoken loyalty that knits together a ship's company. The independent offspring of the ignoble freedom of the slums full of disdain and hate for the austere servitude of the sea.(10-11)

It is a portrait without much light and shade, and Donkin appears later in the same flat, cold light—the eternal agitator as he exists in a conservative imagination; we read of the crew that "inspired by Donkin's hopeful doctrines they dreamed enthusiastically of the time when every lonely ship would travel over a serene sea, manned by a wealthy and well-fed crew of satisfied skippers."(103) But the manner in which Donkin and Wait—the latter without intending much mischief, or doing more than exploit a malingering attitude in order to conceal from himself a terrifying truth—the manner in which these two come near to destroying that "unspoken loyalty" which their fellows acknowledge: this is a matter of far more subtle art. Both men become potentially destructive forces through attaching to themselves an unwholesome because essentially self-regarding sympathy. Donkin comes on board destitute, with "no bed, no blanket," and the crew, as they toss him this and that, are "touched by their own readiness to alleviate a shipmate's misery."(12) When Wait is saved from death through a prodigious exercise of bravery, he responds with gross ingratitude, taunting his rescuers with "funk" because they did not come sooner. But although the crew already hate him, it is in an ambivalent and fascinated way, and when the captain orders him to continue to lie up, they identify themselves with his spurious grievance at once, even to the verge of mutiny. As the mortal

nature of his malady becomes clearer, so does the crew's
attitude become essentially more corrupt:

The latent egoism of tenderness to suffering appeared in the
developing anxiety not to see him die. . . . He was demoralising.
Through him we were becoming highly humanised, tender, complex, execessively decadent: we understood the sublety of his
fear, sympathised with all his repulsions, shrinkings, evasions,
delusions—as though we had been over-civilised, and rotten, and
without any knowledge of the meaning of life. We had the air
of being initiated in some infamous mysteries; we had the profound grimaces of conspirators, exchanged meaning glances, significant short words. We were inexpressibly vile and very much
pleased with ourselves.(138-9)

It is hard doctrine, and driven home by the action. But not
everybody has the same attitude to Wait; and two men, at
very different promptings, brutally tell him he is going to die.
Podmore the cook is a selfless and devoted man, and his
religious fervour prompts him to cry out at the height of the
tempest, "imploring in that storm the Master of our lives not
to lead him into temptation." His religious fervour also fills
him with the conceit of the saved and favoured, and he has
marked down Wait as a brand to snatch from the burning.
The account of his attempt is given in a key of macabre
comedy which Conrad has not commanded before:

"Don't you see the everlasting fire . . . don't you feel it? Blind,
chockfull of sin! Repent, repent! I can't bear to think of you.
I hear the call to save you. Night and day. Jimmy, let me save
you!" The words of entreaty and menace broke out of him in a
roaring torrent. The cockroaches ran away. Jimmy perspired,
wriggling stealthily under his blanket. The cook yelled. . . .
"Your days are numbered! . . . "—"Get out of this," boomed
Wait, courageously.—"Pray with me! . . ."—"I won't! . . ." The

little cabin was as hot as an oven. It contained an immensity of
fear and pain. . . .

But the grotesque scene continues, with the whole crew
crowded outside the closed door:

All hands were there. The watch below had jumped out on
deck in their shirts, as after a collision. Men running up, asked:
—"What is it?" Others said:—"Listen!" The muffled screaming
went on:—"On your knees! On your knees!"—"Shut up!"—"Never!
You are delivered into my hands. . . . Your life has been saved. . . .
Purpose. . . . Mercy. . . . Repent."—"You are a crazy fool! . . ."—
"Account of you . . . you . . . Never sleep in this world, if I . . ."
—"Leave off."—"No! . . . stokehold . . . only think! . . ." Then
an impassioned screeching babble where words pattered like
hail.—"No!" shouted Wait.—"Yes. You are! . . . No help. . . .
Everybody says so."—"You lie!"—"I see you dying this minnyt . . .
before my eyes . . . as good as dead already."—"Help!" shouted
Jimmy, piercingly.—"Not in this valley . . . look upwards,"
howled the other.—"Go away! Murder! Help!" clamoured
Jimmy.(116-7)

Later it is Donkin who sits by Wait—not to save his soul, but
to rifle his sea-chest the moment he is dead. Wait offers
Donkin one of two biscuits (the crew is now on very short
rations) and murmurs something about being ashore in ten
days. Donkin's malignity is stirred:

"Ten days. Strike me blind if I ever! . . . You will be dead
by this time tomorrow p'r'aps. Ten days!" He waited for a while.
"D'ye 'ear me? Blamme if yer don't look dead already."
Wait must have been collecting his strength for he said almost
aloud—"You're a stinking, cadging liar. Every one knows you."
And sitting up, against all probablity, startled his visitor horribly.
But very soon Donkin recovered himself. He blustered,
"What? What? Who's a liar? You are—the crowd are—the
skipper—everybody. I ain't! Putting on airs! Who's yer?" He

nearly choked himself with indignation. "Who's yer to put on airs," he repeated, trembling. " 'Ave one—'ave one, says 'ee—an' cawn't eat 'em 'isself. Now I'll 'ave both. By Gawd—I will. Yer nobody!"

He plunged into the lower bunk, rooted in there and brought to light another dusty biscuit. He held it up before Jimmy—then took a bite defiantly.

"What now?" he asked with feverish impudence. "Yer may take one—says yer. Why not give me both? No. I'm a mangy dorg. One fur a mangy dorg. I'll tyke both. Can yer stop me? Try. Come on. Try."

Jimmy was clasping his legs and hiding his face on the knees. His shirt clung to him. Every rib was visible. His emaciated back was shaken in repeated jerks by the panting catches of his breath.

"Yer won't? Yer can't! What did I say?" went on Donkin, fiercely. He swallowed another dry mouthful with a hasty effort. The other's silent helplessness, his weakness, his shrinking attitude exasperated him. "Ye're done!" he cried. "Who's yer to be lied to; to be waited on 'and an' foot like a bloomin' ymperor. Yer nobody. Yer no one at all!" he spluttered with such a strength of unerring conviction that it shook him from head to foot in coming out, and left him vibrating like a released string.(150-1)

Such prove to be the comforts of the proud and lonely Nigger's last moments on earth. Donkin puts his ear to Jimmy's lips, and hears "a sound like the rustle of a single dry leaf driven along the smooth sand of a beach."(154) Jimmy is asking for the lighting of a lamp which is already burning brilliantly. Donkin reaches for the key of the seachest, knowing that his opportunity has come. As he leaves the cabin with his spoil, he turns for a second and sees Jimmy's eyes "blaze up and go out at once, like two lamps overturned together by a sweeping blow."(155) The Nigger of the *Narcissus* is dead. "I belong to the ship,"(18) he had said on stepping on board. But it is when he leaves her again

—with a weird hesitation, since in the apparatus for committal the carpenter has left an awkwardly protruding nail— that the breeze for which the *Narcissus* has been waiting comes. "The sails filled, the ship gathered way, and the waking sea began to murmur sleepily of home to the ears of men."(161) Old Singleton does not fail to remark this new warrant for an ancient seafaring superstition. We might be less tolerant of it ourselves but for the brilliant authenticity of the grotesque scene leading up to it.

The Nigger of the "Narcissus" was to remain the finest of Conrad's writings centered on the sea. Its fusion of epic and dramatic qualities; its further subtle superaddition, here and there, of an elegiac tone; the controlled richness of its facture as instanced not only in the fullness and precision of its descriptive and emotive prose but also in the fine gradations of its characterization from the roundness of Jimmy Wait, Donkin, Singleton through the substantial forms of Podmore, Belfast, Archie to the softened but authentic outlines—as if in a kind of aerial perspective—of the three officers, the carpenter, the Finn Wamibo, and the twinned and nameless Swedes: all this makes the book Conrad's masterpiece in the strictest sense, since with it he presents his claim, once and for all, to stand with the great writers of English fiction. Compared with it "Youth," which was completed a little more than a year later, is not only a slighter narrative of the sea but also one of markedly lesser resonance. It has an important place, nevertheless, in the development of Conrad's art.

The Nigger of the "Narcissus" purports to be related by a member of the crew: a fact intimated by the use of the word "we" and once or twice of the word "I." The only positive fact we learn of this narrator is that he was one of those who went to the rescue of the Nigger in his deck-house; but we have to conclude, of course, that he is educated and articulate, and that he has strayed into a fo'c'sle through necessities unknown. We catch in his voice no hint of anything dramatic or personative, no suggestion that he has been created to interpose, between the author and ourselves, the artistic illusion of independent observation and comment. Deeply considered though the novel is, there is little evidence that Conrad had at this time given much thought to the problems of "point of view." In the very month of his finishing the book he had received a copy of *The Spoils of Poynton* from its author; he may well have read *What Maisie Knew* almost immediately thereafter; and within a couple of years he is displaying in a letter to Galsworthy a sensitive understanding of James's art.[7] But the period of his actually being influenced by James in technical matters still lies well ahead, and *The Nigger of the "Narcissus"* shows a thoroughly Victorian disregard of centres of consciousness and the like. We find ourselves listening to conversations which the narrator could not have heard, and at times we are even securely planted inside James Wait's head.

The arrival of Marlow on the first page of "Youth" portends a complete revolution in this regard. It is unlikely, indeed, that Conrad was aware of this, since the device with which he starts off is a very simple one. "Marlow (at least I think that is how he spelt his name) told the story, or rather the chronicle, of a voyage,"(3) we read—and then Marlow's voice takes over and continues without interruption until, on the last page of the story, the formal framework is restored in a single, slightly portentous, paragraph. And what we have heard is nothing except the impact of certain early experiences on Marlow (who is now forty-two) himself. The mood invoked, as the Author's Note contrives to imply, is "of wistful regret, of reminiscent tenderness." [8] But the point of major significance is clear. In *The Nigger of the "Narcissus"* we can only imagine the narrator as one who has sat at a desk and written for us. In "Youth" there is again, in theory, such a person: the "I" who began life in the merchant service, who listens to Marlow along with the director, the accountant and the lawyer, and who must be conceived as subsequently recording for us what Marlow had to say. But essentially we are listening to a speaking voice. We are to listen to the same voice in "Heart of Darkness," *Lord Jim,* and *Chance.* In "Youth" it is simply to Marlow himself that things happen. In "Heart of Darkness" and *Lord Jim* they happen chiefly to other people, but a large part of the interest lies in Marlow's essentially dramatic relationship to them. In *Chance* much of this more subtle interest is withdrawn: Marlow records and comments, but his own personality is not really involved, or felt to be at risk. The four Marlow narratives thus vary greatly in density.

"Youth," however, has its own complexity—a fact of which one is aware as soon as one attempts to attach a label to it, whether of kind or of tone. In compass no more than a *conte,* it is in essence *une recherche du temps perdu,* and its note in places is predominantly elegiac. When the luckless *Judea* and its cargo of coal have finally gone down in smoke and flame, and when Marlow, in the 14-foot boat which is his first command, has brought his two men and a bag of biscuits to the coast of Java:

I remember the drawn faces, the dejected figures of my two men, and I remember my youth and the feeling that will never come back any more—the feeling that I could last for ever, outlast the sea, the earth, and all men; the deceitful feeling that lures us on to joys, to perils, to love, to vain effort—to death;

the triumphant conviction of strength, the heat of life in the
handful of dust, the glow in the heart that with every year grows
dim, grows cold, grows small, and expires—and expires, too soon,
too soon—before life itself.(36-7)

But the tone is also lyrical; even in this passage it is subtly
so; and indeed the fusion is percurrent:

O youth! The strength of it, the faith of it, the imagination
of it! To me she was not an old rattletrap carting about the
world a lot of coal for a freight—to me she was the endeavour,
the test, the trial of life. I think of her with pleasure, with affection, with regret—as you would think of someone dead you
have loved. I shall never forget her.(12)

We could, of course, rather quickly have too much of this.
And perhaps there is too much. Yet it is the breadth and
boldness of Conrad's art in this first period of its efflorescence
that sounds in the reiterated apostrophes. There is nothing
sentimental about "Youth." Moreover, the heroic is granted
no admittance whatever. For the young Marlow is not interested in that. He sees the successive perils of sailing in a
ship like the *Judea* as being so much adventure, so much fun
—and so much opportunity for a new second mate to do not
badly, and be pleased with himself in consequence. Moreover, Marlow is not the commonplace gently-bred but tough
junior officer whom we have met in the Creighton of *The
Nigger of the "Narcissus."* Young or middle-aged, he is quite
as intelligent as his creator, and quite as fond of articulate
speech: does he not spend the remains of three months' pay—
after he has had a single splendid night out in London and
bought a railway rug—on a complete set of Byron's works?
And the Byronic is his own note to the extent that he has a
considerable capacity for finding things entertaining and
exhibiting them as that. The rats, which have continued to

live perfectly happily on the *Judea* during her desperate and absurd attempts to sail for Bangkok while leaking like a sieve, promptly and perversely (but, as the event proves, with prescience) desert her as soon as she is "recaulked, new coppered, and made as tight as a bottle":

We had been infested with them. They had destroyed our sails, consumed more stores than the crew, affably shared our beds and our dangers, and now, when the ship was made sea-worthy, concluded to clear out. . . . Rat after rat appeared on our rail, took a last look over his shoulder, and leaped with a hollow thud into the empty hulk.(17)

We can believe in that last look over the shoulder, yet it adds agreeably to the absurdity of the occasion. Mildly shocking things happen on the *Judea*. During one of her misadventures the steward goes "completely and for ever mad."(13) During another of them (the definitive one) Marlow himself is blown sky-high, and his hair, eyebrows, and eyelashes vanish. Her last hours are perpetually attended by effects of farce. "It was our fate to pump in that ship, to pump out of her, to pump into her: and after keeping water out of her to save ourselves from being drowned, we frantically poured water into her to save ourselves from being burnt."(20) As the ship's end draws near, Captain Beard—enjoying, at sixty and in this shocking old tub, the pleasures and responsibilities of a first command—becomes a figure of high comedy. And his crew respond nobly. He drops comfortably off to sleep on the deck of a vessel it may be suicidal not to abandon at once; the men sit round an open case, "eating bread and cheese and drinking bottled stout."(33) All this is the perfect complement to what "Youth" so boldly says again and again:

Oh, the glamour of youth! Oh, the fire of it, more dazzling than the flames of the burning ship, throwing a magic light on

the wide earth, leaping audaciously to the sky, presently to be
quenched by time, more cruel, more pitiless, more bitter than
the sea—and like the flames of the burning ship surrounded by
an impenetrable night.(30)

IV

"Heart of Darkness," "Typhoon," and "The End of the Tether"

"An Outpost of Progress," one of Conrad's earliest short stories, is about two Europeans left in charge of an isolated and unimportant trading station far up an African river. They are well-meaning men, and when their chief native assistant sells the remainder of their staff into slavery in exchange for some ivory, they are at first horrified and indignant. But their morale has already begun to decline, and they soon acquiesce in the situation and take charge of the elephants' tusks so unscrupulously acquired. "It's deplorable," one of them says, "but, the men being Company's men the ivory is Company's ivory. We must look after it." *Tales of Unrest,*(106) The incident accelerates their disintegration. When their stores run out, they have an absurd quarrel over some lumps of sugar, and as a consequence one of them shoots the other and then hangs himself.

Technically, "An Outpost of Progress" is an immature story. The initial situation is stated rather than dramatized, and the conclusion is huddled and melodramatic. Yet the generalized account of Kayerts, Carlier, and their plight is full of point:

They were two perfectly insignificant and incapable individuals, whose existence is only rendered possible through the high organization of civilized crowds. Few men realize that their life, the very essence of their character, their capabilities and their audacities, are only the expression of their belief in the safety of their surroundings. The courage, the composure, the confidence; the emotions and principles; every great and every insignificant thought belongs not to the individual but to the crowd: to the crowd that believes blindly in the irresistible force of its institutions and of its morals, in the power of its police and of its opinion. But the contact with pure unmitigated savagery, with primitive nature and primitive man, brings sudden and profound trouble into the heart. To the sentiment of being alone of one's kind, to the clear perception of the loneliness of one's thoughts, of one's sensations—to the negation of the habitual, which is safe, there is added the affirmation of the unusual, which is dangerous; a suggestion of things vague, uncontrollable, and repulsive, whose discomposing intrusion excites the imagination and tries the civilized nerves of the foolish and the wise alike.(89)

We may view this as looking back at Almayer and Willems, both studies of "perfectly insignificant and incapable individuals" hopelessly outmatched by their savage surroundings. That it also looks forward to "Heart of Darkness" and *Lord Jim* is accented in the description of Kayerts and Carlier after they have condoned the slave-trading:

It was not the absolute and dumb solitude of the post that impressed them so much as an inarticulate feeling that something from within them was gone, something that worked for their safety, and had kept the wilderness from interfering with their hearts. The images of home; the memory of people like them, of men that thought and felt as they used to think and feel, receded into distances made indistinct by the glare of unclouded sunshine. And out of the great silence of the surrounding wilderness, its very hoplessness and savagery seemed to approach them nearer, to draw them gently, to look upon them, to envelop them with a solicitude irresistible, familiar, and disgusting.(107-8)

Carlier (shortly before getting himself killed over the lump of sugar) has declared "the necessity of exterminating all the niggers before the country could be made habitable."(108) This is precisely what Kurtz in "Heart of Darkness" scribbles at the last on the printed page of his edifying report to the International Society for the Suppression of Savage Customs: "Exterminate all the brutes!"(*Youth, and Two Other Stories,* 118)

"Heart of Darkness," in fact, is a reworking of the theme of "An Outpost of Progress," with incomparably enhanced power. Yet, in modified form, the weakness of the first story remains the weakness of the second. In "An Outpost of Progress" too much of the wider significance of the fable is established for us merely in an authorial commentary; what the story "says" is not adequately conveyed as a direct reverberation of the presented facts. In "Heart of Darkness" the commentary, the evaluation, is, indeed, cunningly withdrawn within the framework of the illusion, since it comes to us from the narrator, Marlow, upon whose emotions—and, one may say, upon the very structure of whose personality— the recounted experiences heavily bear. Yet the result renders the same effect of an inadequate immediacy and precision at crucial points in the enacted scene. Kurtz, whose corruption and disintegration while isolated among savages is the formal centre of the story, comes to us a little too much as an interest, an absorption, a nightmare inside Marlow's head.

Consider, for example, how cunningly yet evasively, at the moment at which we feel direct encounter must at last take place, we are offered instead the nameless young Russian in his symbolical harlequin's rags—Kurtz's only disciple, and innocent to the extent of being a kind of Fool of God. It would be inapposite to expect of Conrad an ocular proof of the fallen Kurtz's "monstrous passions," "inconceivable ceremonies," "unspeakable rites," [1] and so on; and indeed Marlow himself is nowhere constrained to witness anything of the sort. The most we see—and that at long range, through Marlow's binoculars—is a row of human heads which the respected correspondent of the International Society for the Suppression of Savage Customs has set up to embellish his residence. Perhaps it ought to be enough. Yet the heavily atmospheric and suggestive way of going about the invocation of "things vague, uncontrollable, and repulsive" (to re-quote the earlier story) is often in danger of getting out of hand, so that "the incomprehensible, which is also detestable,"(50) is urged upon our attention at once too insistently and too vaguely. As Marlow moves, so he gazes: "deeper and deeper into the heart of darkness."(95) In the circumstances, it would no doubt be unreasonable to expect him to see very much. The trouble is, perhaps, that he seems to gain an obscure emotional satisfaction from the gestures of helplessness he is forced to make. Dr. Leavis, here sharpening the indictment and turning it upon Conrad himself, says that "he is intent on making a virtue out of not knowing what he means." [2] It is certainly true that portentousness is throughout the main danger hovering over the story. "Heart of Darkness" remains, nevertheless, one of Conrad's greatest things.

The narrative itself is fairly simple. Marlow is appointed to the command of a river-steamer plying between trading stations far up the Congo. (The river is not actually named.

The "rapacious and pitiless folly"(65) which is to form the background of his story was being perpetrated as he wrote by the servants of an actual European monarch. Conrad maintains an ironical convention of non-reference to this.) The first stages of Marlow's journey acquaint him with the ruthless exploitation of native populations that is going on, and of the utter meanness of its agents. He is the more interested when he hears of Kurtz, a successful trader who has for long been isolated in a remote station, and who is said to possess high ideals and to be a "civilizing genius."(79) The other traders are jealous of Kurtz—so much so that the steamer which Marlow is to take over has been scuttled in order to delay the relieving of Kurtz, who they hope will thus be driven to a breakdown. This has in fact already happened. When Marlow refloats his vessel and gets to Kurtz, it is to find that he has assumed divine attributes and is now mortally ill after for long having indulged himself in unimaginable depravities. He is brought on board the steamer, tries to escape back to his evil courses, is again brought on board, and dies on the voyage down-stream. Marlow later visits in Europe the woman to whom Kurtz has been engaged, and who believes in the unimpaired loftiness of his character. She asks Marlow what had been his last words, and Marlow, although he detests a lie as something holding "a taint of death,"(82) declares that Kurtz had died uttering her name. In fact, his last words had been more to the point, for he had cried out "The horror! The horror!"(149) Marlow regards this as having been "an affirmation, a moral victory!"(151) Kurtz at least dies knowing, so to speak, what he has been about. In terms of Catholic theology—although Marlow is unconcerned with this—Kurtz may be imagined as having achieved an act of contrition.

The portrait of Kurtz, and the enigma of the obscure kinship which Marlow comes to feel with him, derive a large part of their effect from Marlow's contrasting attitude to the other traders. The theatre in which these mean and predatory scoundrels operate is utterly horrifying. Niched in enclaves of supposed civilization "with names like Gran' Bassam, Little Popo; names that seemed to belong to some sordid farce acted in front of a sinister back-cloth"(61); regardlessly implicated in futilities and cruelties of which we are given vivid glimpses in the French man-of-war "firing into a continent,"(62) the chain gang, the Negroes from whom no more labour can be extracted left to die of disease and starvation as if in "the gloomy circle of some Inferno"(66); seeming to exude "a taint of imbecile rapacity . . . like a whiff from some corpse"(76): the "pilgrims," as Conrad calls them, are utterly despicable in a manner that yet remains finite and comprehensible. They represent everything that is hateful in modern acquisitive society; compared with them, the native crew of the steamer (although cannibals and uncommonly hungry) are models of dignity and self-control. But although Marlow is revolted by them, he is not disturbed. Kurtz, although a "hollow man" just as these are hollow men, is a different matter.

Marlow has voyaged thousands of miles to meet the traders, but Kurtz is found at the end of a further journey—a journey that is "like travelling back to the earliest beginnings of the world."(92) And it is now that Marlow is alerted to a danger against which he has never thought to arm himself; the danger to which Kurtz, "an emissary of pity, and science, and progress, and devil knows what else,"(79) will prove to have succumbed. At first it is heard as something in the darkness, far away: "At night sometimes the roll of drums behind the curtain of trees would run up the river and remain sustained faintly, as if hovering in the air high over our heads, till the first break of day."(95) Then it presents itself as a recurrent irruption of a Stone Age, quasi-Dionysiac revel:

But suddenly, as we struggled round a bend, there would be a glimpse of rush walls, of peaked grass-roofs, a burst of yells, a whirl of black limbs, a mass of hands clapping, of feet stamping, of bodies swaying, of eyes rolling, under the droop of heavy and motionless foliage. The steamer toiled along slowly on the edge of a black and incomprehensible frenzy. The prehistoric man was cursing us, praying to us, welcoming us—who could tell? We were cut off from the comprehension of our surroundings; we glided past like phantoms, wondering and secretly appalled, as sane men would be before an enthusiastic outbreak in a madhouse. . . . (95-6)

It was unearthly, and the men were— No, they were not inhuman. Well, you know, that was the worst of it—this suspicion of their not being inhuman. It would come slowly to one. They howled and leaped, and spun, and made horrid faces; but what thrilled you was just the thought of their humanity—like yours—the thought of your remote kinship with this wild and passionate uproar. Ugly. Yes, it was ugly enough; but if you were man enough, you would admit to yourself that there was in you just the faintest trace of a response to the terrible frankness of that noise, a dim suspicion of there being a meaning in it which you —you so remote from the night of first ages—could comprehend. . . . You wonder I didn't go ashore for a howl and a dance? Well, no—I didn't. Fine sentiments, you say? Fine sentiments, be hanged! I had no time.(96-7)

Marlow, in fact, contrives to witness very little in the way of this savage spectacle—and always from the deck of his steamer, where he has a difficult job on hand. Nevertheless, atavistic impulses stir mysteriously in his heart; he feels the "fascination of the abomination"(50); is grateful when his civilized professional sense finds itself responding to the tattered volume he so oddly finds in the wilderness: *"An Inquiry into some Points of Seamanship,* by a man Tower, Towson—some such name."(99) Kurtz, for long held at close quarters with the darkness of native life, has succumbed to it. "The wilderness had patted him on the head . . . it had caressed him, and —lo!—he had withered; it had taken him, loved him, embraced him, got into his veins, consumed his flesh, and sealed his soul to its own by the inconceivable ceremonies of some devilish initiation."(115)

In terms of the surface situation, there is something altogether excessive about this, and it may well be that our acceptance of it today is further impaired by a sense that modern anthropology and psychology have to some extent invalidated Conrad's assumptions about "savages" as representing a direct ancestry upon which we may disastrously regress. Conrad is certainly in difficulty with Kurtz's subjects or worshippers, and shows on the whole great artistic skill in always arresting them as he does on the margins of his picture: an undergrowth now alive with brown limbs, and now empty; a shower of arrows, feeble yet dangerous; "a cry, a very loud cry, as of infinite desolation"(101); "the gleam of fires, the throb of drums, the drone of weird incantations."(144) When he adopts another method, suddenly bringing before us "a wild and gorgeous apparition of a woman" whom we suppose to have been Kurtz's chief companion in his obscure abominations, the effect is rhetorical and unimpressive:

She must have had the value of several elephant tusks upon her. She was savage and superb, wild-eyed and magnificent; there was something ominous and stately in her deliberate progress. And in the hush that had fallen suddenly upon the whole sorrowful land, the immense wilderness, the colossal body of the fecund and mysterious life seemed to look at her, pensive, as though it had been looking at the image of its own tenebrous and passionate soul.(135-6)

We feel at once that this woman—although we can, if we want to, give her some conjectural place in Kurtz's story—has no status in the essential fable. Nor has the other woman, Kurtz's "intended," to whom Marlow finally tells his lie. Marlow makes two remarks about women in the course of the book. They are of the misogynist cast in which he is to abound in *Chance*. "It's queer how out of touch with truth women are,"(59) he says, early on. And, near the end: "They —the women I mean—are out of it—should be out of it. We must help them to stay in that beautiful world of their own."(115) There is only a very shallow truth in these propositions, however "sheltered" the women in question are conceived of as being. What has got them on to Conrad's page is a kind of inattention—and when we pause on the matter we realize that "Heart of Darkness" is a completely a-sexual work, however dark may be the talk of Kurtz's "gratification of his various lusts."(131) We have to account for the fact that this seems, somehow, all to the good; even the mere massed vegetation (on which Conrad has to rely for his *décor* rather heavily, since he is neither here nor elsewhere much of a field naturalist) seems the better for having shed the obtrusively sexual associations which we have remarked in *Almayer's Folly* and *An Outcast of the Islands*. In this there is conceivably a clue to something important.

Henry James occasionally spoke of "horrors"—meaning gross sexual depravities and deviations on which he was by no means uninformed, but to which he would not have dreamed of granting admission in his novels. Horrors in this sense are, of course, to be posited in "Heart of Darkness." And they remain veiled, shrouded in their proper darkness, no doubt because Conrad knows that this is the most effective way of making a flesh-creeping business of them. Yet they are not *merely* veiled; they are also, as it were, *inert;* and this is because Conrad's imagination is not really much compelled by them. When Kurtz cries out "The horror!" he is not merely acknowledging, at an eleventh hour, the degradation inherent in whatever cruel or libidinous practices we choose to imagine for him. This would not make him the "remarkable man" with "something to say" that Marlow has finally to acclaim in him.(151) When, at the end of the story, some emissary of the Company, wishing to get his hands on certain papers, declares that "Mr. Kurtz's knowledge of unexplored regions must have been necessarily extensive and peculiar,"(153) we understand the undesigned reverberation the words carry. Kurtz's evil courses—and this is the final terror of the fable—have brought him to the heart of an impenetrable darkness in which it is yet possible to *see* more than can be seen in daylight by those to whom no such journey has befallen. Kurtz's last words are a statement of the widest generality. They define one tenable view of man's situation in an alien universe. Alternatively, they define the only sense of himself that man can bring back from a wholly inward journey: that into the immense darkness, the unmeaning anarchy, of his own psyche.

It is these further significances—only in the hinterland of Conrad's conscious intentions though they may have been—that largely validate what might otherwise seem disproportioned in Marlow's response to his "pilgrimage amongst hints of nightmares."(62) He calls Kurtz "the nightmare of my choice,"(141) and says that in retrospect his whole experience seems like a dream. Conrad was fond of quoting the title of Calderón's play, *La Vida es sueño*. Even so—and as Professor Guerard remarks [3]—Marlow's emphasis on the dreamlike quality of his narrative would be over-insistent were it not that his voyage, in its symbolical aspect, is into a region to which, in general, it is only dreams and mental illnesses that give us access. From the moment that he encounters, in the continental office of the Company, the two ominous old women "guarding the door of Darkness"(57) as they knit black wool, on through the interview with the doctor who mysteriously insists that "the changes take place inside,"(58) to the first hypnoidal tremor of far-off drums—"sinking, swelling, a tremor vast, faint; a sound weird, appealing, suggestive, and wild—and perhaps with as profound a meaning as the sound of bells in a Christian country"(71)—we are constantly aware of a beckoning across the borders of normal consciousness. The function that Kurtz and his black friends perform in the total fable regarded as a symbolic structure is at least as important in estimating the significance of "Heart of Darkness" as is our sense of the psychological and anthropological "realism" that Conrad achieves. The opening and close of the story on board the yawl in the estuary of the Thames—Marlow's meditation on the darkness which some Roman naval commander must have found here long ago; the concluding vision of the river as still seeming "to lead into the heart of an immense darkness"(162) today—these sombrely-toned termini to "one of Marlow's inconclusive experiences"(51) constitute a simple and superbly executed means of establishing that Kurtz's Congo flows through a darkness we all know.

The only darkness in "Typhoon" is of the material order through which the *Nan-Shan* has to plough during a night in which storm-clouds have driven the last stars from the sky— that and the darkness of the athwartship coal-bunker in which the boatswain has his alarming encounter with what was probably a coal-trimmer's slice, a commonplace iron object rendered lethal by the fact that the obstinate Captain Mac-Whirr is insisting on navigating his vessel ("a full-powered steam-ship," as he points out to his perturbed first officer) through the centre of the disturbance which gives the story its title. The *Nan-Shan*—a good ship and thoroughly up-to-date: built in Dumbarton, indeed, less than three years before—finds herself "looted by the storm with a senseless, destructive fury"(44); she becomes "like a living creature thrown to the rage of a mob: hustled terribly, struck at, borne up, flung down, leaped upon"(47); when she eventually makes the port of Fu-chau—direct, as Captain MacWhirr had intended—she has the appearance of having "been used as a running target for the secondary batteries of a cruiser."(91)

"Typhoon" is primarily the record of these marine extremities, and it was a shade unreasonable in Conrad to declare, with a kind of mildly offended surprise, that at its first appearance the story "was classed by some critics as a deliberately intended storm-piece."(vi) It is assuredly that—and as assuredly one of the best of its kind ever written. Nothing, perhaps, should be excerpted from the story in this aspect by way of mere illustration. The evocation is, above everything else, precise; at the end we feel that we would know a typhoon if we met one, by no means confounding it with a cyclone or a tornado. Yet it is true, of course, that the storm-piece is not the whole thing; as in *The Nigger of the "Narcissus"* it provides opportunity for a study of the *mores* of British seamen under stress. But it is far more a genre-piece, burdened little or not at all by any prompting to universalize its spectacle. That spectacle is almost consistently amusing, and its treatment is high-spirited in a fashion Conrad does not often contrive. We may read it as it was perhaps conceived: as "time off" from a universe inwardly rather than merely meteorologically tormented such as we meet in "Heart of Darkness" and *Lord Jim*.

Yet "Typhoon," although so much lighter in tone than anything round about it in Conrad's work, is in no sense shallow, and it is not in any spirit of mere inclusiveness that it ought to be admitted to an inquiry into the scope of his genius. Critics can even disagree about it, despite the simplicity of its structure and the forthrightness of its statement. For nothing comes to us here through a mind like Marlow's, and there is no bother about a point of view: the author is omniscient; with every appearance of artistic innocence he scurries informatively round the ship and round the globe—so that we learn of the boatswain, for instance, during his difficult half-hour with the two hundred coolies battened below deck, that his wife is a fat woman who with two grown-up daughters keeps a greengrocer's shop in the East-end of London. But does Conrad not, after all, have some of his customary designs upon us? It is the character of Captain MacWhirr—very much the hero, or at least the protagonist of the story—who can occasion debate here.

Are we to regard Captain MacWhirr as a stupid man? Young Mr. Jukes, the chief mate, confidently so describes him in the last words of the narrative. But Jukes himself is not exactly impressive, and it is hard to tell which officer has the better of it in the matter of the Siamese flag, which has to be hoisted in place of the Red Ensign when the *Nan-Shan* is transferred to a foreign register. This transaction leaves Jukes with something like a sense of personal affront, and he is not assisted by what he judges the absurdity of the new emblem:

The first morning the new flag floated over the stern of the *Nan-Shan* Jukes stood looking at it bitterly from the bridge. He struggled with his feelings for a while, and then remarked "Queer flag for a man to sail under, sir."

"What's the matter with the flag?" inquired Captain Mac-Whirr. "Seems all right to me." And he walked across to the end of the bridge to have a good look.

"Well, it looks queer to me," burst out Jukes, greatly exasperated, and flung off the bridge.

Captain MacWhirr was amazed at these manners. After a while he stepped quietly into the chart-room, and opened his International Signal Code-book at the place where the flags of all the nations are correctly figured in gaudy rows. He ran his finger over them, and when he came to Siam he contemplated with great attention the red field and the white elephant. Nothing could be more simple; but to make sure he brought the book out on the bridge for the purpose of comparing the coloured drawing with the real thing at the flagstaff astern. When next Jukes, who was carrying on the duty that day with a sort of suppressed fierceness, happened on the bridge, his commander observed:

"There's nothing amiss with that flag."

"Isn't there?" mumbled Jukes, falling on his knees before a deck-locker and jerking therefrom viciously a spare lead-line.

"No. I looked up the book. Length twice the breadth and the elephant exactly in the middle. I thought the people ashore would know how to make the local flag. Stands to reason. You were wrong, Jukes. . . ."(10)

Jukes, thus put right, has further to suffer a caution against the danger of hoisting the flag wrong way up. A white elephant upside down, Captain MacWhirr points out, would be understood as a signal of distress.

Captain MacWhirr, in fact, even if not stupid, is rather far from being an imaginative man. His letters to his wife consist of sentences like: "The heat here is very great" and "On Christmas day at 4 P.M. we fell in with some icebergs."(5) Nor is he particularly talkative, for the past, to his mind, is done with, the future not here yet, and the present seldom such as to require more than the giving of a few directions or orders. Nor, again, is he much of a reading man; he has not the knack of picking up information from the printed page; from the technical manuals which might tell him a thing or two about typhoons (which are outside his experience, so far) he retires baffled and impatient. The stuff about storm-tactics might have been written by an old woman, he informs Jukes—and adds that there is no way of telling what a gale is made of till you get into it. This is what he does. But when the resulting prospect of disaster is at its nearest, and the general confusion extreme, he knows that the Chinamen (whose chests have broken open and whose hoarded silver dollars are rolling all over the place) must not be left to fight it out, and he sees to it inflexibly that Jukes and the crew should pile in and restore order. What is proper to be done is always quite clear to Captain MacWhirr.

But what some readers feel Conrad to be minded to say about MacWhirr is that his is a fugitive and cloistered virtue. "He had never been given a glimpse of immeasurable strength and of immoderate wrath, the wrath that passes exhausted but never appeased—the wrath and fury of the passionate sea." This has some appearance of being offered as a matter not merely of nautical fact but of spiritual limitation. For on the same page we read:

Captain MacWhirr had sailed over the surface of the oceans as some men go skimming over the years of existence to sink gently into a placid grave, ignorant of life to the last, without ever having been made to see all it may contain perfidy, of violence, and of terror. There are on sea and land such men thus fortunate—or thus disdained by destiny or by the sea.(19)

Yet we are not at all likely to feel, as we finish the story, that the sea has disdained MacWhirr, or that this rhetorical peroration at the close of the first section is being proposed

as a significant theme. It reads much more like an involuntary incursion of the vaguely portentous which is always a
hazard in Conrad's writing, but which is barely evident anywhere else in "Typhoon."

"The End of the Tether" is a tragic story, and in some
respects looks forward to much later developments in Conrad's art. Like the hero of *Lord Jim*, it is true, Captain
Whalley has extremely bad luck. But he is not, like Jim, a
man in whose personality bad luck reveals (or half reveals)
some deep-seated weakness. He is a man of fine, indeed elevated character, who is practiced against and destroyed by
villains. And if he has what theorists of the drama used to
call, after Aristotle, a "tragic" flaw, it is the inverted sort of
flaw which A. C. Bradley attributed to Othello. His very
nobility makes him vulnerable; although too experienced in
the world to credit men in general with much wisdom, he
believes that they harm one another from ignorance and not
from ill will. People may "be silly, wrong-headed, unhappy;
but naturally evil—no. There was at bottom a complete
harmlessness at least." (*Youth, and Two Other Stories*, 215)
These generous persuasions render Captain Whalley unwary.
Driven by an acute necessity which is itself wholly unselfish
in origin, he associates with a man whom he would normally
despise or at least avoid. His necessities sharpen and he puts
his honour as a seaman in hazard. The knavery of his partner
then brings about his death.* Much of this looks past *Lord*

---

* Whalley—one of those Conrad heroes who is very much an English
gentleman—has had a distinguished and prosperous career in Eastern waters.
But misfortunes have overtaken him. His wife is dead; his only daughter has
made an unfortunate marriage; he has lost nearly the whole of a large fortune in a bank smash. Moreover, he is sixty-seven, and the merchants and
shipowners to whom he had been honourably known have departed. "The
piercing of the Isthmus of Suez, like the breaking of a dam, had let in upon
the East a flood of new ships, new men, new methods of trade. It had changed

Jim (Conrad's most recently completed long novel) to *Chance* and *Victory*, in which people tend to be either a little too good or a little too bad, and in which the canons of senti- mental fiction are—perceptibly thought not cripplingly—be- ginning to apply.

The writing of "The End of the Tether" was marked by a misadventure of which both Conrad and Ford have given dramatic accounts. The manuscript of the entire second part perished in a fire on Conrad's desk, and had to be recovered from memory at high speed in order not to miss an instal- ment in *Blackwood's*. The crisis ended with a sleepless Con- rad in a state of "frenetic idiocy" and Ford saddling a horse upon which the stable-boy made a dash to catch the mail train. "That was what life was like with us," Ford records, and the story does suggest the journeyman character of Con- rad's final labour at what he called "my Blackwood stuff." [4] It is not labour that is ever scamped; one has the impression that every paragraph has been carefully wrought; neverthe-

---

the face of the Eastern seas and the very spirit of their life." He sells the last ship he owns to set up his daughter in a boarding-house, and with what is left buys a share in, and the right to command, an old coasting steamer, the *Sofala*. The owner, Massy, sails in her as first engineer; he has made the money to buy her in a lottery; he is a despicable and intolerable character whom no other captain has managed to put up with for more than a single voyage. Whalley, because he must still support his daughter, holds on for three years.

Whalley finds that he is going blind. With the aid of a faithful Serang, who in fact navigates the ship, he conceals this dangerous condition. It is dis- covered by the mate Sterne, a revolting sneak, who plays a treacherous but ineffective part in the subsequent narrative. It has already been discovered by Massy, who is by this time desperately in need of money with which to repair the engines of the *Sofala* and keep her in trade. When Massy fails to get a promise of this from Whalley (whom he cannot believe to be without further resources), he decides that only shipwreck and the recovery of the sum for which the vessel is insured can save him. He deflects the compass of the *Sofala* by hanging close to it a jacket the pockets of which he has filled with scrap iron, and the ship runs upon a reef and sinks. Everybody is saved except Whalley, who realizes how his own deception has been exploited, puts the iron into his own pockets, and is drowned.

less the story does bear signs of having been achieved under distracting pressure. Like *An Outcast of the Islands*, it is rather too long-drawn-out for its theme, and there are many places in which the narrative is impeded rather than fortified by elaborate descriptive passages which often exploit once more the curious dragging rhythms of *Almayer's Folly*:

The guidance of a form flattened and uneven at the top like a grinder tooth, and of another smooth, saddle-backed summit, had to be searched for within the great unclouded glare that seemed to shift and float like a dry fiery mist, filling the air, ascending from the water, shrouding the distances, scorching to the eye. In this veil of light the near edge of the shore alone stood out almost coal-black with an opaque and motionless solidity. Thirty miles away the serrated range of the interior stretched across the horizon, its outlines and shades of blue, faint and tremulous like a background painted on airy gossamer on the quivering fabric of an impalpable curtain let down to the plain of alluvial soil; and the openings of the estuary appeared, shining white, like bits of silver let into the square pieces snipped clean and sharp out of the body of the land bordered with mangroves.(219-20)

Yet the glare "scorching to the eye" is here wonderfully evoked, and has the same relevance—we eventually find—to the theme of the story as it has in the opening paragraph:

For a long time after the course of the steamer *Sofala* had been altered for the land, the low swampy coast had retained its appearance of a mere smudge of darkness beyond a belt of glitter. The sunrays fell violently upon the calm sea—seemed to shatter themselves upon an adamantine surface into sparkling dust, into a dazzling vapour of light that blinded the eye and wearied the brain with its unsteady brightness.(165)

There is a great deal that is made very vivid in "The End of the Tether," including small things like Massy's teeth—

which "gleamed evenly in the shade of the awning like the keyboard of a piano in a dusky room"(226)—and his hands, red as if covered with blood, when he has secured the scraps of rusty iron which are to bring his vessel to its destruction. Yet Conrad's liveliest concern is with some of the characters— with these less in any notable depth than in terms of a brilliantly achieved surface idiosyncrasy.

It is not the good people who are the best realized. Mr. Van Wyk, the cultivated and humane recluse who befriends Captain Whalley on his remote tobacco plantation at Bata Beru, holds some affinity with Stein in *Lord Jim*, but he is quite without the evocative hinterland and the gnomic quality that make Stein memorable. Captain Whalley is, within certain limits, beautifully achieved. "His very simplicity (amusing enough) was like a delicate refinement of an upright character."(290) But he is to some extent withdrawn from us into his own reserve and loneliness as the certainty of his rapidly advancing blindness becomes apparent to him, and we are left with the three variously unamiable men who constitute his sole white companionship on the *Sofala*. The least important of these, the morose second engineer, whose surly taciturnity when sober is only matched by his capacity for night-long sustained and solitary monologue when drunk, is an entertaining essay in the Dickensian grotesque. His fellows, indeed, both have a touch of this. The mate Sterne, that excellent seaman who is determined to get on, and who only in his idlest moods catches himself thinking no harm of anyone, is an answeringly effective study in nervous and ineffective scoundrelism. "His character was so instinctively disloyal that whenever he joined a ship the intention of ousting his commander out of the berth and taking his place was always present at the back of his head, as a matter of course."(239) The opportunity that has come to him when he discovers Captain Whalley's secret is almost too great, too splendid. His head swims before it—which is perhaps why he fails to realize the possibility that Massy, a rather deeper rascal, may have tumbled to the truth already. But Massy himself cannot be judged by any means a first-class villain. His excitable and unreflecting malignity is a handicap. Willems in *An Outcast of the Islands* is within hailing distance of Massy; Cornelius in *Lord Jim* is closer; and if Massy had more stuffing and more intelligence he might begin to measure up to Conrad's more formidable embodiments of evil, "Gentleman" Brown, Ricardo, and Jones. Anti-social man is a subject perennially fascinating to Conrad, and in all his varieties is presented almost invariably with a touch of extravagance or grim farce. Massy, who is at once dangerous, revolting, and extremely absurd, is one example.

Lord Jim

Dr. F. R. Leavis tells us in *The Great Tradition* that *"Lord Jim* is neither the best of Conrad's novels, nor among the best of his short stories."* [1] The remark may seem unaccountable. In point of simple compass, at least, *Lord Jim* * does not in any degree hover between the novel and the "long-short" story; it is quite a long novel by modern standards. Conrad himself, however, is responsible for people saying this sort of thing. His Author's Note leads off with the remark that "some reviewers maintained that the work starting as a short story had got beyond the author's control." And he goes on to acknowledge that, when his subject originally came to him, his "first thought was of a short story," and only later

---

* Jim—we never learn his surname—is a son of the vicarage who has entered the Merchant Service. He is simple, romantic, and sensitive, and his ideal conception of himself prompts him to dream of heroic responses in such moments of crisis as he may have the good fortune to encounter. But deep in Jim there is something which does not answer to his dream, and we have a glimpse of it during his training as a *Conway* boy, when he fails to move promptly enough in a minor but unnerving emergency. Arrived in the Far East, he decides to remain there, at least for a time; and we are given to

did it occur to him that he had found "a good starting-point for a free and wandering tale."(viii)

We have always to reckon with a certain defensive self-depreciation or understatement in Conrad's talk about his writing. He had no fancy for being regarded as a latter-day Captain Marryat, and he took the art of prose fiction quite as seriously as did any of his contemporaries. Nevertheless—perhaps because success was so slow in coming to him—he was chary of claims that might appear pretentious. This is evident on his title-pages. *Lord Jim* ends up as "a Tale"; *Nostromo*, one of the most complex novels in English, is "a Tale of the Seaboard"; *The Secret Agent*, in its sustained ironic presentation so considered a labour of art, is "a Simple Tale." We are not to take quite at its face value the implication that, even on a maturer view, he saw the odd business of Captain Clark and the S.S. *Jeddah* as merely something that could be spun out in a "free and wandering" manner.

As the basis of a short story, indeed, the affair was a gift. The *Jeddah* had sailed from Singapore on 17 July 1880 bound for the port of Jeddah with more than 900 Muslim pilgrims. On 8 August, having met with a stormy passage and

---

understand that such a decision is customarily regarded by sailors in the home service as a little soft. He becomes first mate of a pilgrim-ship, the *Patna*, and the *Patna* meets with what appears to be imminent disaster. Jim knows his duty, but action eludes him. He is in an isolated situation, since the captain and the other European officers are thinking only of saving their own skins. With the pilgrims still unsuspecting or asleep, these men take to one of the boats. Supposing Jim, still on deck, to be the second officer (a man of their own kidney, who has, in fact, died of a heart-attack), they urge him to jump. Jim jumps. He and the other deserters are rescued, and the captain reports the *Patna* as lost. But the *Patna* is towed safe into harbour, and an official inquiry follows. Jim alone stays to face it, and is disgraced. It is at the inquiry that he first comes under the notice of Marlow, the narrator of all but the four opening chapters of the novel.

For a time Jim makes a living as a water-clerk—a kind of chandler's tout or runner—in one Eastern port or another, but always his story catches up with him, and he moves on. Eventually, through the good offices of a rich mer-

begun to leak, she was abandoned by Clark and his European officers; these men were picked up and taken to Aden, where they reported their ship as lost without other survivors; on the very next day the *Jeddah*, safe if far from sound, was towed into Aden by another steamer. It was a wonderful little tale, and we need not be surprised that at first Conrad simply saw it as such—precisely as Henry James at first saw the subject of *The Golden Bowl*, eventually the most elaborate of his novels. Both Conrad and James, beginning with their plot, went on to consider the characters proper to it, which is at least the Aristotelian order of proceeding in the evolution of a story. And Conrad's Note is finally forthright enough. He saw that the substantial interest of his narrative must inhere in the disposition of one of the deserters. Perhaps—but this was to come in the evolving of the novel—this deserter could feel disgrace and therefore seek rehabilitation, or feel guilt and therefore seek atonement. Or perhaps neither of these things would quite hold; perhaps there would have to be acknowledged some complexity of motives, some mystery of the heart, not finally to be pronounced upon even by the most concerned and penetrating of observers.

---

chant, Stein, he is established in a remote trading post, Patusan in Borneo. (We are thus back in the world of *Almayer's Folly* and *An Outcast of the Islands*.) Jim now appears to have been tempered into a man of resource, judgment, and inflexible courage. He has become the virtual ruler of a native state, enjoys the close friendship of its king's son, Dain Waris, and has taken a devoted Eurasian girl, Jewel, as mistress. But eventually there comes catastrophe. A small band of hunted desperadoes take refuge in Patusan. They are ruthless and unscrupulous, and it seems to be Jim's plain duty to destroy them. But their leader, "Gentleman" Brown, sensing something of Jim's nature and even of his history, makes a cunning appeal to him in the name of a shared outlawry. Jim hesitates, and then decides to let them go. It is perhaps an irresponsible decision, as being dictated less by his duty to his mistress or to the people in his care than by a strained notion of personal honour. He thus loses his grip on the situation; Dain Waris and many others are massacred by Brown's men in sheer vindictiveness; and at the end Jim walks deliberately to his death at the hands of Dain Waris's father.

Certainly a good deal of space would be required for the un-
folding of an inner drama of this sort. And as soon as there
was formulated the question "What happens to such a man
afterwards?" it became inevitable that the narrative should
fall into two more or less sharply accented parts. It can be
argued with some cogency that the later chapters of *Lord Jim*
are inferior to the earlier. The contention that they represent
an infelicitous expatiation impairing the integrity of the
whole seems far less tenable.

Conrad was in London when the *Jeddah* scandal occurred,
and he must have read the abundant newspaper accounts of
it with interest. Three years later, when he arrived in Singapore for the first time, he was to find the *Jeddah* in harbour
there, and its story must surely have been rekindled in his
mind. But a further fifteen years elapsed before he began his
novel. Whether this long period was in any significant sense
one of gestation, whether he pondered the episode's possi-
bilities at all, it is impossible to say. But we do know the
manner in which he was eventually to modify the circumstances of the case, and it is interesting to approach *Lord Jim*
by way of the salient facts of Captain Clark's actual misadventure.

When the *Jeddah* set out from Singapore on her fateful
voyage, the Europeans on board were Captain Clark and his
wife, the first and second officers, and the chief engineer. The
native crew numbered 45, and there were 953 adult pilgrims,
together with an unspecified number of children as well. The
Jeddah was not an old ship; she had been built at Dumbarton on the Clyde only eight years before; she was in no
way unseaworthy. Almost from the first, however, she met
heavy weather, and by 3 August, her seventeenth day out,
she was in something like a hurricane. The boilers began to
move in their fastenings, and there was delay in dealing with

them; on 6 August, the weather still increasing in severity, the vessel had to be stopped for repairs; she began to leak, and by that evening all hands and passengers were working at the pumps and bailing. But by this time the movement of the boilers was out of control, and the engine-rooms (in the words of the official report) "became untenable and a wreck." [2] The passengers—and manpower must have been in inexhaustible supply—continued to pump until midnight; and then some degree of disorganization, not easy to estimate, set in. Clark gave the order to man a boat or boats, and the bulk of the crew then seem to have behaved in such a manner that the passengers, whether unreasonably or not, "entertained the idea that the boats were going to leave the ship." [3]

The *Jeddah* affair now takes on some appearance of muddled and macabre comedy; and for this the first officer, whose name was A. P. Williams, was largely responsible. Determined to get away, he played upon Clark's fears for the safety of his wife, declaring that the passengers—who had in fact so far shown no sign of violence—were determined to murder her. Clark, who must be described as easily alarmed, caused the starboard lifeboat astern to be manned, and his wife to be transferred to it through a porthole. It was then boarded by the chief engineer and himself, and lowered to the water—Clark's intention being thus ignominiously to await events. Some of the pilgrims, disapproving (as they well might) of this spectacle, began to pelt Clark's boat with boxes, pots, and pans; others, finding the second engineer also to have boarded a boat, bundled him, with others of the crew, unceremoniously back on deck; yet others, observing the second officer similarly attempting to get away, cut the falls of his boat, with the result that it fell bow first into the sea, so that all who had boarded it perished. Williams, who had either fallen or been pitched into the water, was picked up by Clark's boat in sufficiently good trim to open fire on the *Jeddah* with a pistol. It was amid scenes like these that the greater part of the crew of the pilgrim-ship deserted her. When the confusion caused by this exodus had abated, the passengers returned to the pumps, managed by their exertions to gain upon the leak, managed further to set some sail and gain smooth water, and eventually attracted the attention of the steamship which was to bring them into Aden (as we have seen) on the day following the arrival of the miserable Clark and his associates, replete with their tale of the largest calamity.

The official inquiry into this sequence of events found in them "the most extraordinary instance known to the Court of the abandonment of a disabled and leaking ship at sea by the master and Europeans, and almost all the crew." The strictures upon Clark are at first mild in tone. He "showed a want of judgment and tact to a most serious extent" and had been "misled in regard to the real intentions of the pilgrims." Finally, however, he is indicted as having "shown a painful want of nerve as well as the most ordinary judgment"; he was guilty of "gross misconduct," and of "great cruelty" in so representing matters when picked up that no thought of searching for the *Jeddah* was entertained by his rescuers. Much is blamed upon "the officious ill-advice of his chief officer . . . who may be said to have more than aided and abetted the master in the abandonment of his vessel." But for Williams's "officious behaviour and unseamanlike conduct," Clark would probably have done his duty by remaining on the ship. Williams, in fact, had done what he could to "demoralize" Clark.[4] After all this, we may feel the culprits to have been dismissed with some leniency. Clark's certificate was suspended for three years; at the end of that period he returned to Singapore, and there seems even to have been some thought of restoring him to the command of the *Jeddah*. Williams got off with a reprimand. The son of a west-country parson of good family, he appears to have been a man of strong character and little sensibility. After the inquiry at Aden he returned at once to Singapore, faced up to whatever met him there, and for a time contrived to continue at sea. Eventually he took work as a ship-chandler's water-clerk and prospered in various commercial situations. A photograph, taken together with his Eurasian wife and perhaps dating from his early forties, shows a portly figure with a hint of swagger or grossness which is accented by his appearing in full evening-dress.[5] He is reported as a bankrupt, however, in 1914, and he died two years later. He caused an anchor to be carved on his headstone. It may be supposed to have been a symbol of fidelity to the sea.

Here, then, is the material for what Conrad first thought to write: the story, as he says, of "the pilgrim ship episode; nothing more."(viii) He composed, he records, only a few pages on this plan. It was when he returned to them later— we do not know after what interval—that he became aware of his larger theme: "the acute consciousness of lost honour."(ix) Yet it seems likely that from the start his transforming imagination was at work on the *Jeddah* affair. The *Jeddah* was a well-found ship, cast in hazard through a combination of bad seamanship and violent storm. The *Patna* is old and in poor shape, "eaten up with rust worse than a condemned water-tank"(13); she meets with mysterious misadventure on a calm sea, her hull striking and passing over some submerged object never to be identified; it is a single large flake of falling rust that brings home to Jim the extremity of danger made the more unnerving by the unflawed tranquillity of the natural scene. On the *Jeddah* there was a long

and mounting appreciation of peril, frenzied effort among all
on board, the crash of tremendous seas, a final pervasive confusion in which many people behaved with varying degrees
of culpability. On the *Patna* the pilgrims are asleep throughout the action, with only such exceptions as the man who
reaches out a hand to Jim and asks for water. The *Jeddah*
had as its captain the calamitously uxorious and feeble Clark.
The *Patna* is commanded by "a sort of renegade New South
Wales German"(14) so monstrous in physical appearance as
to suggest "a trained baby elephant."(37) All these more or
less superficial changes made by Conrad represent a great
gain in art. But it is in the character and situation of Jim
himself—simple and outward-seeming yet remote within his
romantic dream, justly contemptuous of his fellow officers
yet in a fatal instant implicated for ever in their ignominy—
that the genius of the book declares itself. The creative
process is the more impressive when we come to realize that
Jim was not, so to speak, *pure* creation. There is considerable
evidence that Conrad had to find his way to him—it was a
strange kind of exploring—through the figure of the deplorable A. P. Williams.

According to one testimony, Conrad used to see Williams
in Singapore, thought to inquire how one who was plainly a
gentleman came to be working as a ship's runner, and was
thereupon told the story of the *Jeddah*. If this were all, we
might say that Conrad's imagination had immediate free-
play. But Conrad almost certainly had other sources of information: for example, in 1882 Williams served as first officer on the *Vidar*, as Conrad did five years later; the *Jeddah*
affair was notorious; and it is improbable that one of its
central figures was not for long talked about on any ship on
which he had sailed. There are sufficient parallels between
Williams and Jim—for instance, upbringing in a country

rectory—to make it arguable that Conrad in fact met Williams, conversed with him, and held him at least casually in mind while writing his novel. What is certain is that the novel found itself when the historical Williams was jettisoned and Tuan Jim introduced in his place.

For the later part of *Lord Jim*, as for the earlier, there is source-material available for study. But the situation is different. We can compare the story of the *Patna* with that of the *Jeddah* much as we can compare *Othello* with Cinthio's tale or *Macbeth* with Holinshed's chronicle: here indisputably is what the artist started from, and there is at least a limited sense in which we may instruct ourselves in his craft by watching him at work. Patusan, although it is simply the Sambir of *Almayer's Folly* and therefore modelled upon the remote Bornean trading-post, Berau, which Conrad visited four times in 1887, takes us to more debatable ground. Here, indeed, Conrad certainly encountered Jim Lingard, nephew and protégé of that almost legendary Captain Lingard who had first opened up the Berau region. This young man, not long out from England, was sufficiently impressive to have received the Malay title of "Tuan Jim," and he had a Sea Dyak as a mistress and a notably faithful native servant as a bodyguard. These are interesting facts, particularly when we know that the whole Lingard family and its connections for long occupied a substantial place in Conrad's imagination. But there is another and very significant source for the Patusan episode. Conrad put a good deal of reading into it.

He had spent, according to Dr. Sherry's calculations, perhaps twelve days all told at Berau. He could therefore have gained no intimate acquaintance with its people, even had he tried to do so. And quite probably he did not—since it is possible to feel that, during the whole of his period in the

Far East, he showed less curiosity about its native inhabitants than would have been advantageous to a future novelist. But if he found in books much to make up for deficiencies here, he found there other things as well. Prominent among Europeans who had set their mark upon the islands of the Malay Archipelago was Sir James Brooke of Sarawak, and Conrad seems to have read whatever he could about him. But in doing so he would only have been reinforcing what he had already heard, since the astonishing career of the White Rajah was writ large upon the memory and imagination of the region. "Misunderstood and traduced in life," Conrad was to declare of him in *The Rescue*, "the glory of his achievement has vindicated the purity of his motives." [6] It was an achievement on a spectacular scale: Brooke became ruler of a native state, amassed a great fortune, and founded what was in effect a dynasty. Lord Jim does one of these things. It is conceivable that, but for Brooke, Conrad would not have framed Jim's story precisely as he did.

In all this there is material upon which conjecture and asseveration flourish. The character of Conrad's hero is very commonly declared to be baffling or at least elusive—we shall find that Marlow himself sets a dogged example here—and it is tempting to suppose that the novelist's intentions can be elucidated, or his weaknesses excused, by turning to the original or originals whom he may have had in mind. Thus Dr. Sherry believes that there is something to explain about Jim, and that he can explain it. "There is a change," he writes, "in the character of the hero in *Lord Jim* once he goes to Patusan. This change is not simply the result of his more active role. It obviously involved a change in Conrad's conception of his hero, and it marks a weakness in the book as a whole. It is apparent that the change in character depended upon a shift from A. P. Williams to some other source." [7]

And later: "I believe it was Jim Lingard's position in the area which led Conrad to conclude Lord Jim's early adventures in the pilgrim ship *Patna* with a final period in the jungle. . . . But Conrad could know little about Jim Lingard or his way of life, and he was therefore forced to make the source a composite one. Thus he drew upon the inspiration of Brooke for the success of his hero, and upon travellers' tales for the incidents and details of his life." [8]

But it is necessary to distinguish here. The travellers' tales are extant, and we can watch Conrad dipping into them and be sure of what he is about. Of Lingard and Brooke, on the other hand, as of Williams as well, we can say only that Conrad's interest in their histories and personalities almost certainly finds some reflection in his novel. And in judging of the consistency or inconsistency of Jim's character, the novel itself affords the only evidence upon which it is legitimate to draw. We may merely be prejudicing the case if we approach it with these widely differing real-life figures in our heads.

Let us consider, then, the Jim who is Conrad's creation. We see him on his training-ship simply as a boy subject to a momentary failure of nerve. He has been indulging in romantic reverie, and when suddenly confronted by actual danger he is taken by surprise and cannot adjust to it in time. We realize, of course, that the incident is ominous. One of Marlow's first perceptions is to be that this stolid-seeming young officer is "an imaginative beggar,"(83) and that such a man may be afraid of an emergency he can all too vividly evoke even while not, perhaps, being afraid of death. Imagination, Conrad says earlier, is "the enemy of men."(11) We may recall Dr. Johnson declaring that it "preys upon human life."

On the *Patna* Jim has got himself companions who represent "everything vile and base that lurks in the world we

love."(21) It is at a moment when he has drawn utterly apart
from this disagreeable reality to luxuriate in valorous dreams
that crisis strikes again, and this time in monstrously magni-
fied form. And Jim now doesn't merely fail to jump where
he should; he jumps where he should not. Looking back on
it, he sees his disaster as "awfully unfair,"(128) and in a way
we are constrained to agree with him—telling ourselves that,
had a single one of his fellow-officers made a single move to
do the right thing, Jim would have had no problem. The
breaking-strain imposed on him was as grotesquely severe as
it was utterly unheralded. It is true that no experienced seaman would ever entrust a deck to him again. But the facts
are not such that we need be surprised on finding that a lack
of physical courage never conditions any subsequent act of
Jim's life; nothing of the sort, certainly, enters into the final
catastrophe precipitated by "Gentleman" Brown. It seems
not difficult for Jim to become an exceptionally daring water-
clerk, or to do every intrepid thing that he does in Patusan.
At the simple level of his first misadventures he is not to be
betrayed anew. These are facts of the narrative, and neither
Marlow nor anybody else expresses the least surprise in face
of them. There seems to be no reason why we should do so
either. Deep in Jim the old vulnerability no doubt remained,
and fate might have been shown as searching it out with a
cunning overgoing even that deployed on the pilgrim-ship.
But this would scarcely have made for the kind of interest
Conrad is concerned to pursue.

The nature of that interest, however, is elusive. We may
at times suppose that there is being exhibited to us simply a
young man whose first big disaster makes and tempers him.
Before it happens, he is beginning to reveal himself as a mis-
fit at sea; he has taken to it after "a course of light holiday
literature"(5); the spirit of its service escapes him; soon he

will go soft, and the chasm will widen between the actual
man and his reveries of heroic action. Once in the boat with
his fellow-criminals, however, he knows passionately what he
hates; alone among them, he faces up to formal judgment;
thereafter, his single wish is for rehabilitation—is for what he
calls, however inadequately, "a second chance."(179) Opportunity comes to him in Patusan, and he seizes it with magnificent firmness. In the end he dies vindicating what Marlow
calls at the start "a fixed standard of conduct."(50) For
Brown, like himself, is a disgraced gentleman, and he sees his
own code of behaviour as requiring him to take a risk and
let the beaten man go. When catastrophe results, when he
realizes that the order he has created in Patusan must inevitably perish, he walks willingly to what he conceives of as
a just death, casting round about him—we are twice told—"a
proud and unflinching glance."(416)

Many first readings of *Lord Jim* probably leave some such
preponderant impression as this, which is perhaps why the
book is the most popular Conrad ever wrote. Yet it is dis-
tinguishable almost from the first moment of Marlow's entering the book as narrator that he is going to invite us to
consider something more. Jim is an enigma, and Jim has
high representative significance. It is on these two linked
facts that the deeper emphasis of the novel is placed.

Jim has Marlow wondering from beginning to end.[9] The
note sounds in the first sentence Marlow utters, and is present
in the last paragraph he writes: "He is gone, inscrutable at
heart. . . ." Again and again the point is driven home. "I
don't pretend I understood him."(76) "I cannot say I had ever
seen him distinctly."(221) "I am not certain of him."(330)
"It is impossible to see him clearly."(339) The constant refrain tends to inhibit us in our own exploration of the case—
for if so acute and favoured an observer as Marlow is con-

tinually producing gestures, murmurs, even cries of bewilderment, will it not be merely discreet to remain modestly
bewildered ourselves? But Marlow's uncertainty is, in a last
analysis, before Marlow, which is perhaps a way of saying
that it is our own uncertainty before ourselves. "I was bound
to him," Marlow says of Jim, "in the name of that doubt
which is the inseparable part of our knowledge. I did not
know so much more about myself."(221) And further: "It is
when we try to grapple with another man's intimate need
that we perceive how incomprehensible, wavering, and misty
are the beings that share with us the sight of the stars and the
warmth of the sun. It is as if loneliness were a hard and
absolute condition of existence."(180) Thus, at his point of
deepest meaning, Jim is the clouded mirror of our secret
life. And perhaps the cloud—with mist, vapour, moonlight,
shadow, veiled presences it is among the novel's recurrent
symbols—is of our own creating; it poses agonizing doubt but
defers final judgment. What is the truth about ourselves?
That we are capable of facing the truth about ourselves—or
that we are not?

The theme of *Lord Jim*, then, may perhaps be defined as
the difficulty of distinguishing and acknowledging what Conrad elsewhere calls "the humble reality of things," [10] of contemplating with any confidence or comfort those areas of
human experience in which judgment in terms of fixed
standards seems, in face of the plain human plight, inadequate or inappropriate. What may fairly be called the book's
refrain leads us this way. When, upon an early view of Jim,
Marlow says: "He came from the right place; he was one of
us,"(43) the statement is a very simple one. Jim is an English
gentleman, brought up within a tradition from which men
emerge acknowledging personal honour as absolute. Just this

(which asserts, of course, an extra measure of dereliction in Jim's case; more is required of him than of "a sort of renegade New South Wales German") is reiterated again and again: "He was of the right sort; he was one of us."(78) But before we have reached the end of the story we have come upon the phrase altogether too often to continue receiving it merely in this primary sense. Jim is one of us because we are all one. We are one with him, and if we are honest we shall acknowledge the fact—as did Captain Brierly, the successful and impeccable seaman who committed suicide after sitting as one of Jim's judges. The repeated phrase, moreover, gathers various ironies to itself. Thus, turning the page from Marlow's second and apparently uncoloured use of it, we find Jim urging upon Marlow his view of himself:

He discovered at once a desire that I should not confound him with his partners in—in crime, let us call it. He was not one of them; he was altogether of another sort. I gave no sign of dissent. I had no intention, for the sake of barren truth, to rob him of the smallest particle of any saving grace that would come in his way. . . . No man ever understands quite his own artful dodges to escape from the grim shadow of self-knowledge. (79-80)

But if Jim *was* one of them, then Marlow must ask himself whether he is one of them too; must suggest to his reader that the reader is one of them too. And it is not quite a matter merely of the risk or potentiality of failure, haunting as the sense of that may be. It is not a matter of having to say "There but for the Grace of God go I," but rather of what, in our fallen humanity, we *are*. Near the end of the book, and addressing an unnamed correspondent, Marlow writes: "You maintained that we must fight in the ranks or our lives don't count."(339) In fact, we cannot fight anywhere else. There are only the ranks. "We exist only in so far as we hang together."(223)

Like the surviving officers of the *Patna*, we are all in the same boat. This does not mean that, by a grim paradox, there is necessarily no escape for us from the prison of self; that there is no reality beyond that humblest one of each man's hungry egoism. We are a mixed lot. Indeed, each of us is a mixed lot, which is one reason why we can fascinate and bewilder one another. It is this complexity that Marlow has to acknowledge in one of the topic places in the book:

I was made to look at the convention that lurks in all truth and on the essential sincerity of falsehood. He appealed to all sides at once—to the side turned perpetually to the light of day, and to that side of us which, like the other hemisphere of the moon, exists stealthily in perpetual darkness, with only a fearful ashy light falling at times on the edge. He swayed me. I own to it, I own up.(93)

And what Marlow has just been witnessing in Jim is "a dispute with an invisible personality, an antagonistic and inseparable partner of his existence." Indeed, it is more; it is "a subtle and momentous quarrel as to the true essence of life."(93) Jim is fascinating to Marlow because he is neither securely aware nor fatally ignorant of what he has done. At the inquiry he understands that facts have "surged up all about him to cut him off from the rest of his kind," and he is likened to "a creature that, finding itself imprisoned within an enclosure of high stakes, dashes round and round, distracted in the night, trying to find a weak spot, a crevice, a place to scale, some opening through which it may squeeze itself and escape."(31) Sometimes Jim seems very close to successful self-deception, and it is then that we recognize in his story "a hint of a destructive fate ready for us all."(51) He can speak as from "some conviction of innate blamelessness"(79); what he has lost is obscured by what he has been cheated of obtaining, so that he cries out "Ah! What a chance

missed!"(83); he can insist that it was not Jim—not the real
Jim—who jumped: "it was their doing as plainly as if they
had reached up with a boathook and pulled me over."(123)
Or he is a young fellow in a scrape, a scrape which Marlow is
to reprehend solemnly while being disposed through his
maturity and better sense of proportion simply to hide a
smile. If Jim can never face his father again it is because of
a mere insuperable difficulty in communication; "the poor
old chap," he says, "wouldn't understand."(79)

In all this, it may be seen, Jim is "trying to save from the
fire his idea of what his moral identity should be."(81) "He
made so much of his disgrace while it is the guilt alone that
matters,"(177) Marlow says—thereby almost, as it were, re-
signing Jim to judgment. But always, within Marlow's fine
intelligence, there is a balance to be held; and sometimes he
is able to hold it because he can watch as well as listen:

> "Come—I carried it off pretty well," he said, wheeling suddenly.
> "Something's paid off. . . ." He paused; the rain fell with re-
> doubled violence. "Some day one's bound to come upon some
> sort of chance to get it all back again. Must!" he whispered, dis-
> tinctly, glaring at my boots.(178-9)

The glare contradicts the assertions, and it is the glare that
is authentically related to "the true essence of life." *Lord
Jim*—at least the recesses of the book—will make little impression on us unless we agree with this, or imaginatively suspend
our disagreement. Jim has not lost a position, a prestige, that
he can get back—like an athletic record, or a boy's place at
the top of his form. He has done something that is in effect
treason to his kind. Marlow sees this as a simple fact on the
record. And it is impossible, Marlow says, to lay the ghost of
a fact. You can face it or shirk it, and Marlow finds it hard to
tell which of these courses Jim pursues. Facing the ghost, we

may ourselves interpret, implies acknowledging what has raised it. This in Jim's case has been that underlying egoism in his romantic dream which has made his treason possible. Rehabilitation will be meaningful for him only if it is concomitant with a radically changed relationship to other people.

It is such a changed relationship that the second part of the novel appears to present to us. Or at least in Patusan—and it is a start—Jim has found "a totally new set of conditions for his imaginative faculty to work upon."(218) In furthering the order and prosperity of this remote place he is giving himself to an impersonal purpose, and if charged with having run away he can now surely say: "From no man—from not a single man on earth."(75) But Marlow has long ago reflected that there is one exception to this kind of boast which may hold true of the bravest of us. And perhaps Tuan Jim is still fleeing from himself. Indeed, he is certainly doing this if he is still the self-absorbed young man who had so little known himself on the bridge of the *Patna*, "penetrated by the great certitude of unbounded safety and peace."(17)

"I am trusted,"(247) he says to Marlow, his achieved empire around him. More than this is true. He is admired and loved. He is the chivalrous protector of a devoted mistress, and his consciousness that his existence is absolutely necessary to this girl brings him more of our respect than anything else in his story: "I believe I am equal to it," he says soberly."(304)

But is he? "I shall be faithful,"(334) he says, referring to all that has passed into his trust in Patusan. Again there is a doubt. At one point it appears to Marlow that Jim is "approaching greatness as genuine as any man ever achieved."(244) But Jim is perhaps unchanged—as Marlow, in his heart, knows from the first may be his fate. ("As if the initial word of each

our destiny"—so the first part of the novel concludes—"were
not graven in imperishable characters upon the face of a
rock."(186) The outward man, indeed, seems transformed.
He can now, as matter of course, act with an utter disregard
of his personal safety. And this intrepidity brings its rewards:
"He, who had been too careful of it once, seemed to bear a
charmed life."(285) But is not the inward man the Jim we
have first known? Patusan remains simply the place where *he*
is trusted, and it ceases to exist for him when this ceases to be
so. He had loved the land and the people, but "with a sort of
fierce egoism, with a contemptuous tenderness."(248) He has
no further obligation to a world which, although of his own
making, had fallen in ruins about him. "There was nothing
to fight for"(410)—once there was no further question of
fighting for Jim.

But however all this may be, Conrad cannot be found as
recording any final verdict against his hero. For one thing,
Jim does have atrociously bad luck. The men with whom he
ships on the *Patna* prove to be not merely craven scoundrels
but monsters by whom any youth in his early twenties might
well be unnerved and unmanned. It is, of course, very bad to
desert a sinking ship and its helpless passengers, and perhaps
Conrad feels that he must dissuade us from turning down
our thumb on Jim out of hand. So—unfairly, it may be—he
uses a device as old as *Macbeth*, where the early irruption of
something preternatural in the soliciting of the weird sisters
subtly serves to soften, or even confuse, our sense of Macbeth's culpability within the boundaries of our own familiar
and ponderable world. The captain of the *Patna*, "like a
clumsy effigy of a man cut out of a block of fat"(23) and the
very "incarnation of everything vile and base that lurks in
the world we love,"(21) performs, along with his answeringly
grotesque subordinates, a similar function. A fate that throws

"one of us" amid such cattle plays with loaded dice. And the dice are again loaded when we come to Brown.

Brown is a brilliant imaginative achievement, a singular instance of a writer's rising to a stiff challenge at the crisis of a tale. If Brown had failed, the whole book would have failed. And we can see Conrad remarking what he must not too much rely on. Brown is rumored to be the son of a baronet, and through his fatal colloquy with Jim there runs a "subtle reference to their common blood."(387) But this theme of *sahib* calling to *sahib* (which Kipling would have jumped at in such a situation) is only cautiously deployed. The "sickening suggestion of common guilt"(387) is more important. But what is chiefly played upon is something— again as in *Macbeth*—involving unnatural knowledge. Brown is both intelligent and intuitive; we are successfully convinced of his possessing these qualities; yet we may resent their exploitation as unashamedly novelistic if we are not here prepared a little to depart from the canons of realistic fiction. Brown has no previous knowledge whatever about Jim. But he manages to ask him why *he* came here; to indicate his own wretched followers and exclaim: "There are my men in the same boat—and, by God, I am not the sort to jump out of trouble and leave them in a damned lurch"(382); to say that he is in Patusan because he "was afraid once in his life,"(383) and that when "it came to saving one's life in the dark, one didn't care who else went—three, thirty, three hundred people."(386) This sinister clairvoyance, implausible when we pause upon it, serves the same purpose as the physical grotesquerie of the *Patna*'s officers; it piles up against Jim more than a man might fairly reckon on. It may conceivably have the further function of an expressionist device conveying something too abstract for effective direct statement: that sort of unconscious rather than reflective identification with an adversary which totally inhibits action—as when Hamlet proceeds effectively against everybody except Claudius, who has achieved Hamlet's own unacknowledged goals. In Brown, Jim confronts egoism naked and confessed, and he is powerless before it. Something like this, for what it is worth, is now the accepted psycho-analytic explanation of the dénouement of *Lord Jim*.

But if *Lord Jim* ends with an open verdict, it is not really because any unfair appeal has been made to our sympathy. It is of the essence of Conrad's theme that what has come into Marlow's life with the arrival of Jim is a spectacle fascinating and disquieting because enigmatical. Some readers feel that this is not enough; that Marlow is a kind of shield or carapace getting in the way of their legitimate endeavour to pin Conrad down; that the whole technique of the book, indeed, is based upon an abnegation of both moral and artistic responsibility. They will point to the insistent way in which, at crucial moments, the import of events, the movement towards clarity of vision and objectivity of judgment, are faded into a mounting and elusive rhetoric. For example, there is the place where Marlow takes Jim's case to Stein, the successful merchant and eminent lepidopterist. In the course of this, in one of the novel's main digressions, we are offered Stein's whole history, and with the plainest intention of building up his authority as one deeply read in human nature. Stein pronounces Jim to be "romantic."(212) "What's good for it?" Marlow asks, as if romanticism is an acknowledged malady. Stein replies that the question is not how to get cured, but how to live, and continues:

"A man that is born falls into a dream like a man who falls into the sea. If he tries to climb out into the air as inexperienced people endeavour to do, he drowns—*nicht wahr?* . . . No! I tell

you! The way is to the destructive element submit yourself, and
with the exertions of your hands and feet in the water make the
deep, deep sea keep you up. . . . In the destructive element im-
merse." . . . He spoke in a subdued tone, without looking at me,
one hand on each side of his face. "That was the way. To follow
the dream, and again to follow the dream—and so—*ewig—usque
ad finem*. . . ."(214-5)

This must be considered as oracular in the Delphic fashion,
since competent critics have arrived at radically differing in-
terpretations of it. Nor does Marlow, although the words
remain to haunt him, extract anything very precise from
them; his comment, in fact, is pitched in very much the same
key:

> The whisper of his conviction seemed to open before me a
> vast and uncertain expanse, as of a crepuscular horizon on a plain
> at dawn—or was it, perchance, at the coming of night? One had
> not the courage to decide; but it was a charming and deceptive
> light, throwing the impalpable poesy of its dimness over pitfalls
> —over graves. (215)

We are tempted to feel that there is something a little
facile about the eloquence; a shade of routine in the gesture
that resigns the writer and ourselves to mystery. And this
holds of the final paragraphs of the novel, in which, amid
studied cadences and calculated repetitions, Jim "passes away
under a cloud, inscrutable at heart," with his ideal of conduct
"shadowy" and the final opportunity that has come to him
"veiled."(416) Does Conrad lean too heavily upon that elu-
siveness of the spirit, that final impenetrable enigma of
human personality, which lies undoubtedly at the centre of
his design? If he appears to do so, the reason may lie in two
conditions that he imposes upon himself in the later course
of the novel. The first of these is his not really knowing quite
enough about his scene and its peoples. The second will

serve to introduce an aspect of *Lord Jim* perennially fascinating to students of the Novel: the book's structure.

If we compare the Malayan stories of Conrad with the
West African stories of Joyce Cary, we shall probably feel
Cary's indigenous inhabitants to be portrayed with far greater
understanding than Conrad's. Cary had been a colonial
administrator, whereas Conrad was only a seafarer. Moreover, we receive a strong impression that, while in the East,
Conrad subscribed somewhat unreflectingly to the dominant
European view of race relationships. ("He was still one of
them, while Jim was one of *us*,"(361) Dain Waris's fellow-
countrymen are represented as reflecting.) This made for a
certain lack of attention. Moreover, Conrad, although he was
to declare that he for long carried about the world with him
"the hallucination of the Eastern Archipelago," and although
it was as an exotic novelist that he became famous, had no
great fondness for remote places and primitive peoples. For
him civilization was something that had begun in the Mediterranean basin, and as one moved away from that one
moved towards darkness. His essential feeling here is perfectly conveyed in Marlow's description of his taking final
leave of Patusan:

> The boat fairly flew; we sweltered side by side in the stagnant
> superheated air; the smell of mud, of marsh, the primeval smell
> of fecund earth, seemed to sting our faces; till suddenly at a bend
> it was as if a great hand far away had lifted a heavy curtain, had
> flung open an immense portal. The light itself seemed to stir, the
> sky above our heads widened, a far-off murmur reached our ears,
> a freshness enveloped us, filled our lungs, quickened our thoughts,
> our blood, our regrets—and, straight ahead, the forests sank down
> against the dark-blue ridge of the sea.(331)

Marlow rejoices that ahead lies "the energy of an impeccable
world"(331)—and it is the world that European men have

created and now carry about with them. But if Conrad had no absorbed attention to give to remote societies, he knew where to turn for information about them when it was required. Much reading, it seems, did not prevent him from frequently getting small things wrong. This is unimportant in itself, but is significant when we are considering what happens to our sense of Jim in the later pages of the novel.

For we are regularly aware of a certain thinness in Jim's relations with the people—or rather peoples—of Patusan which may be explained by his creator's need to work to some extent from second-hand. Perhaps the mediocre rendering of much of Jim's romance with Jewel is otherwise to be accounted for; it is superior, but not much superior, to that of Dain and Nina in *Almayer's Folly*; we simply have to remember, no doubt, that Conrad seldom scores high marks on sex.[11] But it should be otherwise, we feel, with Jim's close friendship with Doramin's son, Dain Waris. This bond, although stated, remains substantially unrealized in the novel, and so, in consequence, does an important hinted facet of Jim's character. We see him acquiring a confessor in Marlow and a patron in Stein; even with Jewel, despite the uncertainty of treatment, we see a relationship touching in its very limitation (as of a good-hearted prefect and his fag); but if Jim is to be capable of making a *friend*, the fact is so important that it ought to be brought home to us. But it is not. For one thing, we simply see too little of Dain Waris. He is a "distinguished youth" (which a young Bostonian might be in Henry James) and he owns "a European mind" and "a polished, easy bearing."(261-2) ("You meet them sometimes like that," Marlow says—meaning natives in general—"and are surprised to discover unexpectedly a familiar turn of thought, an unobscured vision, a tenacity of purpose, a touch of altruism.") If Jim is not quite so real to us in Patusan as he has been on board the *Patna* or before his judges, it is partly because of this uncertainty of relation and implication with his final background.

More important than this, however, is the manner in which the final catastrophe is narrated. Conrad appears to have felt that, alike for the opening and the close of his story, the speaking voice of Marlow would be too leisured and reflective an instrument. This must be why the novel begins as straight narrative, with the start of Marlow's yarn deferred until the fifth chapter. But the end had to be differently contrived, since Marlow could scarcely be withdrawn altogether after commanding our attention for hundreds of pages. What was wanted was *compressed* Marlow, or the familiar voice in some way constrained a little to speed up. So Conrad adopts the expedient of setting Marlow to work with a pen. A written narrative, together with a covering letter, occupies the last ten chapters.

This device makes possible one notable effect, to which we shall come. But it also deprives Marlow of a certain degree of authority. He has left Patusan ("The boat fairly flew . . ."), where he has been visiting Jim, and he knows that he will never return, and probably never see the young man again. Nor does he. So, for our benefit, or that of his unnamed correspondent, he must pick up the rest of the story where he can. We are not without a feeling as we read that this is a politic withdrawal, the distancing it effects reflecting an uncertain command of the detail of Tuan Jim's empire. We are conscious, too, of a new degree of manipulation on the writer's part; Conrad has to work hard, and contrive several stiff coincidences, in order that Marlow may gain access to his material. And, even so, Marlow is now confessedly making quite a lot up—writing "as though I had been an eyewitness,"(343) he says. All these circumstances may be esti-

mated as interposing between Jim and ourselves the thick-
ness of one more veil than Conrad, perhaps, supposed to be
present. But in imaginative fiction of any depth there has
always to be a delicate balance between the writer's intuitive
penetration into his characters and the nescience which he
must confess to sharing before the frontiers of their final
mystery. On this tightrope *Lord Jim* is a performance by one
of the great virtuosos of modern English literature.

In point of formal structure *Lord Jim* is chiefly distinguished by the multiplicity of its time shifts. The most
obvious employment of this device is in the creation of
suspense. Thus the first three chapters conduct us rapidly
from Jim's boyhood (although with a preliminary later
glimpse of him as water-clerk) to the deck of the *Patna*, introduce us briefly to those physical and moral grotesques, the
captain and the second engineer, and close upon the small
ominous shock which accompanies the vessel's passing over
some submerged object. Chapter 4 takes us straight to the
court of inquiry, and in its first sentence we learn that Jim
has to answer "pointed questions."(28) We learn that the
Patna had been holed and seemed about to sink, and that
Jim's subsequent conduct—whatever precisely it may have
been—has placed him in a morally untenable position, so
that he himself feels it to have "cut him off from the rest of
his kind."(31) But our knowledge of the full agony and irony
of his situation (the survival of the ship, and thus the lost
chance to have played, and himself survived in, a heroic role)
is deferred. For in Chapter 5, Marlow begins to speak, and he
is not in the least disposed to carry on the straightforward
narrative. Dipping back in time, he describes the arrival of
the *Patna*'s officers in the eastern port where the inquiry is
to be held, and the fat captain preparing to tell his story in

the harbour office—to tell it, we are casually informed, "in the innocence of his heart."(37) Later, we visit the chief engineer, who has had to be put in hospital with delirium tremens. He says: "I saw her go down," and Marlow records himself as ready to vent his indignation "at such a stupid lie."(51) The engineer (who believes that there are millions of pink toads under his bed) adds that the *Patna* was full of reptiles, and that "we had to clear out on the strict Q.T."(53) An acute reader will now be groping towards the truth, but he has to wait thirty pages for so much as a further oblique intimation of it, and fifteen more for its formal and weighted statement: "And still she floated! These sleeping pilgrims were destined to accomplish their whole pilgrimage to the bitterness of some other end."(97) In all this we have to notice that we are ourselves, so to speak, the only people 'being kept in the dark, since Marlow's hearers must be presumed already to know the brute facts about the *Patna*, and it is only briefly that her officers are exhibited as ignorant of whatever those facts may be. This lends some plausibility to the deviousness of Marlow's communication.

The contriving of mere suspense is a basic part of the story-teller's armoury, which is never to be despised even in the most sophisticated estimation of fiction. And it is still, perhaps, something to be called suspense that the time shifts in *Lord Jim* induce at a higher level. The turns and twists—the shuttle-like motion—of Marlow's yarn represent the casting hither and thither of a mind concerned less with mere dramatic effects to be secured by reassorting temporal sequences than with the immediate admission to consciousness of matter freshly discerned as here holding a relevant place in that attempted elucidation of Jim's mystery which is Marlow's central concern. That the mystery is also *his*, Marlow's, mystery (as it was Brierly's, too) is with us a felt fact which

makes us the more willing to follow what may sometimes
seem the merely arbitrary casting around of his mind. Marlow has to be careful. He must not—by moving on too rapidly
in desregard of this conceivably significant circumstance or
that (or this conceivably significant mere rumination or that)
—proceed too hastily to judgment. The constant halting of
the temporal sequence as Marlow's mind is beckoned to this
or that builds up a kind of inner tension echoing that outer
tension which makes us ask: "What really happened on the
Patna?" or "What finally happened in Patusan?"

It is only as we near the end of the book that we realize
this last question as one to which Marlow himself has as yet
no answer. "And later on," we read at the end of Chapter 4,
"many times, in distant parts of the world, Marlow showed
himself willing to remember Jim, to remember him at length,
in detail and audibly."(33) "To this day I don't know, I can
only guess,"(79) he says three chapter later—but he is saying
it, as he so often does, of Jim's inner mind, not of his final
fortune. Three pages later we hear of the "unforeseen conclusion of the tale"(82)—but this is merely on the *Patna*'s
staying afloat. In the last, and enormously long, paragraph of
Chapter 21 something perplexing happens to the tenses of
Marlow's verbs. Jim has established himself in Patusan:

> I ought to be delighted, for it is a victory in which I had taken
> my part; but I am not so pleased as I would have expected to be.
> I ask myself whether his rush had really carried him out of that
> mist in which he loomed interesting if not very big, with floating
> outlines—a straggler yearning inconsolably for his humble place
> in the ranks. And besides, the last word is not said,—probably
> shall never be said.(224-5)

We may reflect that the verbs are Conrad's as well as Marlow's—and Conrad's English grammar is always liable to
fatigue. But "I ought to be delighted," at least, is correct—

for Marlow's knowledge, as he talks, turns out to extend only
to that point, a little more than a hundred pages ahead, in
which he says good-bye to Jim on the shore of Patusan. " 'I
shall be faithful,' he said, quietly."(334) Within a few hundred words of this, Jim disappears for ever from Marlow's,
and our own, direct view. For Marlow's yarn is over; he has
told all he knows; and "there was only one man of all these
listeners who was ever to hear the last word of the story."(337)
This is the man who receives a written communication from
Marlow more than two years later.

Lord Jim is commonly described as being in two parts,
and we have seen that these are sometimes regarded as insufficiently integrated. It is really in four parts. Employing
the old terms appropriate to tragedy, we may say that the
first four chapters afford a swift *protasis;* the *epitasis,* com-
prising Marlow's oral narrative, is in two movements, the
first downward to the point at which Jim is beginning to
drift, and the second upward as he rebuilds his life in
Patusan; the *catastrophe* is heralded by another break in the
manner of narration, and is compressed, although not dras-
tically, so as to take on something of the character of an
epilogue. From the first still night on the Arabian Sea, with
its moon "like a slender shaving thrown up from a bar of
gold,"(17) to those final moments when the sky over Patusan shows "blood-red, immense, streaming like an open
vein,"(413) the execution of this plan in all its larger dimensions is unfaltering and superb. Conrad's art has entered its
all-too-brief major phase.

CHAPTER

VI

Nostromo (i)

Few great novels yield less to brief summary than does
*Nostromo.** The fact signals at once the large strength and
the cardinal weakness of the book. It is a philosophical and
political novel containing situations of wide representative
significance, and at the same time there is plenty of action
and some marvellous suspense. But the narrative line—if we
can speak of narrative line in a structure allowing so little to
free linear movement—seems at times inadequate to support
all that is hung on it, and, moreover, the book's conclusion
disappoints expectation. But when one has said so much (and
it is, of course, a good deal), one is dispensed from almost

* Costaguana is a South American state in which all semblance of public
order intermittently vanishes beneath one or another corrupt and brutal
dictatorship. In its occidental province, Sulaco, lies a great silver-mine which
an Englishman, Charles Gould, has inherited from a father who has died
worn out by his long struggle against venal and rapacious governments. The
son, who has at least powerful material weapons in the mine's outpouring
silver and in the backing of great financial interests in the United States,
dedicates himself to a continuation of the struggle to achieve a rational political and economic evolution for the country; by this idea he becomes progressively obsessed, to the detriment of any harmonious development of his

any further need to speak in dispraise of *Nostromo*. Conrad found imaginative creation desperately arduous. Yet there are few English novels into which we feel sheer creative power as flowing more abundantly.

While the standing of the novel as Conrad's masterpiece is generally apparent, the two limiting conditions here mentioned are sometimes overemphasized by its critics. It is true that this long story does not quite sustain itself to the end at its own highest level. But when Professor Guerard, in his major study of Conrad, suggests that little of the essential *Nostromo* would be lost "if we simply lopped off those last two hundred and sixty pages," [1] we must feel that the concept of essentiality thus invoked suggests a somewhat ruthless crash-course in Masters of the Modern European Novel. Again, the difficulty of getting on terms with the Costaguanan scene at the start can be exaggerated. "The plight of the

own personality, and in particular of his relationship with his wife. A point comes at which Gould makes a bold and dangerous move, throwing the resources of the mine uncompromisingly behind Don Vincente Ribiera, a "President-Dictator" disposed to develop a liberal constitution and admit further North American influences. Unfortunately Ribiera, although a doctor of philosophy from Cordova University, is not up to his job; he is overthrown by a section of the army, bolts over the mountains to Sulaco on a mule which drops dead beneath him as he arrives, and has to be hurried out of the country by sea. Sulaco is likely to be occupied by the forces of the victorious and reactionary General Montero. The city falls into the hands of the mob. The upper classes—the remnants of a Spanish American aristocracy, abundant in political eloquence but with no instinct for effective political action—harangue each other and compose proclamations behind the barricaded doors of their club. Gould decides, as a first measure of prudence, that a very large consignment of silver must be smuggled out in a lighter to the Golfo Placido, where it can be picked up by a European steamer and got away.

This task is given to two men. Nostromo, the Capataz de Cargadores, is a son of the people, daring, resolute, and judged incorruptible because his enormous vanity makes him faithful to an idealized image of himself which he has to project upon the public regard: he is admired and trusted by Gould, whose mirror-image in a sense he is. Martin Decoud is a Europeanized Costaguanan aristocrat, intelligent, intellectual, detached, and chiefly con-

reader"—as Mr. Guerard puts it—before "the disruptions of chronology and bedeviling distortions of emphasis" amid which Conrad winds his way into his tale can be unduly stressed. It is no doubt true that a "lazy reader" will find "the first sixty pages constitute an almost impenetrable barrier," [2] and true as well that no two endeavours to determine the book's time-scheme are ever likely to arrive at quite the same result. But it is equally true that no more bafflement need attend a first reading than we should feel in making a preliminary survey of any actual scene of some social or political complexity.

And here, as Mr. Guerard ably exhibits, is just what Conrad is about. We arrive in Sulaco, we have leisure for a brief topographical inspection, and then we are listening to an old gentleman of inexhaustible local knowledge (he turns out to be the superintendent of the Oceanic Steam Navigation

---

cerned to secure the love of Antonia Avellanos, the child of a diplomat who has suffered torture and extreme privation under a former tyranny, and now a woman passionately devoted to the cause of Costaguanan regeneration and liberty. These two men take the silver out to sea by night, and hide it on an island, the Great Isabel. Decoud remains there alone. Nostromo, returning to Sulaco, is further employed on a dangerous mission the success of which shifts the balance of military advantage, saves the city, and finally enables the occidental province to pursue a plan of secession adumbrated in the astute planning of Decoud, and which is to lead eventually to stable government and a rapidly developing (perhaps strangling) material progress.

But meanwhile Decoud has broken down under the strain of a few days' solitude on the Great Isabel and committed suicide. Matters have so fallen out, moreover, that the silver is believed to have been lost at sea. Nostromo keeps quiet about it, for he persuades himself that his merits have not been given their due, and under this affront to his vanity his celebrated incorruptibility disintegrates. He gradually enriches himself from the hidden treasure over a period of years. But a lighthouse is built on the Great Isabel, and Nostromo's access to the silver is thus threatened. He contrives that the light be put in charge of Giorgio Viola, once one of Garibaldi's "immortal thousand," so that he may continue his visits under pretence of courting one of Viola's two daughters. He becomes betrothed to the elder, enters into an intrigue with the younger, and is finally shot dead by Viola as a consequence of mistaken identity.

Company) who has a taste for yarning to newcomers about Costaguana's turbulent history. We are aware at once that anything we hear from Captain Mitchell is likely to be substantially affected by the limitations of his own vision. But Captain Mitchell is almost immediately withdrawn, and we are making what we can of an obscure political convulsion by watching how it impinges upon the little hotel run by Giorgio Viola. We learn that he is a Genoese, that his wife is a native of Spezzia, and that the mainstay of their staff is a certain Luis, who is "a cinnamon-coloured mulatto."(18) We get much precise information of this kind, but its larger context remains fragmented and obscure, so that we realize we are to be very much on our own, and that the shifting points of view and rapid time-shifts with which we are involved are simply so many demands upon our active participation in the task of exploring Costaguana and ordering in our minds as we can the fragmentary evidences pouring in on us. The technique of fiction thus brought to bear is no doubt subtle and sophisticated. Nevertheless, as common readers we are steadily catered for with adequate consideration. Nothing could be farther from the truth than the proposition that *Nostromo* was designed by Conrad as a stiff exercise for some graduate seminar. No sooner have we landed in the occidental province than its reality is all round us. We have only to look, and listen, and learn.

As with *Lord Jim*, the sources of *Nostromo* afford a study of considerable interest. South and Central America had been little more to Conrad than landfalls uncertainly glimpsed, although in one letter he records two or three days ashore in Puerto Cabello and La Guayra, together with "a few hours in a few other places on that dreary coast of Venezuela." It appears assured that he did not at first propose to make so unfamiliar a terrain the setting for more than a short story. When the difficulties of the larger project into which he was led thickened around him he appealed to his friend R. B. Cunninghame Graham, who was, among other things, as authentic an Anglo-South American as Charles Gould of the San Tomé Mine:

> And if you will *mettre le comble à vos bontés* you may render me a service by coming to see me here. (I speak not of heartfelt pleasure—*cela va sans dire*), I want to talk to you of the work I am engaged on now. I hardly dare avow my audacity—but I am placing it in South America, in a Republic I call Costaguana.[3]

This was written early in May 1903; a further appeal, this time merely implicit, followed three months later:

> I am dying over that cursed *Nostromo* thing. All my memories of Central America seem to slip away. I just had a glimpse 25 years ago,—a short glance. That is not enough *pour bâtir un roman dessus*. And yet one must live.
>
> When it's done I'll never dare look you in the face again.[4]

It is now known that Conrad made considerable use of books in filling in the background of *Nostromo*, and Cunninghame Graham probably put them in his way. But for the story itself—so far, at least, as it concerns the stolen silver— he must have possessed a literary source anterior to this correspondence. According to his own account, he had heard, when a very young sailor in the Gulf of Mexico, "the story of some man who was supposed to have stolen single-handed a whole lighter-full of silver, somewhere on the Tierra Firme seaboard during the troubles of a revolution"(vii); and long afterwards had come upon a full account of the incident "in a shabby volume picked up outside a second-hand book-shop."(viii) The coincidence is possible—and if Conrad is romancing, it is not about the "shabby volume," since this has recently been traced and described by Mr. John Halverson and Professor Ian Watt.[5] It substantiates Conrad's statement that the theft it records was committed by "an unmitigated rascal, a small cheat, stupidly ferocious, morose, of mean appearance, and altogether unworthy of the greatness this opportunity had thrust upon him."(viii) But Nostromo, Conrad goes on, "is what he is because I received the inspiration for him in my early days from a Mediterranean sailor."(xii) As it happens, there is a pointer of great significance here to the whole inspiration of the novel in its largest dimensions. The immediate fact is that Conrad's mind, faced with the business of creating wild exploits on and around his Placid Gulf, cast back to the early period of his own life when he had been involved in those gun-running adventures of which he gives an account, in part probably fictitious and in part certainly true, in the later sections of *The Mirror of the Sea*. His hero in those days was a certain Dominic Cervoni, the resourceful *padrone* of the unlawfully employed *Tremolino*, and with a grand air of being "darkly initiated into the most awful mysteries of the sea."[6] Conrad was to call the romantic largeness of this man time and again to the aid of his invention. He uses him here to elevate what he calls "a vagrant anecdote completely destitute of valuable details"(vii):

It was only when it dawned upon me that the purloiner of the treasure need not necessarily be a confirmed rogue, that he could be even a man of character, an actor and possibly a victim in the changing scenes of a revolution, it was only then that I had the first vision of a twilight country which was to become the province of Sulaco, with it high shadowy Sierra and its misty Campo for mute witnesses of events flowing from the passions of men shortsighted in good and evil.(ix)

We have here a key to the whole creative process underlying *Nostromo*. It has been claimed that this novel marks a
turning-point in Conrad's career as a writer because in it he
is breaking away for the first time alike from the high seas
and from the Malay Archipelago, the only two theatres
within which his invention could fortify itself from any store
of personal experience. It is true that he felt these two sources
of inspiration to have been exhausted, at least for a time,
and that he must venture farther afield in the future. He is
doing this in *Nostromo*, and one consequence is a running
into the kind of difficulty which produces his appeal to
Cunninghame Graham. But reflection suggests to us that, at
a deeper level, *Nostromo* shows Conrad exploring personal
experience of the most poignant kind. The mind turning
back to those dark nights on the Mediterranean filled with
wild adventurings in the Carlist cause is also a mind turning
back to the Poland of Apollo Korzeniowski. Just as Nostromo's
character and interest are enlarged by the imaginative reference back to Cervoni, so is Costaguana's history elevated—
and, for the writer, charged with emotion—through a similar
implication with the land of Conrad's birth. *Nostromo*, indeed, is the first of three novels, each essentially political in
theme, which are very far from being objective exercises in
the craft of fiction.

At the same time, the element of mere research is not to
be minimized. When writing his Malayan stories, Conrad
had accustomed himself to the use of literary sources. Wal-
lace's *The Malay Archipelago*, the Brooke journals, books
with titles like *Perak and the Malays, My Journal in Malayan
Waters, Life in the Forests of the Far East* were regularly
consulted. Now it was the turn of *The War between Peru
and Chile*, and *Venezuela: or, Sketches of Life in a South
American Republic*, and *Seven Eventful Years in Paraguay*.

His habitual reliance upon factual sources when assembling
proper names is particularly evident here, and in one instance
is of substantial interest. It appears that in Valencia (which
suffered more than any other /Venezuelan city from the
ravages of revolution) there had lived a certain Antonia
Ribera, a reigning beauty who joined to her outward charms
considerable learning, an emancipated outlook, and a particular interest in politics and diplomacy. Conrad borrowed
her surname, a little changed, for his hapless President-
Dictator, and a good deal more than her Christian name for
his heroine, Antonia Avellanos. Yet in his Author's Note he
is quite specific about Miss Avellanos. He modelled her, he
says, on his first love, a young Polish patriot whom he and
his school-fellows had revered as "the standard-bearer of a
faith to which we all were born but which she alone knew
how to hold aloft with an unflinching hope!"(xiv) There is
no certain evidence as to this girl's identity; she may or may
not have been the future Baroness Janina de Brunnow, about
whose romantic relationship with Conrad an uncertain family
tradition exists.[7] But we need not doubt that genuine memories of this kind were vividly in his mind as he wrote
Nostromo, or even his further hinted assertion that the
levity with which this stern young "Puritan of patriotism"
used to charge him as a boy is mirrored in Miss Avellano's
attitude to "poor Decoud."(xiv) And the larger point is
obvious. What energizes *Nostromo*, adding a further dimen-
sion to a South American scene itself created with an astonishing solidity and immediacy in the round, is its emotional
hinterland in the Poland of Conrad's youth. Don José Avellanos, an impoverished aristocrat elevated in political and
moral feeling but inept in action, who has suffered atrociously under a barbarous regime and achieved some literary
distinction with his eloquent *History of Fifty Years of*

Misrule, is close enough to Conrad's father for the purposes of at least semiconscious imaginative identification. At the same time the parallel here, as also in the broad political situation, is a long way from being oppressively close. In *Nostromo* Conrad contemplates the Polish spectacle only across a substantial aesthetic distance. It is a subject he was never anxious to obtrude. Up to 1914, Mr. Najder tells us, he mentioned Poland in his published work only three times.[8]

Nostromo was begun in January 1903 and finished, despite various tribulations and one or two attempts at more rapid money-making, in just twenty months. Conrad's letters at this time are even more than usually filled with cries of despair. However much we discount these as the expression of an excitable and even hysterical temperament, it remains evident that his actual situation was grim. He was constantly disabled by severe attacks of gout, and his wife suffered the accident which crippled her for life. He had no money, the tradesmen were at the door, his banker wrote disagreeable letters so that he didn't dare to draw a cheque. (He was now forty-six.) Then his bank actually failed. This was a not uncommon hazard at the time; for example, Rudyard Kipling's bank had failed only a decade before. Unlike Kipling, Conrad had only an overdraft at risk, but the incident must have been upsetting, all the same. In the midst of all this, *Nostromo* seemed to him a hand-to-mouth affair. It begins as a substantial short story. Three months later, he is hoping to finish it in a further three months—although at the same time he expresses himself to H. G. Wells like this:

I, my dear Wells, am absolutely out of my mind with the worry and apprehension of my work. I go on as one would cycle over a precipice along a 14-inch plank. If I falter I am lost.[9]

Two months after this, he is reporting himself as having produced 42,000 words, which he supposes have brought him to the half-way mark, although in fact more than three-quarters is yet to write. At this point he told Galsworthy that he felt "half dead and wholly imbecile." [10] When the book was actually finished, he wrote to Garnett requesting congratulations "as upon a recovery from a dangerous illness"; [11] to Ford declaring that he was without elation or even relief; to William Rothenstein saying that he had been working practically night and day for a month with the tenacity of despair; and to Galsworthy reducing this unintermitted labour to a fortnight, but adding an encounter with a maniacal dentist, a fit of amnesia, and a motor-accident which had resulted in his being surrounded by a cursing and howling mob. It is scarcely surprising that so unfortunate a man should cry out: *"Mes nerfs sont tout à fait détraqués!"* [12]

These are all matter of private communication. In *A Personal Record* Conrad has provided a more decorous and not less impressive account of his struggle to write his greatest novel:

I was just then giving up some days of my allotted span to the last chapters of the novel "Nostromo," a tale of an imaginary (but true) seaboard, which is still mentioned now and again, and indeed kindly, sometimes in connection with the word "failure" and sometimes in conjunction with the word "astonishing." I have no opinion on this discrepancy. It's the sort of difference that can never be settled. All I know, is that, for twenty months, neglecting the common joys of life that fall to the lot of the humblest of this earth, I had, like the prophet of old, "wrestled with the Lord" for my creation, for the headlands of the coast, for the darkness of the Placid Gulf, the light on the snows, the clouds on the sky, and for the breath of life that had to be blown into the shapes of men and women, of Latin and Saxon, of Jew and Gentile. These are, perhaps, strong words, but it is difficult to characterise otherwise the intimacy and the strain of a creative effort in which mind and will and conscience are engaged to the full, hour after hour, day after day, away from the world, and to the exclusion of all that makes life really lovable and gentle—something for which a material parallel can only be found in the everlasting sombre stress of the westward winter passage round Cape Horn. For that too is the wrestling of men with the might of their Creator, in a great isolation from the world, without the amenities and consolations of life, a lonely struggle under a sense of over-matched littleness, for no reward that could be adequate, but for the mere winning of a longitude. Yet a certain longitude, once won, cannot be disputed. The sun and the stars and the shape of your earth are the witnesses of your gain; whereas a handful of pages, no matter how much you have made them your own, are at best but an obscure and questionable spoil. Here they are. "Failure"—"Astonishing": take your choice; or perhaps both, or neither—a mere rustle and flutter of pieces of paper settling down in the night, and undistinguishable, like the snow-flakes of a great drift destined to melt away in sunshine.[13]

This rather sombrely tinted sketch of the artist's vocation is undoubtedly very authentic to Conrad. Yet we must reflect that it was a vocation which he had gone a long way to find; that "the common joys of life that fall to the lot of the humblest of this earth" may indeed have been in some degree renounced during the journey, but are scarcely to be described as something he had been cheated of; and that he almost certainly derived far more of solace than of frustration from his exhausting labours. H. G. Wells, an observant friend of no very sympathetic complexion, expresses the fact of the matter succinctly:

He had set himself to be a great writer, an artist in words; and to achieve all the recognition and distinction that he imagined should go with that ambition, he had gone literary with a singleness and intensity of purpose that made the kindred concentration of Henry James seem lax and large and pale.[14]

The writer of *Nostromo*, in a word, was wholly an artist. Although far from unsociable, he made his friends and acquaintances almost wholly among literary people. Unlike James, he seems not to have been much attracted by the wealthy, nor does he seem to have had an ambition to move in any class of English society equivalent to that into which he had been born in Poland. He had married a good cook, and it is recorded that he often seemed mildly surprised that two attractive small boys had been the result. Domestic life on inadequate means harassed him, but he permitted no aspect of it to become absorbing. The key to *Nostromo*'s being triumphantly achieved amid so many discouragements and distresses lies simply in the fact that its author was a fiercely dedicated man.

We may return to the structure of the book. The opening chapter, which is very short, contrives both to evoke the physical theatre of the action and to offer a subtle adumbration of its theme. Sulaco appears a fortunate place. Set amid the luxuriant beauty of orange gardens, it has found "an inviolable sanctuary from the temptations of a trading world in the solemn hush of the deep Golfo Placido as if within an enormous semicircular and unroofed temple open to the ocean."(3) Nevertheless we are made aware at once of something sombre in the scene, for we are told at the end of the first paragraph that the lofty mountains surrounding the Gulf are "hung with the mourning draperies of cloud." Then immediately we have the legend of Azuera, that isolated patch of blue mist which is in fact a waterless peninsula, a wild chaos of stony levels and vertical ravines, amid which a

vast treasure of gold is popularly supposed to lie. Three men
—two of them gringos—and a donkey once set out in search
of it; they were never seen again; nevertheless it is known
that the gringos at least, "spectral and alive,"(5) dwell to this
day among the rocks, souls unable to tear themselves away
from their bodies mounting guard over a fabulous spoil. The
story—spare and vivid as the *exemplum* told by Chaucer's
Pardoner to the Pilgrims—suggests that "the temptations of
a trading world" are not absent from Sulaco, after all. Perhaps it is some resulting human spectacle that the surrounding mountains are mourning over. Meanwhile, with just this
glimpse of men going about such labour as seems good to
them, we are returned to the natural scene: a tremendous
cloudscape in ceaseless mutation from morning through noon
to night:

At night the body of clouds advancing higher up the sky
smothers the whole quiet gulf below with an impenetrable darkness, in which the sound of the falling showers can be heard beginning and ceasing abruptly—now here, now there. Indeed, these
cloudy nights are proverbial with the seamen along the whole
west coast of a great continent. Sky, land, and sea disappear together out of the world when the Placido—as the saying is—goes
to sleep under its black poncho. The few stars left below the
seaward frown of the vault shine feebly as into the mouth of a
black cavern. In its vastness your ship floats unseen under your
feet, her sails flutter invisible above your head. The eye of God
Himself—they add with grim profanity—could not find out what
work a man's hand is doing in there; and you would be free to
call the devil to your aid with impunity if even his malice were
not defeated by such a blind darkness.(6)

But by daylight there are the three islets called the Isabels.
From the Great Isabel—an emerald green wedge of land a
mile long, with a spring of fresh water in a ravine—one can

glimpse two miles away, and through an opening in the coastline so abrupt that it might have been chopped with an axe, the harbour of Sulaco. It is an oblong, lake-like piece of water. Beyond that is the town: "tops of walls, a great cupola, gleams of white miradors in a vast grove of orange trees." And then there is the vast Sulaco plain, which "passes into the opal mystery of great distances overhung by dry haze."(8) The authority of this writing cannot be conveyed in summary. There is no comparable opening in the entire range of English fiction, unless it be Hardy's evocation of Egdon Heath in *The Return of the Native*.

Four further short chapters follow. From the Great Isabel one can just distinguish the jetty of the Oceanic Steam Navigation Company; its activities are described, and we learn that to the commanders of its ships its superintendent in Sulaco, Captain Mitchell, is known as "Fussy Joe." Captain Mitchell's voice is heard, disapproving of "frequent changes of government brought about by revolutions of the military type."(11) He recalls one such occasion when "poor Señor Ribiera," a displaced dictator, had come pelting over the mountains, found that the news of his fall had preceded him, and been saved and got away only by the resolution of Nostromo, Capataz de Cargadores, a protégé of whom Captain Mitchell is inordinately proud. The mob had been in control of the town, but Nostromo and his men had repulsed it from the harbour. Even "the little hotel kept by old Giorgio" was saved. This is the end of Chapter Two. Although we do not know it, Captain Mitchell's reminiscences, represented as habitual rather than as being offered on a specific occasion, have taken us straight to the brief period of time in which the central action of the novel is conceived as having taken place. In Chapter Three the time is unchanged, and we are given a picture, direct and unmediated, of Giorgio Viola preparing to defend his hotel, his wife, and his two daughters from the rioters. Conrad somewhere speaks of his endeavour to use "the power of the written word, to make you hear, to make you feel . . . to make you *see*." [15] Here, in Viola's shuttered room, we do not merely see "the coloured lithograph of Garibaldi in a black frame on the white wall"; we also mark that "a thread of strong sunshine cut it perpendicularly."(21) The whole chapter is astonishingly concrete and immediate. At the same time we learn something of what certain people think of each other. Signora Viola wishes that their lodger, Gian' Battista (who is Nostromo), were coming to their aid—but "he thinks of nobody but himself."(20) In fact, Nostromo turns up noisily, and at the head of his men, in the last paragraph.

Chapter Four, which carries straight on, is a little longer. Still centred on "this memorable day of the riot,"(26) it plays freely round the figure of Giorgio on other occasions. We see him cooking for his guests, the foreign engineers who, on British capital, are building Costaguana's National Central Railway. In Italy he had cooked for Garibaldi himself—riding with the staff and holding rank as a lieutenant the while. And at once, briefly, his whole career and character are opened to us:

He had lived among men who had declaimed about liberty, suffered for liberty, died for liberty, with a desperate exaltation, and with their eyes turned towards an opressed Italy. . . . The Spirit of self-forgetfulness, the simple devotion to a vast humanitarian idea which inspired the thought and stress of that revolutionary time, had left its mark upon Giorgio in a sort of austere contempt for all personal advantage. . . . This stern devotion to a cause had cast a gloom upon Giorgio's old age.(29-31)

Long ago, Giorgio had been given a Bible in Italian through the good offices of the British and Foreign Bible Society. It is by means of something tacked on to this information (and here we have quintessential Conradian technique) that we are afforded a first and momentary glimpse of the principal personages in the book:

> He carried it with him into battles. Now it was his only read-
> ing, and in order not to be deprived of it (the print was small)
> he had consented to accept the present of a pair of silver-mounted
> spectacles from Señora Emilia Gould, the wife of the Englishman
> who managed the silver mine in the mountains three leagues
> from the town. She was the only Englishwoman in Sulaco.(30)

Chapter Five makes the first time-shift—very clearly and explicitly. Eighteen months before the revolution the reper-cussions of which in Sulaco we have been glimpsing, "the Excellentissimo Señor don Vincente Ribiera, the Dictator of Costaguana" has appeared there to grace the turning of the first sod in what he calls the "progressive and patriotic under-taking"(34) of building the railway. This is, of course, the benevolent and scholarly despot whom—peering into the future with Captain Mitchell (or rather, long afterwards, peering with him into another past)—we have observed flee-ing into Sulaco and being hurried out of the country with the help of the intrepid Nostromo. But now there is a grand party for Ribiera and his suite on board the O.S.N.'s steamer *Juno*. It is an upper-class affair—for in Costaguana, with Ribiera in power, the old aristocracy, the Blancos, are for the moment on top. The Minister of War, General Montero, is not a Blanco, but a low fellow who has made his way by insolent effrontery. We cannot be going wrong in seeing him as a villain, since Conrad had surprisingly small use for subtlety when such are in question; we know General Mon-tero as instantly as we know, say, Don John in *Much Ado about Nothing*.

The *Juno* does not, for the moment, detain us long. There is an English financier aboard, much inclined to admire Mrs. Gould, the only woman in Sulaco sufficiently advanced to appear on such public occasions. But as he is floating the railway, he is interested in its construction, and suddenly we have accompanied him to a surveying camp established at the highest point to which the line will climb. So the tinsel of the *Juno* junketing (with Captain Mitchell in his glory upon so historic an occasion) is magnificently juxtaposed with the unchanging natural face of the occidental province:

He spent the night there, arriving just too late to see the last dying glow of sunlight upon the snowy flank of Higuerota. Pillared masses of black basalt framed like an open portal a portion of the white field lying aslant against the west. In the transparent air of the high altitudes everything seemed very near, steeped in a clear stillness as in an imponderable liquid; and with his ear ready to catch the first sound of the expected diligencia the engineer-in-chief, at the door of a hut of rough stones, had contemplated the changing hues on the enormous side of the mountain, thinking that in this sight, as in a piece of inspired music, there could be found together the utmost delicacy of shaded expression and a stupendous magnificence of effect.

Sir John arrived too late to hear the magnificent and inaudible strain sung by the sunset amongst the high peaks of the Sierra. It had sung itself out into the breathless pause of deep dusk before, climbing down the fore wheel of the diligencia with stiff limbs, he shook hands with the engineer.(40)

Looking at Higuerota, the engineer murmurs to his employer that one can't move moutains. Sir John agrees—which means that more landowners must be persuaded to negotiate with the railway. For this, the powerful and respected Charles Gould is the man. There is some talk about Gould, some about Holroyd, the American capitalist behind the San

Tomé mine, and some about Nostromo, who is acting as
camp-master for Sir John. Commendations of Nostromo conclude the chapter. Conrad here perhaps gives the effect of
having to work rather hard to keep his magnificent Capataz
de Cargadores securely in the picture.

Chapter Six is a shade longer than the five preceding
chapters taken together, and a complex structure in terms
both of time and place. Nostromo provides the backward
link: one man who fails to think highly of him is Dr.
Monygham. But Dr. Monygham's is a bitter and eccentric
character, and his only known devotion is to Mrs. Gould.
Years ago, "in the time of Guzman Bento,"(45) he had been
mysteriously implicated in a conspiracy which was betrayed.
We hear no more of this now—we shall have to wait hundreds
of pages for more—but on Guzman Bento there is sufficient
information at once. Under his monstrous tryanny an uncle
of Charles Gould's had been shot, and this is one reason why
the Blancos, families of pure Spanish descent, regard Gould
(although he is more English-looking than a casual tourist)
as one of themselves. Don José Avellanos, the Goulds' "neigh-
bour across the street," is accustomed "to declare in Doña
Emilia's drawing-room that Carlos had all the English qualities of character with a truly patriotic heart."(50) A description of Gould going about the business of the reviving mine
in the early days of his married life suggests somebody at
once very much at home in Sulaco and surprisingly new to
it. Then—because "Mrs. Gould knew the history of the San
Tomé mine"(52)—there comes the whole story of his father's
being compelled by a rapacious government to take up the
Concession, of the long series of irritated and desperate and
despairing letters to his son during the boy's ten years'
schooling in England, of the boy's growing determination to
to fight "the grotesque and murderous bands that played

their game of governments and revolutions after the death of
Guzman Bento"(56)—so that "by the time he was twenty
Charles Gould had, in his turn, fallen under the spell of the
San Tomé mine."(59) Upon this theme there follows, in
natural chronological sequence, Gould's engagement to his
future wife in Italy, and her participation in his concentrated thought upon this family problem. "They discussed
it because the sentiment of love can enter into any subject
and live ardently in remote phrases. For this natural reason
these discussions were precious to Mrs. Gould in her engaged
state."(60) Then comes the news of the elder Gould's death,
and then his son's resulting sense of dedication. "Her lips
were slightly parted as though in surprise that he should not
be looking at her with his usual expression. His usual expression was unconditionally approving and attentive."(62)
Hard upon this, Gould leaves his *fiancée* "for a few days, to
find an American, a man from San Francisco, who was still
somewhere in Europe."(64) The young heir to the precarious
Gould fortunes is making his first contact with the Holroyd
organization and finance capital.

We are now half-way through Chapter Six, and advance
upon "the latest phase in the history of the mine."(66) It is in
essence, we are told, the history of Mrs. Gould's married life.
A twelve months' bride, she is seen in her Sulaco house,
entertaining her first visitors from abroad. One of them is no
less a personage than Holroyd himself, but for the moment
we learn less of him than of the house, which Mrs. Gould
loves. The visitors go away, and the young husband and wife
converse. Mrs. Gould is amused by Holroyd, who confuses
his financial ambition with an aspiration to spread a purified
form of Christianity in Costaguana and elsewhere. For
Charles Gould thoughts of this kind are irrelevant; he is still
thinking of his father, and of his mission. Having thus ad-

vanced to a point at which the Goulds are established in Sulaco, the recital dips back by the space of a year to show in detail the means by which this was brought about. For half-a-dozen pages Gould is shown using "his lever to move men who had capital."(75) Then we are returned over the same year's space to observe this process continuing during Holroyd's visit to Sulaco, after which we are back with the Goulds continuing their discussion following upon Holroyd's departure behind Mrs. Gould's white mules. There is nothing arbitrary in this twelve months' loop in the narrative, since it exhibits the tightening grip of those "material interests" which Gould is to believe he can harness to his ideal purpose of vindicating his father by having his mine bring order to Costaguana. He tells his wife of his faith now:

"What is wanted here is law, good faith, order, security. Any one can declaim about these things, but I pin my faith to material interests. Only let the material interests once get a firm footing, and they are bound to impose the conditions on which alone they can continue to exist. That's how your money-making is justified here in the face of lawlessness and disorder. It is justified because the security which it demands must be shared with an oppressed people. A better justice will come afterwards. That's your ray of hope." His arm pressed her slight form closer to his side for a moment. "And who knows whether in that sense even the San Tomé mine may not become that little rift in the darkness which poor father despaired of ever seeing?"

She glanced up at him with admiration. He was competent; he had given a vast shape to the vagueness of her unselfish ambitions.(84)

In fact, we are here in the presence of what will become a divisive force between husband and wife. And it is the one point at which Gould is perhaps not without some intuition of this. The chapter ends:

"What should be perfectly clear to us," he said, "is the fact that there is no going back. Where could we begin life afresh? We are in now for all that there is in us."

He bent over her upturned face very tenderly and a little remorsefully. Charles Gould was competent because he had no illusions. The Gould Concession had to fight for life with such weapons as could be found at once in the mire of corruption that was so universal as to almost lose its significance. He was prepared to stoop for his weapons. For a moment he felt as if the silver mine, which had killed his father, had decoyed him further than he meant to go; and with the roundabout logic of emotions, he felt that the worthiness of his life was bound up with success. There was no going back.(85)

Chapter Seven is short, and confined entirely within the first phase of the Goulds' venture. We see Charles Gould "stooping for his weapons" as he is received by, and conveys the routine bribe to, some insufferable "provincial Excellency."(90) But in the main it is a background chapter. Mrs. Gould, travelling about Sulaco with her husband in the search for labour, observes the land and its poverty-stricken common people. In the great country-houses of the surviving Blancos she learns more of Costaguanan history: "stories of political outrage; friends, relatives, ruined, imprisoned, killed in the battles of senseless civil wars, barbarously executed in ferocious proscriptions, as though the government of the country had been a struggle of lust between bands of absurd devils let loose upon the land with sabres and uniforms and grandiloquent phrases."(88)

Chapter Eight, which concludes Part I of *Nostromo*, is almost as long as Chapter Six, but less complex in structure. An important function of its earlier part is to mark the passing of a considerable period of time between the reopening of the San Tomé mine by Charles Gould and that cutting of the first sod for the National Central Railway which in turn preceded (by eighteen months, as we know) the fall of Señor don Vincente Ribiera. To mark this, and also to set the *entire* action of the novel securely in a historical past, a first-person narrator makes a curiously casual appearance in the first paragraph:

> Those of us whom business or curiousity took to Sulaco in these years before the first advent of the railway can remember the steadying effect of the San Tomé mine upon the life of that remote province. The outward appearances had not changed then as they have changed since, as I am told, with cable cars running along the streets of the Constitution, and carriage roads far into the country. . . .
>
> Nobody had ever heard of labour troubles then. . . .(95)

The Cargadores, in fact, were effectively controlled by the strong-arm methods of Nostromo. These are immediately described in some detail. But if the dock-hands can be knocked about, it is otherwise with the workers of the mine; should one of these, distinctively garbed, come down from the mountain he is unlikely to be "beaten to within an inch of his life on a charge of disrespect to the town police,"(97) or even lassoed on the road by an army recruiting party. For the mine (unlike Sulaco's dilapidated Aristocratic Club, of which there is a rapid glimpse) is becoming a power in the land. In a series of vigorously realized passages, we see various aspects of its growing life in action. One consequence of this long process has already been exhibited: when the railway is to be begun and Sir John arrives from Europe for the occasion, he is quickly made aware that the effective ruler of the occidental province is the Englishman who controls the mine. And with Sir John we return to the celebrations on board the *Juno*—which we may recall leaving when in full swing nearly eighty pages back. The President-Dictator Ribiera is making a speech, surrounded by a gratified *entourage* of well-bred Blancos. Mrs. Gould, clear-eyed, judges her husband's nominee as Head of State (for Ribiera is virtually that) to be more pathetic than promising. And General Montero, who feels insufficiently deferred to, makes a brutal and aggressive speech—even (to the horror of Don José Avellanos, formerly accredited as Minister Plenipotentiary to the Court of St. James's, and of the other Blancos) mentioning the crude fact that Sir John is putting up "a million and a half of pounds."(120) We are obliged to feel that Conrad likes the General no better than do the assembled Don Antonios and Don Francescos. He might almost be writing about some Russian overlord amid a Polish gentry:

The white plume, the copery tint of his broad face, the blue-black of the moustaches under the curved beak, the mass of gold on sleeves and breast, the high shining boots with enormous spurs, the working nostrils, the imbecile and domineering stare of the glorious victor of Rio Seco had in them something ominous and incredible; the exaggeration of a cruel caricature, the fatuity of solemn masquerading, the atrocious grotesqueness of some military idol of Aztec conception and European bedecking, awaiting the homage of worshippers.(122)

The note of the "ominous" is certainly not muted. And on it the first part of *Nostromo* comes to a close. Or not quite—for, once more, there is Nostromo himself to remember. So we see him in a public encounter with his current mistress—first taunting and then contemptuously placating her. And we hear, finally, the voice of Captain Mitchell yet again. He is recalling, once more, the fatal day upon which Don Vincente's mule perished beneath him:

"It was history—history, sir! And that fellow of mine, Nostromo, you know, was right in it. Absolutely making history, sir."(130)

Unfortunately—Captain Mitchell adds—something else happened as well:

"It was a fatality. A misfortune, pure and simple, sir. And that poor fellow of mine was right in it—right in the middle of it! A fatality, if ever there was one—and to my mind he has never been the same man since."(131)

It is round Captain Mitchell's "fatality" that the rest of the novel is to revolve.

CHAPTER

VII

Nostromo (ii)

The second part of *Nostromo* is substantially longer than the first, and the third is nearly as long as the first and second put together. At the end of the first part, therefore, we are less than a quarter of the way through the novel. Even so, the reader may feel himself to have been denied a good deal of information which he is entitled to by this time. It is not that the first 130 pages are dilute or in the slightest degree tedious. On the contrary, they create with a prodigal power an entire South American world: *Cosas de Costaguana*. All critics are agreed on the overwhelming success of Conrad's impressionistic method in transporting us with all our senses into this distant country. But already it is not merely a matter of the conjuring up of an exotic spectacle in hallucinatory clarity. There has been a dynamic yet analytical presentation of men in society: men circumstanced not at all as we are, and confronting political situations unfamiliar to us—but whose world, nevertheless, has as immediate a relevance for us as has that of Shakespeare's history plays. Moreover, a remarkable diversity of characters have come very much alive: not merely the Goulds, but Dr. Monygham (of whom there has been only a glimpse), and Don Pépé, guardian of the mine (whom we have not even had occasion to mention), and General Montero, so splendidly unspeakable, and old Giorgio Viola, the Garibaldini. (Giorgio above all, perhaps; for he is a secondary character who has from the first that excess of life beyond the requirements of circumstance which is a hallmark of major fiction.) We may, indeed, feel in these characters a tendency to live a little too much on their own. Even what we can dimly see as likely to build up between Charles and Emilia Gould seems essentially an absence of relationship. It is possible that we are here in contact with some difficulty confronting Conrad as he works at his book.

But what the reader is chiefly unprovided with at this point is any secure sense of the nature and dimensions of such action as may be conceived to have taken place. Costaguana has suffered one of its recurrent revolutions, and it has been of a sort not likely to favour Charles Gould of the San Tomé mine and his Blanco friends. In Sulaco itself there have been riots—we have not been put in a position to say how severe or of what continuance—and also something which Captain Mitchell calls a "fatality," and to which he ascribes some alteration for the worse in his right-hand man, Nostromo. This is really as much as we know.

It seems very probable that, here at the end of Part I, Conrad is still feeling his way into his story. He had conceived it as being about Nostromo—who in his first source was a paltry rascal, but whom he had seen the possibility of endowing at least with a certain romantic *panache* borrowed from the Mediterranean and from Dominic Cervoni. Nostromo, during certain public disorders, was to steal and secrete some silver, and was subsequently to enrich himself slowly from the hidden hoard. There can be little doubt that, even when there was added to this the conception of a man whose integrity is a mere function of his vanity, the theme must quickly have come to seem not quite adequate as the mainstay of a long novel. Moreover, almost from the start, we are obliged to sense Conrad as having to work hard at Nostromo; this climaxes at the end of Part I, where the encounter with Paquita, the "pretty Morenita,"(127) rings curiously false. The fact is—it has to be faced up to for the rest of the book—that the magnificent Capataz de Cargadores is in danger of becoming a figure merely Conradesque, as more than one Cervoni-character actually does become in the fiction of Conrad's decline. He belongs to an area of experience to which the imagination of the mature novelist no longer readily kindles.[1] But at least the impressionistic method results in Conrad's retaining great freedom of manoeuvre at this stage. And major characters of whom we have as yet heard no word are now to present themselves.

Part II opens *before* Part I—at least it does this if we regard Part I as starting with the arrival of the fugitive Ribiera in an already disordered Sulaco. For now what we hear of is "the endangered Ribiera Government,"(136) and what we watch through a sequence of six chapters of varying length is the circumstances surrounding the departure of a supporting Ribierist force from the occidental province. Its new rifles have been brought into Sulaco by Martin Decoud, a young Costaguanan aristocrat long resident in Paris, who is frivolous, sceptical, and non-political, and who has himself accompanied his rifles only because he is in love with Antonia Avellanos, the fanatically patriotic daughter of Don José. We may feel that there is a little too much of romantic facility in this conception, and that these new characters are far from attracting us; Miss Avellanos is forbidding, and Decoud's

temperament and attitudes are chronicled in a flatly descriptive idiom which seems designed to leave him the benefit of
a few doubts. In the six short chapters which these two largely
dominate, however, they establish a firm claim to our regard.
Decoud is honest about himself; his moral feelings are essentially uncorrupted; despite his air of disengagement, he can
apply his intellect with a formidable clarity and rapidity to
the practical issues of Sulaco's survival. Miss Avellanos meets
him fairly. The scene in which—to the scandal of the Blanco
ladies—they talk side by side on the balcony of the Casa
Gould, their elbows touching, actualizes their relationship
very fully.

They have to compete with other newcomers at this point:
General Barrios—plebeian, naively boastful, a compulsive
gambler whose god is a bottle—the by no means inconsider-
able or wholly unattractive commander of the army of
Sulaco: Don José's awkwardly fanatical missionary brother-
in-law, Father Corbelàn, full of an impolitic insistence that
the Church must recover its stolen properties; Señor Hirsch,
the comically craven Jewish hide-merchant from the neigh-
bouring port of Esmeralda (whom so dreadful a fate awaits).
Moreover there is now a gathering narrative momentum—
and Decoud and Miss Avellanos are soon swept apart by it.
There is one flash-back to the barbarities inflicted upon Don
José and his friends by the bestial Guzman; it has the function of emphasizing what may happen again if Ribiera fails.
Apart from this, there is an unbroken chronological progression up to the point at which Decoud confides to Mrs. Gould
the news that Ribiera *has* failed, and his conviction that only
a separatist policy can save the occidental province—and possibly bring Antonia safe into his arms. Upon this there
follows a device unrealistic in itself but justified as increasing
the pace. Decoud writes, and we read, a long letter to his

sister in Paris. Ribiera has appeared on his moribund mule, and Nostromo has rescued him and then led the resistance to the mob. Word has come on the telegraph that Ribiera is being pursued across the almost impassable mountains by a small force led by Pedro Montero, brother of the General and lately a servant in a Paris legation. Word has come, too, that the garrison at Esmeralda, supposed faithful to the Blanco interest, has revolted and is on the way to Sulaco in a troopship. Charles Gould has agreed that a great consignment of silver must be got out to sea. Nostromo is the man for the job, but Decoud will go with him in the hope of being picked up by an O.S.N. steamer and put in contact with Barrios, whose army must be brought back to free and defend the newly independent Occidental State. Decoud writes his letter from Giorgio Viola's hotel. It is close to the harbour and he has more or less gone into hiding in it; as a consequence, he is there during Mrs. Viola's last hours. Nostromo has fetched Dr. Monygham to the dying woman; he will not waste time fetching a priest; Mrs. Viola's last words to him are of a kind which we may well believe will colour his mind:

"Get riches at least for once, you indispensable, admired Gian' Battista, to whom the peace of a dying woman is less than the praise of people who have given you a silly name—and nothing besides—in exchange for your soul and body . . . They have turned your head with their praises . . . They have been paying you with words. Your folly shall betray you into poverty, misery, starvation. The very leperos shall laugh at you—the great Capataz."(256-7)

This prophetic interlude a little holds up the action—but it is without the break of a chapter-heading, nevertheless, that Nostromo and Decoud, together with their unsuspected fellow-traveller, the blindly terrified Hirsch, are out on the

Golfo Placido with the silver-laden lighter. The remaining forty pages of Part II constitute one of Conrad's greatest triumphs as a teller of tales. It is sometimes maintained that he is seldom at his best in the direct description of action. But the art here seems unerring. There is just enough of digression and reflection to enhance rather than impair the suspense. The apartness of Decoud and Nostromo—thus arbitrarily associated together and isolated in an impenetrable darkness—is conveyed by the reflections of each on the other. The brief retrospective account of Hirsch's day of imbecile panic, in itself an admirable stroke of the macabre, is made the occasion of the stiffest dramatic irony in the book: "Nature, who had made him what he was, seemed to have calculated cruelly how much he could bear in the way of atrocious anguish without actually expiring."(274) When the point of view abruptly switches to Colonel Sotillo on the invisible troopship, there is a brief glance at his character and career, and at the recent circumstances which have prompted him to turn Monterist and make this dash to Sulaco in quest of the silver. But then the direct narrative is immediately resumed. The collision takes place; Hirsch, howling, make his bizarre exit on the troopship's anchor; the crippled lighter is got safely to the Great Isabel; the final manoeuvring is rapidly but plausibly achieved. "Manoeuvring" is perhaps the fair word.[2] Decoud's object in accompanying Nostromo has been to find means to get down the coast to Cayta and contact Barrios; he meant, we have been told, "to put into that attempt all the desperation of which he was capable"(282); and his resolution now to remain in hiding on the Great Isabel is not quite accounted for by the fact that, in the city, the arrival of Pedro Montero will mean that there is a prescription hanging over his head. But at least Part II ends with the situation very clear-cut. Decoud is alone, at

least for days, on the island, and is in a state of physical and
emotional exhaustion. The treasure has been rapidly but
effectively buried there. Nostromo—who is coming to feel
that he has received too much payment only in fair words—
has sunk the empty and damaged lighter and swum ashore.
Those in Sulaco who know enough to entertain any conjecture at all, may well suppose that the lighter went to the
bottom after collision with the troopship. In the city the state
of affairs is desperate. When Pedro Montero and his few
followers arrive over the mountain, they will find Sotillo
and a large body of troops prepared to support them.

Nostromo, sub-titled "A Tale of the Seaboard" is now a
little more than half told. The narrative current has been
gathering strength, and some critics see this as putting the
book in danger of drying out into shallows, of ending its
course as a straight adventure story. Mr. Guerard, as we have
seen, inclines to this view. "The essential creative fact," he
writes, "is that Conrad had, by page 304, discovered and
explored his material." [3] We can only read on and form our
own conclusion. Perhaps it is relevant to remember that
Conrad's moral vision is habitually implicated with the life
of action.

At the opening of Part III Sulaco is preparing "for the
coming of the Monterist *régime,* which was approaching . . .
from the mountains, as well as from the sea."(307) Nevertheless, so far as the narrative is concerned, the tension must be
eased for a little after the breathless series of events on the
Placid Gulf. So Dr. Monygham and the chief engineer hold
a leisured conversation, partly on the attitude of the Europeans in the political crisis, and partly on Nostromo and his
relationship to the Violas; briefly inset in this is another
imperfect glimpse of what happened to Dr. Monygham under

Guzman Bento. Then the scene switches to Captain Mitchell, pacing his wharf and wondering whether Sotillo is really on his way. For a few pages there is a subtle shift to the later Mitchell reminiscing again ("We have been infested here with mosquitoes before the late improvements,")(325) and suddenly Sotillo and his force have arrived, Mitchell is seized, and there follows the serio-comic interview which centres in Sotillo's undignified covetousness in the face of his captive's presentation gold watch. Dr. Monygham has been seized, too, and is present when the wretched Hirsch reiterates his story of the collision and the presumed loss of the silver. Before Monygham and Mitchell are released by the indecisive Sotillo (who is an entirely convincing compendium of brutality, cowardice, cupidity, and incompetence), they are shut up together for a time, and Monygham says enough to show how he is prepared to exploit his own popularly discredited character in a dangerous double game against the Monterists. Meanwhile in the city the Ribierists have made their last desperate throw. It has an ironic ring. A large stretch of wooded country is controlled by Hernandez, a celebrated robber. The party which was to bring the rule of law to Costaguana creates him a general out of hand—and now the Blanco ladies and children, together with the dying Don José Avellanos under the care of his daughter, stream out of the town to place themselves within his protection. His extreme piety, fortunately, is vouched for by Father Corbelàn.

The exodus of the gentry and the arrival of Pedro Montero and his followers are vigorously realized episodes—simple action-pieces set on either side of a long and complex chapter which contrasts the characters of Gould and Decoud, depicts the abject behaviour of the rump of Blanco politicians, shows Gould seizing on the separatist plan as the only remaining hope, includes an unexpected and shattering retrospect in which the breaking of Dr. Monygham under the tortures of Guzman Bento's expert Father Beron at last appears in full, and ends with a crashing of bells throughout Sulaco as Montero rides through the gates. There is a great deal of careful observation, as when Charles Gould makes his way home through the disordered city:

Charles Gould turned towards the town. Before him jagged peaks of the Sierra came out all black in the clear dawn. Here and there a muffled lepero whisked round the corner of a grass-grown street before the ringing hoofs of his horse. Dogs barked behind the walls of the gardens; and with the colourless light the chill of the snows seemed to fall from the mountains upon the disjointed pavements and the shuttered houses with broken cornices and the plaster peeling in patches between the flat pilasters of the fronts. The daybreak struggled with the gloom under the arcades on the Plaza, with no signs of country people disposing their goods for the day's market, piles of fruit, bundles of vegetables ornamented with flowers, on low benches under enormous mat umbrellas; with no cheery early morning bustle of villagers, women, children, and loaded donkeys. Only a few scattered knots of revolutionists stood in the vast space, looking all one way from under their slouched hats for some sign of news from Rincon. The largest of those groups turned about like one man as Charles Gould passed, and shouted, "*Viva la Libertad!*" after him in a menacing tone.

Charles Gould rode on, and turned into the archway of his house. In the patio littered with straw, a practicante, one of Dr. Monygham's native assistants, sat on the ground with his back against the rim of the fountain, fingering a guitar discreetly, while two girls of the lower class, standing up before him, shuffled their feet a little and waved their arms, humming a popular dance tune. Most of the wounded during the two days of rioting had been taken away already by their friends and relations, but several figures could be seen sitting up balancing their bandaged heads in time to the music. Charles Gould dismounted. A sleepy mozo coming out of the bakery door took hold of the horse's bridle; the practicante endeavoured to conceal his guitar hastily; the girls, unabashed, stepped back smiling; and Charles Gould, on his way to the staircase, glanced into a dark corner of the patio at another group, a mortally wounded Cargador with a woman kneeling by his side; she mumbled prayers rapidly, trying at the same time to force a piece of orange between the stiffening lips of the dying man.

The cruel futility of things stood unveiled in the levity and sufferings of that incorrigible people. . . .(363-4)

"Bundles of vegetables *ornamented with flowers.*" Alike in the sharp image and the extended descriptive passage in which it is set we have a gauge of the unfaltering march of the realizing imagination which is the chief distinguishing characteristic of *Nostromo* as a whole. It continues through a short chapter in which we are taken out to the mine, watch an emissary from Pedro Montero propose to its Gubernator, Don Pépé, that it should be treacherously yielded up, and then hear Don Pépé and his friend Padre Romàn discuss plans for that total destruction of the workings upon which Gould has determined in a last extremity. Montero and Gould meet, and then Gould and Dr. Monygham. It is Dr. Monygham's conviction that the sending away of the silver was a mistake. Sotillo, who is merely avaricious, might have been bribed with it; even now, he can perhaps be diverted by some mere hope of recovering it. "Let me try to serve you," he tells Gould sombrely, "to the whole extent of my evil reputation. I am off now to play my game of betrayal with Sotillo, and keep him off the town."(410)

We have now come to the main turning-point of the novel. Nostromo has been asleep since his swim ashore. He wakes up:

Nostromo woke up from a fourteen hours' sleep, and arose full
length from his lair in the long grass. He stood knee deep amongst
the whispering undulations of the green blades with the lost air
of a man just born into the world. Handsome, robust, and supple,
he threw back his head, flung his arms open, and stretched himself with a slow twist of the waist and a leisurely growling yawn
of white teeth, as natural and free from evil in the moment of
waking as a magnificent and unconscious wild beast. Then, in
the suddenly steadied glance fixed upon nothing from under a
thoughtful frown, appeared the man.(411-2)

Everything at this point marks Conrad's undeviating determination to end his story as he had first conceived it. The
corruption of the San Tomé silver is wide-spreading. It can
be subtle and slow. But the victim upon whom its power is
centred must be the incorruptible Capataz de Cargadores.
Characteristically, the significance of Nostromo's return as
from the dead is marked by its being framed within superb
passages of natural description; the one of the seascape at
sunset ("The great mass of cloud filling the head of the gulf
had long red smears amongst its convoluted folds of grey and
black, as of a floating mantle stained with blood")(411); the
other of the hovering of a vulture, a rey-zamuro, hopefully
above the sleeping man. And then, before the full suspense
of the quickening action is resumed, there comes the first of
a number of passages intimating and analyzing the crumbling
integrity of this man of intensely subjective nature. More
space is given to this than to the answering disintegration of
Martin Decoud at which we shall presently arrive.

    The remaining action—so far as the main story goes—to be
given full narrative treatment centres in the Custom House,
and oscillates (in a strikingly effective short-term way) in
time. There Nostromo finds the dead body of the tortured
Hirsch suspended from its beam. The dead body of the tor-

tured Hirsch so remains—we never hear of its being cut down—and serves as a kind of dreadful punctuation mark in the long colloquy between Nostromo and Dr. Monygham—who knows, despite his deep antipathy towards the Capataz, that here is the only man who can reach General Barrios and save Sulaco (and Mrs. Gould, who is from first to last Dr. Monygham's real concern). But, half-way through this, there is a short backward dip to pick up the troubles of that sadly infirm Monterist, Colonel Sotillo. Hirsch is still alive, and we see his torment and death actually take place. This is the novel's direst stroke. In its sinister darkness the whole poised fate of Sulaco and its struggling factions turns shadowy.

Chapter Nine ends with that fate undetermined, and with no more than a hint that Nostromo is going to answer a last appeal to his vanity. Chapter Ten opens as if a straight chronological progression were to be preserved:

The next day was quiet in the morning, except for the faint sound of firing to the northward, in the direction of Los Hatos. Captain Mitchell had listened to it from his balcony anxiously. . . .(473)

But here the slipping in of a verb in the pluperfect tense is the prelude to the most astonishing tour de force in all Conrad's writing. Within this same paragraph we are taken back —or forward—to the Captain Mitchell of the second chapter of the novel, entertaining any visitor who will listen to him to an account of the stormy events preceding the triumphant emergence of the independent Occidental State of Sulaco. The day of the firing at Los Hatos had been a memorable day. Towards dusk, he had seen "that poor fellow of mine— Nostromo. The sailor whom I discovered, and, I may say, made, sir. The man of the famous ride to Cayta, sir. An historical event, sir!"(473) And as Captain Mitchell leads his

visitor around—a view of the Plaza ("twice the area of Tra-
falgar Square")(476), a dive into the cathedral, lunch at the
Amarilla Club, dinner at the Miraflores—nearly everything is
tidied up for us amid a convincing appearance of merely
random communication. We learn things important and unimportant: that the tablet to the memory of "poor Decoud"
was erected by "his betrothed Antonia Avellanos"(478); that
Nostromo, "perfectly fearless and incorruptible,"(483) was
got out of Sulaco on his mission to Barrios on a charging
railway engine; that the gentleman in the long-tailed black
coat is the famous Hernandez, Minister of War; that Don
Carlos Gould had been rescued by Don Pépé and a force
from the mine just as Pedro Montero was about to have him
shot; that Dr. Monygham, who for days had successfully kept
Sotillo fishing for silver in the harbour, was similarly rescued
by the troops of Barrios as he was standing with a halter
already round his neck; that General Montero and Sotillo
were both assassinated; that Pedro Montero now keeps a
brothel in one of the southern ports. We have no sense of
being offered a huddled-up ending in all this, since beneath
Captain Mitchell's pompous manner the narrative continues
to thrust vigorously at all our senses. At the same time, its
distancing over a period of years tempers what might otherwise be a spate of melodrama.

There remain some episodes which it is not within Captain
Mitchell's power to recount. So, still within the bounds of
this chapter, we are taken back to the moment at which
Nostromo, from on board Barrios's transport, leaps into the
sea on spying the drifting dinghy which he recognizes as that
left on the Great Isabel with Decoud. He rows to the island,
comes to realize that Decoud must be dead, and knows that
the treasure is his, if he cares to take it. Within this episode,

and for only five pages, the narrative moves back by a few days to a direct account of Decoud's suicide.

To the final three chapters of *Nostromo* it is possible to ascribe the character of an epilogue; yet to the extent to which the novel is indeed Nostromo's story they are rather the climax of the whole. Chronogically, they afford our latest, as well as final, glimpse of the surviving characters. Captain Mitchell has retired from the service of the O.S.N. and gone home to England; Father Corbelàn is Sulaco's first Cardinal-Archbishop; his niece, Antonia Avellanos, is a stately lady over whom some shadow of political fanaticism lies: she has persuaded herself that it was Decoud's vision that Costaguana should be a single state again in the end. The Goulds have been abroad for a year; on their return Charles Gould is instantly absorbed in the vast complex of the San Tomé mines (gold, silver, copper, lead, cobalt), so that Dr. Monygham, now Inspector-General of State Hospitals, is more than ever painfully aware of Mrs. Gould's loneliness; it is no doubt prompted by this that he delivers one of the final judgments of the book—a judgment answering Charles Gould's faith in the influence of his mine, as expressed to his bride long ago:

"There is no peace and no rest in the development of material interests. They have their law, and their justice. But it is founded on expediency, and is inhuman; it is without rectitude, without the continuity and the force that can be found only in a moral principle. Mrs. Gould, the time approaches when all that the Gould Concession stands for shall weigh as heavily upon the people as the barbarism, cruelty, and misrule of a few years back."(511)

On this indictment the book's main burden closes. We have still to hear the end of Nostromo's history. It is like an extended *exemplum*—as the legend of the gringos of Azuera at the beginning of the novel is a brief *exemplum*—of the malign lure of wealth. The comparison, indeed, is made explicitly:

> He could never shake off the treasure. His audacity, greater than that of other men, had welded that vein of silver into his life. And the feeling of fearful and ardent subjection, the feeling of his slavery—so irremediable and profound that often, in his thoughts, he compared himself to the legendary Gringos, neither dead nor alive, bound down to their conquest of unlawful wealth on Azuera—weighed heavily on the independent Captain Fidanza, owner and master of a coasting schooner . . . Nostromo, the miscalled Capataz de Cargadores.(526-7)

There is a good deal of this. We may feel that Conrad is once more having to work a little too hard with Nostromo. Or we may feel that it is the destruction of a man of the people, large in nature even if large in vanity too, more defenceless than his superiors because uninstructed, that Conrad is concerned to assert as the very deepest evil of a mountingly acquisitive society. It is perhaps a weakness of this final, and substantially extended, movement of the book that in the rivalry of Giorgio Viola's two daughters, and in the intrigue and misapprehension on the Great Isabel which follows, an extraneous element is introduced, and at the end mere accident is substituted for the fatality of the silver. It is certain that the introduction, at the eleventh hour, of an element of direct sexual encounter such as Conrad rarely succeeds with is far from felicitous. The love passages with Giselle Viola ring as false as does the episode of the "pretty Morenita" at the end of Part I. Linda Viola is another matter; her passion has dignity and pathos; the tone of the novel deepens to a satisfactory close in the final pages in which she is left alone with her father, the old Garibaldino who has fired the fatal shot in defence, as he thinks, of his daughter's honour.

The "meaning" of *Nostromo*, the interpretation of experience which it presents, has been felt by some of the novel's most perceptive critics as particularly bound up with the character and fate of Martin Decoud. In one aspect he is almost a choric character; his voice is distinguishably related to Conrad's voice as that comes to us in the whole timbre of the book. Yet Decoud is unsympathetically presented at the start, and his end is a defeat.

We cannot tell how deeply Conrad meditated Decoud's suicide. Had Decoud lived, Nostromo's story could scarcely have been brought to the conclusion which its creator had from the first designed for it. We have already seen signs of Conrad's clinging to Nostromo as his subject with tenacity—whether or not the "tenacity of despair" [4]—even while more significant interests appeared to be growing beneath his hand. But even if the death of the only other witness to the preservation of the silver was in the first instance no more than an adjunct of the main plot, it does not necessarily follow that an urgent imaginative pressure was absent from its eventual contriving. The tone of *Nostromo* is pervasively sceptical, yet it is the novel's assertion that scepticism is not an amour. Amid the solitude of the Great Isabel, Decoud, the arch-sceptic, is confronted in its full rigour with the logical consequence of that noninvolvement in the moral universe—as contrasted with the merely sensational universe —which the sceptical attitude implies. Such passivity is death. "In our activity alone do we find the sustaining illusion of an independent existence as against the whole scheme of things of which we form a helpless part."(497) It is thus that Decoud drifts into self-annihilation:

Decoud lost all belief in the reality of his action past and to come. On the fifth day an immense melancholy descended upon him palpably. . . . The vague consciousness of a misdirected life given up to impulses whose memory left a bitter taste in his mouth was the first moral sentiment of his manhood. But at the same time he felt no remorse. What should he regret? He had recognized no other virtue than intelligence, and had erected passions into duties. Both his intelligence and his passion were swallowed up easily in this great unbroken solitude of waiting without faith.(497-8)

It is legitimate to see in Decoud's plight at least a broken reflection of a dilemma urgent in the experience of his creator. Conrad was a sceptic in the sense of being a man temperamentally vulnerable to sombre views and intellectually persuaded of the vanity of most human wishes. He once commended scepticism to Galsworthy in the largest terms as "the tonic of life, the agent of truth—the way of art and salvation," [5] and to Cunninghame Graham he wrote that "the attitude of cold unconcern is the only reasonable one." [6] This is perhaps a little coloured by something no more substantial than current post-Flaubertian aesthetic fashion; it is a view of the artist's stance equally sweepingly subscribed to by James Joyce's Stephen Dedalus. It is certainly true, however, that faith came hardly to Conrad. On the other hand he was very susceptible to *les valeurs idéales,* and once even declared that all his gifts were dedicated to their celebration. Few English writers, indeed, have written better and more movingly of courage, endurance, and fidelity.

It may well be that the contradiction between these attitudes is more apparent than real, and that Conrad's underlying thought cannot be charged with incoherence. Ideals may be extremely treacherous and corrosive, as Charles Gould's story shows. But nobody can get on without them, least of all the man who confronts the void, the bleak fact that the theatre of our destiny is a neutral and disregarding universe. Life without values simply does not work; simply ushers a man out, as Decoud is ushered out. We survive as human beings only by creating faith, by transmuting behaviour into conduct. This is the burden of Conrad's "high and impersonal discourse" in his greatest novel.[7]

CHAPTER
VIII

The Secret Agent

It is not at all difficult to write a reasonably adequate brief synopsis of *The Secret Agent*,* and this in itself is an indication that the novel notably differs from its immediate predecessors, *Lord Jim* and *Nostromo*. The structure is altogether simpler and the action more concentrated. When Conrad later attempted a dramatic version, the result was a failure. But his inexperience as a playwright was responsible, and a skilful adapter might well have produced a successful stage piece taking few liberties at least with the main outlines of the book. Nobody in his senses would try to dramatize *Nostromo*. *Lord Jim*, indeed, has been made into a film. But so have the Ten Commandments.

---

* Mr. Verloc is the owner of a small shop in Soho, where he deals in pornographic writings and other dubious wares, but this is merely a cover for his activities as a secret agent. He works for various revolutionary, anarchist, and terrorist organizations whose members frequent his unobtrusive premises. At the same time he is retained by officials in the London Embassy of a great power (clearly Russia) to inform against these people and their more or less ineffective plots. He also makes himself quietly useful to Chief Inspector Heat of the Special Crimes Department of the metropolitan police.

The extent to which Conrad is breaking new ground in *The Secret Agent* becomes apparent when we examine the temporal dimensions of the narrative, which is deployed in thirteen chapters of very varying length. In Chapter 1 Mr. Verloc leaves his house and household, which are briefly described, having received his summons from the Embassy. In Chapter 2 he arrives there, is given his monstrous instructions by Mr. Vladimir, and returns home, a much injured man and citizen. A few days pass, and in Chapter 3 we have our only meeting with Mr. Verloc's revolutionary associates as a group; Mr. Verloc is moody and baffled among them, and he so continues when he retires with his wife to the sanctity of their bedchamber. There is a further small passage of time. In Chapter 4 the abortive attack upon Greenwich Observatory has just been made, and Ossipon, who assumes that it is Mr. Verloc who has been killed, gives the news allusively to the Professor, the bomb's manufacturer. In Chapter 5 the Professor, having parted with Ossipon, has his chance encounter with Chief Inspector Heat, returning from the scene of the explosion; and Heat goes straight from this to report to the Assistant Commissioner. The interview is continued in Chapter 6, after we have been introduced in a brief digression to the drawing-room of the great lady who is befriending

---

These various loyalties aside, Mr. Verloc is a respectable member of the lower-middle class, supporting not only his wife Winnie but also Winnie's mother and mentally-defective brother Stevie. He believes that the charms of his person and the rectitude of his conduct alike endear him to his wife. In this he is mistaken, since Winnie, although a loyal and uninquiring spouse, has married much against inclination and solely to secure a future provision for Stevie, who is the emotional centre of her life.

Mr. Verloc's diplomatic employers become dissatisfied with the extent of his services, and demand that he assist in stirring up English public feeling against the revolutionary groups by engineering some senseless outrage which can be attributed to them. Mr. Verloc makes a tool of Stevie in this project; there is an accident; Stevie is blown to unidentifiable fragments by a bomb. But Winnie, fearful that Stevie may at some time or other get lost, has sewn

the "ticket-of-leave apostle" Michaelis. Having dismissed Heat, the Assistant Commissioner walks across to the House of Commons to report to the Home Secretary, returns to his office, goes out to dine in an Italian restaurant, and then walks through Soho to inspect, from across the road, "the humble abode of Mr. Verloc's domestic happiness."(151) This is Chapter 7. We are half-way through the book; it is just after nightfall; within a few hours the action will have concluded, and both Mr. Verloc and his wife will be dead.

Chapter 8 presents us with the only substantial time-shift in *The Secret Agent*. If we have been reading with attention, we now suspect, although we do not positively know, that it is Stevie who has been killed by the bomb. But, if this be so, here is Stevie oddly alive again—until we realize that we have been taken back some weeks (but not before the day upon which we first joined the Verlocs in Chapter 1). Winnie's mother, so as not to strain the already well-nigh transcendent benevolence of Mr. Verloc, has nerved herself to withdraw into an almshouse. Winnie and Stevie accompany her in a cab. When they return home, it is to find Mr. Verloc still of a gloomy and baffled mind. He announces that he will be making one of his periodic trips to the Continent on the morrow. This, we shall realize later, is in the vain hope of

---

an address on the collar of his coat, and this enables Heat to connect the crime with Mr. Verloc's shop. Heat is not anxious to incriminate or incommode so valuable an informer as Mr. Verloc, but his hand is in some degree forced by his more scrupulous superior, the Assistant Commissioner. In the issue, Winnie learns with brutal abruptness that her brother is dead and that her husband has been the instrument of the fatality. Mr. Verloc, thus awkwardly situated in point of marital harmony, behaves with such complacent obtuseness that Winnie is driven to a frenzy and kills him. She tries to escape under the protection of a young revolutionary, Ossipon, who has for long exercised a half-acknowledged physical attraction over her. But when Ossipon glimpses the full story, he is terrified, steals all her money, and deserts her on a boat train. She drowns herself by jumping overboard from a channel steamer.

enlisting foreign aid in the alarming business of leaving a time-bomb at the Observatory. Chapter 9 continues within this time-shift, for it opens with Mr. Verloc "returning from the Continent at the end of ten days."(182) Mr. Verloc listens to Winnie's anxiously stressing the extent of Stevie's devotion to him, and he begins to take Stevie for walks. Then he sends him to stay (outside London, but not very far from Greenwich) with the ticket-of-leave apostle, who is writing his autobiography in the seclusion of a cottage loaned to him by the Assistant Commissioner's great lady. The chapter continues at a mounting pace. Mr. Verloc is perturbed, and it appears that he has taken all his money out of the bank. A stranger calls, and Mr. Verloc is suddenly in a panic. We realize that this is the Assistant Commissioner, and that the hour must just have elapsed in which we left him—having dined on fraudulent Italian fare—outside the humble abode of the secret agent. The time-shift, or flash-back, is over, and here is a hurrying present. Mr. Verloc and the Assistant Commissioner depart together, and almost at once Chief Inspector Heat arrives. He has some conversation with Winnie and then—overheard by Winnie—with Mr. Verloc, who has again returned to the shop. Winnie is in possession of the truth.

Chapter 10 is short; it drops the tension and slows the pace. The Assistant Commissioner goes straight to the Commons and makes a further report to the Secretary of State: this clears up any confusion in which we may ourselves remain. He returns home, changes his clothes, and proceeds to the house of Michaelis's patroness, with whom his wife has been dining. There he encounters Mr. Vladimir, the Hyperborean inventor of the Greenwich plot. The two men leave the house together, and the Assistant Commissioner makes it clear to Vladimir that he understands the rôle he has played.

They part at half-past ten. Chapter 11, the longest in the book, involves a very small flash-back. It begins at approximately eight o'clock and ends at ten minutes to nine. The fifty minutes thus enclosed are those in which Winnie is wrought up to the killing of her husband: they constitute, as Dr. Leavis has roundly and truly said, one of the most astonishing triumphs of genius in fiction.[1] In Chapter 12 Winnie, rushing from the shop, falls into the arms of Comrade Ossipon. At half-past ten Ossipon cleverly tumbles out of the train at Waterloo station, and Winnie is carried away to what is in fact her death; it is the exact hour at which the Assistant Commissioner and Vladimir are parting outside the Explorers' Club. Chapter 13, which affords a short conclusion, describes a meeting between Ossipon and the Professor. Some weeks may have elapsed, since Ossipon's copy of the newspaper carrying the story of the drowning is "much folded," and he has of late been finding himself nervously out of sorts and indisposed to his customary amatory conquests.[2] It will be Ossipon's destiny, we are told, to walk the gutter with a sandwich-board. But the incorruptible Professor, the dedicated destroyer, is left on the pavement. He passes on "unsuspected and deadly, like a pest in the street full of men."(311)

The masculine impetus and linear clarity of *The Secret Agent* in its narrative aspect make it immediately and deceptively readable as a superb example of the *roman policier*. One may find oneself thinking of the prolific Belgian writer, M. Georges Simenon, with his astonishing gift for the evocation of low life and criminal practice. There are readers too fastidious for M. Simenon, and so there were for *The Secret Agent*, which was widely censured at the time of its publication for the sordid nature of its concerns. Even Thomas

Mann, although he thought sufficiently well of the novel to write a preface to the German translation, viewed it as essentially a thriller into which was interestingly transfused Conrad's hatred and fear of Russia.[3] And Conrad himself was sensitive about this. In point of any popular success, his career was still a failure; in framing the story he had probably not been without the fond hope of achieving some wider appeal; at the same time he knew that it had emerged "from a mood as serious in feeling and thought" as any in which he had ever written.(xiii)[4]

He was also rather comically nervous about the company which the novel might suggest that he had kept, and he extended this solicitude to Ford Madox Ford, who had discussed with him the actual "blood-stained inanity" at Greenwich and added the appalling words: "Oh, that fellow was half an idiot. His sister committed suicide afterwards."(x) His informant, Conrad hastens to tell us, had actually seen even less of anarchists and their like than he had. And although the book had been *Verloc* while he wrote it, and was *The Secret Agent* when published, he maintained that it was essentially the story of Winnie Verloc (to whom he could justly attribute, we may reflect, "a life of single purpose and of a noble unity of inspiration")(242). He further insisted that he had no more knowledge of the philosophy of anarchism than he had personal acquaintance with its exponents. "The whole thing is superficial and it is but a tale," he wrote to Galsworthy. He "had no idea to consider Anarchism politically."[5]

There is something uneasy in these disclaimers, and in others which can be gathered from his correspondence. It is as if he distrusts the very intensity of his reaction to the underworld of fanaticism and violence which he sees or imagines. "Ferocious imbecility"(34) is the hallmark of revolutionaries and counter-revolutionaries alike; and when he comes to describe the exploitation of political passion by, for example, the "moribund veteran of dynamite wars,"(48) Karl Yundt, the pen seems to tremble in his hand as he writes:

He took the part of an insolent and venomous evoker of sin-ister impulses which lurk in the blind envy and exasperated vanity of ignorance, in the suffering and misery of poverty, in all the hopeful and noble illusions of righteous anger, pity, and revolt. The shadow of his evil gift clung to him yet like the smell of a deadly drug in an old vial of poison.(48)

Conrad's morally revolting characters always tend to be physical grotesques, and this reaches an extreme in *The Secret Agent*. Of Yundt himself we learn that "an extraor-dinary expression of underhand malevolence survived in his extinguished eyes," and that his "thrusting forward of a skinny groping hand deformed by gouty swellings suggested the effort of a moribund murderer summoning all his re-maining strength for a last stab."(42) Of Michaelis, who is viewed not altogether without sympathy, we read that he "had come out of a highly hygienic prison round like a tub, with an enormous stomach and distended cheeks of a pale, semi-transparent complexion, as though for fifteen years the servants of an outraged society had made a point of stuffing him with fattening foods in a damp and lightless cellar."(41) Ossipon, although attractive to Mrs. Verloc, has crinkly yellow hair, a red face, almond-shaped eyes, and "a flattened nose and prominent mouth cast in the rough mould of the negro type."(44) The Professor is even more unlovely; "his flat, large ears departed widely from the sides of his skull"; his cheeks—also "flat"—"of a greasy, unhealthy complexion, were merely smudged by the miserable poverty of a thin dark

whisker."(62) These and similar descriptions go a little beyond what may be called the routine macabre of crime fiction. Taken together, they constitute something excessive to
which Conrad is driven as he responds to his theme. The "in-
spiring indignation and underlying pity and contempt"(viii)
of which he speaks in his Note have nothing factitious about
them, and we must suppose the emotion which we can sense
behind them to derive, once more, from sources deep in his
Polish background.

There is a point in Chapter 7 in which his attitude is made
explicit. The Assistant Commissioner is making his first
report to Sir Ethelred, the Secretary of State. Conrad is on
unfamiliar ground here. Sir Ethelred, the "big and rustic
Presence,"(136) and his private secretary, the "nice and privi-
leged child"(135) called Toodles, are both stereotypes of the
ruling-class Englishman whom their creator may have picked
up from political novels such as Trollope's. We are aware, for
example, of a false note when the Assistant Commissioner is
exhibited as "pressing deferentially the extended hand"(221)
of Sir Ethelred. (Conrad himself, it appears, was liable to do
this; his manners had an Oriental tinge disconcerting to
those who expected to meet a sea-dog of the old school.) It is
the more surprising, therefore, that the Assistant Commissioner reads Sir Ethelred a lecture:

In principle, I should lay it down that the existence of secret
agents should not be tolerated, as tending to augment the positive dangers of the evil against which they are used. That the
spy will fabricate his information is a mere commonplace. But
in the sphere of political and revolutionary action, relying partly
on violence, the professional spy has every facility to fabricate
the very facts themselves, and will spread the double evil of emu-
lation in one direction, and of panic, hasty legislation, unreflecting hate, on the other.(139)

The terrorist and the policeman against whom the terrorist pits himself, we are told elsewhere, come from the same basket, and in the protecting of public order moral considerations and the rule of law are liable to go by the board. Another detail of mere physique intimates this horror of a pervading corruption. The grotesquerie we have noted in Conrad's evil characters is occasionally a matter of skeleton-like emaciation or meagre proportions, as with the second engineer on the *Patna* or the Professor here in *The Secret Agent*. More commonly, as with the *Patna*'s captain, the spectacle is of revolting obesity. Mr. Verloc himself approximates to Michaelis here; he is "burly in a fat-pig style,"(13) and he fails to realize that his growing corpulence may have affected the physical appeal he supposes himself to exert over his wife. But Mr. Verloc's antagonist, "the valuable and trusted officer" Chief Inspector Heat, suggests to the dispassionate scrutiny of the Assistant Commissioner a physiognomy "marred by too much flesh"(116): the symbol, like the thing itself, is an infection that spreads. And indeed precisely the same sort of irony is mounted against Heat as against Mr. Verloc. The one is "the excellent husband of Winnie Verloc"(240); the other "a kind man, an excellent husband, a devoted father"(119)—and if he is prepared unscrupulously to frame the harmless Michaelis, we are nevertheless asked to observe "the public and departmental confidence he enjoyed acting favourably upon an amiable nature."(119)

But our main point here is simple. *The Secret Agent* has the speed and directness of a very good thriller largely because it is not bedevilled by doubt; Marlow is in abeyance; there is nothing equivocal in the book's moral stance. Winnie Verloc, Winnie's mother, and Winnie's brother are several types of that humbleness, innocence, helplessness which must perpetually suffer in a world in which a mere mean and obtuse egoism, as in Mr. Verloc, or various corruptions of political feeling, as in a majority of the other characters, operate in disregard of those moral imperatives which alone give dignity to human life. Yet, at the same time, some extraordinary tension attends Conrad's contemplation of his scene. And this is responsible for the novel's most immediately striking characteristic, its style.

The style, or some aspect of it, alarmed Galsworthy while the work was in progress, and he would appear to have thought it tactful to blame the trouble on French masters. Conrad always much deferred to Galsworthy (the reason, according to Ford, being that he mistakenly regarded Galsworthy as a man of property) and he accepted the criticism in a manner characteristic of him:

As to the beastly trick of style, I have fallen into it through worry and hurry. I abominate it myself. It isn't even French really. It is Zola jargon simply. Why it should have fastened on me I don't know. But anything may happen to a man writing in a state of distraction.[6]

We cannot tell just what is in question here. It can hardly be the ironic mode as a whole, which Conrad had chosen with the greatest deliberation, and which he was to take satisfaction in having maintained consistently through the whole book. But it is true that some of the vehicles of ironic method become unsafe when systematically employed in realistic fiction. For example, there is the simple device of dramatic irony. When Winnie Verloc, anxious as she regularly is that Stevie should stand well with her husband, says "You could do anything with that boy, Adolf,"(184) a grim shadow from the future is present potently enough. But when Mr. Verloc, in the last minutes of his life, strays from his common idiomatic road to asseverate "Strike me dead if I ever would have thought of the lad for that purpose,"(257) we are aware that this is not precisely Lady Macbeth considering what can be done with a little water, or her husband urging Banquo not to fail the feast.

But it is where the main burden of the irony is carried that the chief hazard lies. The method here is closely akin to that of mock-heroic. The meanness of mean things is pointed, or their moral bearing seemingly obscured, by exhibiting them in language, or amid images and allusions, of incongruous associations. The writer thus gives himself the air of going astray in his judgments; we are all the time silently putting him right as we read; and this involvement of ours as from a plane of superior perceptiveness constitutes part of our pleasure. At the same time we know that it is all a game, and that the writer is playing it with a dexterity which sets him, rather than ourselves, in a magistral and dispassionate station above his comedy. But this, of course, need not be all. We may realize that there is yet a further deception at work, and that the writer is, in a sense, guarding some privacy of his own by simulating an impassivity, a neutrality, which he is far from feeling. The whole technique of inflation, although it can pay rich dividends, is always in some danger of turning ponderous, of seeming inflexible, of striking a facetious or whimsical note. "Winnie did not expect from her husband in the daily intercourse of their married life a ceremonious amenity of address and courtliness of manner."(190) "At that moment, to an impartial observer, Mr. Verloc would have appeared more than human in his magnanimity."(188) "The usual serenity of the eminent specialist."(85) "The ticket-of-leave apostle of humanitarian hopes."(105) "Mr. Verloc lay very still meanwhile, simulating sleep for reasons of his own."(285) One cannot open the book at any page without being made aware of the pervasive irony as at work—now muted and now commanding, now striking in this direction· and now in that.

Many readers must be uneasy with it at the start. The technique is obtrusive, and its steady march through shabby scenes and amid malignant passions seems bookish and chilly. Yet it quickly makes its way with us. Conrad was to speak to his publisher of an "ironic treatment applied to a special subject." [7] But the notion of application is fallacious, or at least inexact. The ironic mode is not a grace or an embellishment; it has the essential function of creating an aesthetic distance between Conrad and the raw spectacle which he is contemplating. In Chapter 5 the spectacle becomes literally this, for Heat has to inspect those slivers and gobbets of Stevie that a resolute constable has scraped together with a shovel:

No physiologist, and still less a metaphysician, Chief Inspector Heat rose by the force of sympathy, which is a form of fear, above the vulgar conception of time. . . . The inexplicable mysteries of conscious existence beset Chief Inspector Heat. . . . And meantime the Chief Inspector went on peering at the table with a calm face and the slightly anxious attention of an indigent customer bending over what may be called the by-products of a butcher's shop with a view to an inexpensive Sunday dinner.(87-8)

It is all in a paragraph—and the ironic astringency enables Conrad to combine a preserved decorum with a designed effect of brutal shock.

There are two places in particular in which the operation of the method may usefully be considered more at large. The first is the journey in the cab. In this Dr. Leavis marks an "obvious and unfortunate indebtedness to Dickens." [8] The

indebtedness is certainly there. The last drive of Mrs. Verloc's mother through "the early dirty night, the sinister,
noisy, hopeless, and rowdy night of South London"(159);
"the modest assemblage of seven people, mostly under
age," (156) who see it begin; the cab "like a mediaeval device
for the punishment of crime, or some very new-fangled invention for the cure of a sluggish liver"(163); the alarming
cabman who eventually softens into offering Stevie a certain
amount of philosophical communication: all these are Dickensian enough. Nevertheless, the episode is remote from
pastiche. The old lady's almshouse, we learn, "by the exiguity
of its dimensions and the simplicity of its accommodation,
might well have been devised in kindness as a place of training for the still more straightened circumstances of the
grave."(160) Dickens could have produced something like
this, but the language would not have been quite the same.
And this is a matter of ironic method. Macbeth's "Fail not
our feast" is ironic in all but the basic sense of the word;
Macbeth doesn't *know* that, although Banquo himself won't
turn up, Banquo's ghost may. But irony—εἰρωνεία—means
something more than ignorance; it means the feigning of
ignorance for a rhetorical or dialectic purpose. And Conrad's
way of describing the almshouse to which Winnie's mother is
retiring subtly involves this; here is a manner of speech so
remote from the humble old woman's world that it must
surely proceed from a mind without understanding of her or
sympathy with her. But this, of course, is precisely not the
case. Conrad, and Conrad alone, understands what she is
about, and he is admitting us to the privilege of understanding it, too. Winnie, a loving daughter, doesn't understand;
she knows merely that her mother's resolution instances the
general proposition that in this world things do not stand
much looking into. Stevie doesn't understand; he realizes

only that the horse is a suffering creature—and then, in a sudden vast extension of knowledge, that the cabman who whips the horse is a suffering creature, too. But the fact is that Winnie's mother (we have to keep on calling her this, because she is to pass from our ken without a name) is sacrificing herself for her son. Even the superhuman benevolence of Mr. Verloc must not be tried too far, so she has decided to remove herself from within his bounty. She knows that in this she is sacrificing not only herself but her daughter as well, since Winnie will be unjustly aspersed as turning her out. She loves her daughter equally with her son; but her son, being unfortunately "peculiar," is the more nearly helpless of the two. She has made a moral decision and—on the basis of information so limited as again to involve an ironic acting in the dark—she has made it rightly. There are two rays of light in this dark book: the mother's selfless devotion to Stevie, and the sister's. It is one of these that is being exhibited with incomparable poignancy in the episode judged by Dr. Leavis to be "unfortunate."

The death of Mr. Verloc is yet more remarkable. It would be hard to find anywhere in English fiction so tight and economical a weaving together of character and circumstance in the interest of tragic effect. Neither Mr. Verloc nor Winnie has any notion of what is happening until it happens; and Mr. Verloc's transition from ignorance to knowledge—if indeed it ever comes—has to be concentrated in a split second of time. Yet a high lucidity and a terrifying impression of inevitability accompany the entire march of this humble domestic disaster in the little parlour where "the gas-jet purred like a contented cat."(231) Almost every word or action of Mr. Verloc's is an unconscious incitement; we are fascinated as by the spectacle of a man in utter blindness baring his own breast to the knife. Winnie, correspondingly, is like a player unskilled in some subtle game; through move after move which she is helpless to analyze she is driven into a corner.

But nothing in the tautness with which the thing is achieved makes us feel that we are in the presence of a trick —of a result obtained too patly through the employment of loaded dice. In this the Verloc's fatal encounter is distinguishably superior to one at which we have glanced earlier, that between Lord Jim and "Gentleman" Brown. We can believe in Brown as a ruffian sufficiently intelligent to have acquired expertness in reading an adversary's mind; nevertheless, some of the most devastating things he says strike us as mere gifts of fortune, and the effect of this is to tip Jim's disaster—as with some victim of Thomas Hardy's—at least a shade too much in the direction of hard luck. But whenever Mr. Verloc says a luckless thing, the lucklessness goes deep into his being as it has been progressively revealed to us.

Since there was an actual attack upon Greenwich Observatory, *The Secret Agent* may be regarded as being, in the most unassuming sense, founded on historical circumstance. But it also possesses a firm substructure in the facts of English lower-middle-class life at the opening of the twentieth century. Conrad's grip of this is surprising; he manages to bring off something that Henry James, for example, quite fails to do in the early part of *The Princess Casamassima* twenty years earlier. Once the lodging-house in "the Belgravian mansion"(39) is abandoned, and Winnie, together with her mother and brother, pass within the protection of Mr. Verloc, their dependence upon that excellent husband and modest householder becomes absolute. Hence the doctrine "of his supreme wisdom and goodness inculcated by two anxious women"(235) in the groping mind of Stevie. And Winnie (apparently more than her mother) has come to accept the doctrine herself—although always, maybe, with that reservation that "things do not stand much looking into."(177) Mr. Verloc is another who accepts it; during the years of his marriage it may be said, indeed, to have exercised an elevating influence upon his character. Just as from his employment as a double agent he derives his sense of dignified vocation as a protector of society, a humble guardian of opulence and luxury, so his status as an irreproachable family man conduces to his preserving the note of reasonableness and forbearance in trying situations. After the unforeseen and alarming termination of Stevie's existence, he nourishes no resentment against his wife, officious as she has been in sewing that fatal label into the boy's overcoat. "Mr. Verloc was a humane man; he had come home prepared to allow every latitude to his wife's affection for her brother."(233)

Economic compulsion has imposed upon Winnie the necessity of striking a bargain, and one which no prompting of the flesh or allurements of the eye are going to make her risk breaking:

Mrs. Verloc pursued the visions of seven years' security for Stevie loyally paid for on her part; of security growing into confidence, into a domestic feeling, stagnant and deep like a placid pool, whose guarded surface hardly shuddered on the occasional passage of Comrade Ossipon, the robust anarchist with shamelessly inviting eyes, whose glance had a corrupt clearness sufficient to enlighten any woman not absolutely imbecile.(243)

But if Winnie is armoured against present passion, she is finally helpless before passion engendered and nurtured long ago. Stevie's father had been capable of brutal violence against his half-witted son, and it had been the small Winnie who had often intercepted it on her own person. "The protection she had extended over her brother had been in its origin of a fierce and indignant complexion."(246) All her life Winnie has been, in effect, hitting out in defence of Stevie. And now here in the room with her is virtually Stevie's murderer. Lately she had been coming to think of the two of them as almost like father and son—but now she is made aware (it is one of her husband's chief triumphs of obtuseness) that it was Stevie's indoctrination as an anarchist that had been going on, and that the feasibility of this had been put in Mr. Verloc's head by herself in her anxious insistences on the boy's devotion to him.

It does not occur to Mr. Verloc to see Stevie as very important. Being humane, he is at first concerned about the likely effect for a time upon his wife's health and spirits of this unfortunate affair. But it is only marginal, after all, to what are now his, and therefore his wife's, immediate concerns. His unflawed sense that she has much to be thankful for produces the major stroke of irony in the novel: "Do be reasonable, Winnie. What would it have been if you had lost me?"(234) And presently he is going on to matters on which it is natural that deeper feelings should be exercised. Mr. Verloc has, after all, been a much wronged man of late, and the merest proprieties of family life require that his wife should be brought to sympathize with him. Has he not been sparing her much knowledge of the hazardousness of his honourable calling? This emerges when he comes to reflect indignantly on the appalling levity and callousness of Mr. Vladimir:

"You don't know what a brute I had to deal with. . . . A silly, jeering, dangerous brute, with no more sense than— After all these years! A man like me! And I have been playing my head at that game. You didn't know. Quite right, too. What was the good of telling you that I stood the risk of having a knife stuck into me any time these seven years we've been married? I am not a chap to worry a woman that's fond of me. . . . There isn't a murdering plot for the last eleven years that I hadn't my finger in at the risk of my life. There's scores of these revolutionists I've sent off, with their bombs in their blamed pockets, to get themselves caught on the frontier. The old Baron knew what I was worth to his country. And here suddenly a swine comes along an ignorant, overbearing swine."(237-8)

At this point in his complaint to the sister of the dead Stevie Mr. Verloc, who had despatched Stevie, bomb in tin can, against the walls of the Observatory, pauses for the modest refreshment of three glasses of tap-water. "It was a silly, murderous trick," he then says, "to expose for nothing a man —like me."(239) The theme of revenge and of the relief to be obtained through the inflicting of physical violence is one with which he continues intermittently to edify his wife until she kills him. His last note of all, however, is of a different order. Women who are incapable of responding to the dictates of reason may often be diverted by the softnesses of love. Assuming "a peculiar tone,"(262) Mr. Verloc, in the exercise of a just marital authority, summons Mrs. Verloc to the sofa upon which he is reposing. Within seconds he is dead.

This tremendous scene, perhaps the greatest triumph of Conrad's art, is finally and with a crowning irony reduced to the dimensions of a peep-show or a sixpenny *frisson* at a fair. Mr. Verloc has been rather fond of wearing his hat indoors as well as out—an eccentricity condonable in a person of simple station who has much frequented café society when abroad. His hat is the last that his wife sees of him:

Then all became still. Mrs. Verloc on reaching the door had stopped. A round hat disclosed in the middle of the floor by the moving of the table rocked slightly on its crown in the wind of her flight.(265)

And the hat appears again twenty pages later. Comrade Ossipon, "the robust anarchist," glancing into the parlour, is terrified by the spectacle of Mr. Verloc—"simulating sleep for reasons of his own." But what brings to Ossipon "the true sense of the scene" is the hat:

Black, and rim upward, it lay on the floor before the couch as if prepared to receive the contributions of pence from people who would come presently to behold Mr. Verloc in the fullness of his domestic ease reposing on a sofa.(285)

What is offering is an entertainment, we are being told ("but a tale," as Conrad had written to Galsworthy). We may toss it a penny, if we so please.

CHAPTER

IX

Under Western Eyes

The political theme explored first in *Nostromo* and then, at once on a narrower basis and nearer home, in *The Secret Agent* remains Conrad's central concern in *Under Western Eyes*. But he is far from repeating himself. It is with a rather surprising boldness that the new book breaks new ground.

In *Nostromo* the corrupt state called Costaguana is imaginary and somewhat generalized in conception; it stands for any society in which weak government and aggressive material interest are at unequal grips. *The Secret Agent* is set in England, a country in which, in Conrad's eyes, the rule of law is absolute, and revolutionary activity less a menace than a revolting comic turn. *Under Western Eyes* * is about

---

* Kirylo Sidorovitch Razumov is the illegitimate son of Prince K——, by whom he is unacknowledged save to the extent of being supported as a student at the University of St. Petersburg. Only once has he been admitted fleetingly to his father's presence and been conscious of some faint gleam of affection, although no hint of the relationship had been allowed utterance. Razumov is clever, ambitious of intellectual distinction, aloof from his fellow-students, and very lonely.

He comes back to his room one day, his mind much occupied with a prize essay which he hopes will gain him a silver medal. He finds an older student,

Russia; all its characters except the English narrator are Russians; it opens, with superb authenticity, in a city where bombs are employed not to scar the walls of observatories but to blow to pieces undesirable Minister-Presidents and anybody in unfortunate proximity to such. Conrad—boldly, it may be repeated—has committed himself to depicting the political passions in an area where his own political passion is deep-rooted and ever green, yielding none of its leaves to the severing winds of expatriation, distance, time.

He hated Russia and all things Russian—including, it is perfectly fair to say, that greatest of visionary Russians, Dostoevsky, without whose anatomy of the Slavonic mind he could scarcely have written *Under Western Eyes*, but whom he described as a "grimacing, haunted creature" who had produced in *The Brothers Karamazov* something "terrifically bad and impressive and exasperating . . . like some fierce mouthings from prehistoric ages." [1] But if he regarded Russia as exhibiting simply the spectacle of a "Slavo-Tartar Byzantine barbarism," [2] it was nevertheless to the heart of that spectacle that he had now deliberately turned his attention. As before, he was anxious to dissociate himself from any too

---

Victor Haldin, waiting for him. Haldin, a passionate revolutionist, has just assassinated Mr. de P——, a savagely repressive Minister of State. Haldin has only a slight acquaintance with Razumov, but he has interpreted his reserve as a sign of strong character, courage, and idealism answering his own, and on this account he now appeals to him to aid his escape. Razumov, although horrified, agrees to help, and goes off to make some arrangements about hiring a sledge. But there is a hitch; his resolution falters; he walks the streets until he has persuaded himself that he owns a political philosophy which obliges him to give Haldin up. He then takes his story to Prince K——. The Prince, although shocked that his son should present himself at all, listens carefully, and acts swiftly. Haldin is captured, tortured, and hanged.

Razumov finds himself admired by his companions at the University, and in more specifically revolutionary circles as well, as Haldin's close associate in the killing of the detested Mr. de P——. He also finds that the authorities are not blind to the usefulness of this, and presently he is sent as a government spy to Geneva, which is a centre of anti-Czarist intrigue. There, he finds to

specific political interest. His novel was "an attempt to render not so much the political state as the psychology of Russia itself"(vii) and was the result "not of a special experience but of general knowledge, fortified by earnest meditation."(viii) He confessed, indeed, that personal memories as well as simple moral feeling imposed upon him, on this occasion, a special need of detachment; and he seems even to have attributed to a successful maintenance of this detachment the novel's failure to become a popular success. He had been uneasy before the suggestion of an element of political animus in *The Secret Agent*; he flared up when Edward Garnett offered a similar criticism of the new book; Garnett is so Russianized that only what smells of cabbage-soup secures his respect, and Conrad doesn't at all care for being "charged with the rather low trick of putting one's hate into a novel." [3]

It is notable that Conrad does not here deny the hate in itself. Indeed, he could scarcely have done so, since in 1905 he had contributed what he called "a political article" to the *Fortnightly Review* in which the passion is made evident enough. "Autocracy and War" sees in the Russo-Japanese

---

his dismay, live the mother and sister of Haldin, not themselves implicated in revolutionary activities, but sharing Victor Haldin's passionately held liberal convictions. The ladies have learnt from an English paper of Haldin's death, and now the younger understands that there has come to Geneva the man whom she believes to have been his closest friend and courageous associate in danger. Razumov's false position is hateful to him from the first, and is intolerable when the girl discovers a passionate admiration for him, and he finds that he is in love with her. He confesses the full truth first to Miss Haldin and then to the assembled revolutionists—with the result that their professional executioner, Necator, bursts his eardrums with two skilled blows, thus rendering him stone-deaf for life. He staggers away, is knocked down by a tramcar, and finally returns as an obscure cripple to Russia in the care of Tekla, a poor woman who has long been a sort of domestic slave or serf in the *entourage* of Peter Ivanovitch, a prominent revolutionist of repellent character. Upon the death of her mother, Miss Haldin also returns to Russia, to pass her life in charitable labour in slums and jails.

conflict a portent of the approaching doom of the existing Russian state:

And above it all—unaccountably persistent—the decrepit, old, hundred years old, spectre of Russia's might still faces Europe from across the teeming graves of Russian people. This dreaded and strange apparition, bristling with bayonets, armed with chains, hung over with holy images; that something not of this world, partaking of a ravenous ghoul, of a blind Djinn grown up from a cloud, and of the Old Man of the Sea, still faces us with its old stupidity, with its strange mystical arrogance, stamping its shadowy feet upon the grave-stone of autocracy, already cracked beyond repair by the torpedoes of Togo and the guns of Oyama, already heaving in the blood-soaked ground with the first stirrings of a resurrection.

Never before had the Western world the opportunity to look so deep into the black abyss which separates a soulless autocracy posing as, and even believing itself to be, the arbiter of Europe, from the benighted, starved souls of its people. This is the real object-lesson of this war, its unforgettable information.[4]

But Conrad is far from supposing that the approaching end of Czardom will bring an end of tyranny. Evil must succeed upon evil in Russia through any foreseeable future:

A brand of hopeless mental and moral inferiority is set upon Russian achievements; and the coming events of her internal changes, however appalling they may be in their magnitiude, will be nothing more impressive than the convulsions of a colossal body. As her boasted military force that, corrupt in its origin, has ever struck no other but faltering blows, so her soul, kept benumbed by her temporal and spiritual master with the poison of tyranny and superstition, will find itself on awakening possessed of no language, a monstrous full-grown child having first to learn the ways of living thought and articulate speech. It is safe to say tyranny, assuming a thousand protean shapes, will remain clinging to her struggles for a long time before her blind multitudes succeed at last in tramping her out of existence under their millions of bare feet.[5]

It is a sombre vision, and unrelieved at the end. "Millions of bare feet" struck Conrad with no enchantment. He was incapable of seeing a populace other than as a rabble, and owned an almost hysterical fear of the mob.

We ought not to be too impressed by the intemperance and tendentiousness of "Autocracy and War." Mr. Najder, the best authority, stresses its "Polishness." The whole piece, he says, "reads like a literal translation from a late-romantic Polish writer; in a word, like a translation from Apollo Korzeniowski." [6] But even if—as is no doubt the case—Conrad was capable of much more detachment than this excited tirade suggests, it remains true that he faced an uphill task in proposing to depict, with anything of the repose of art, "senseless desperation provoked by senseless tyranny"(viii) in Russian hearts. When he himself sums up his theme, it is with a kind of breathlessness suggesting the most barely controlled emotion:

The ferocity and imbecility of an autocratic rule rejecting all legality and in fact basing itself upon complete moral anarchism provokes the no less imbecile and atrocious answer of a purely Utopian revolutionism encompassing destruction by the first means to hand, in the strange conviction that a fundamental change of hearts must follow the downfall of any given human institutions.(x)

The content of this, as of many similar passages, is negative and despairing. The movement is enraged and vehement.

Under Western Eyes was originally called *Razumov* (as *The Secret Agent* had originally been called *Verloc*). The title finally chosen, however, is ceaselessly played upon throughout the narrative. There comes a point at which we tire of this as we read—feeling, perhaps, that a tragic action ought to be equally moving whether contemplated from London or Peking. We may tire, too, of the nameless English teacher of languages, long resident in Geneva, who tells the story with the assistance of Razumov's improbably copious diary. The function of this intermediary presence is never wholly clear. Nothing happens to him, outwardly or inwardly, as a consequence of his exposure to the events he describes. If he discovers a romantic attachment to the book's heroine, Natalia Victorovna Haldin, this is of an order so elderly and ineffective as to hold no interest for us, or for her. He hints nothing of Marlow's complexity of response to experience; and although, on the other hand, he has often been described by critics of the novel as obtuse, there is no marked indication that anything of the kind is in Conrad's head.

If the Western world is being posited as intrinsically superior to the Russian—and much is said in the book the burden of which seems precisely this—there is yet a great deal in that world that Conrad doesn't like at all: the efflorescence of the *Burgerzeit* in Britain, France, Germany, Switzerland leaves this uprooted Polish aristocrat decidedly cold. But it is the city of Geneva, and not the narrator, which has to carry the burden of this subsidiary distaste. Thus Razumov, in a boiling Russian rage which at least has something large about it, notes "the green slopes framing the Petit Lac in all the marvellous banality of the picturesque made of painted cardboard, with the more distant stretch of water inanimate and shining like a piece of tin"(288); and when he choses a place in which to write his first report as a police spy, it is the small artificial island, graced by a bronze effigy of Rousseau, which he judges "naïve, odious, and inane."(290) Hypocritical respectability and inexpressible dreariness are declared, again and again, to be the keynote of this "passionless abode of democratic liberty,"(357) "indifferent and hospitable,"(338) whose Boulevard des Philosophes is, significantly, so wide, empty, dead, and desolating.

But the narrator, although long domesticated amid all this commonness, is not represented as partaking of it, and if there are occasions upon which he is unaware of what is happening, this is because he is proceeding on civilized assumptions which are betrayed by the event. He must be viewed, in fact, either as a device for securing dispassionateness or as a device for obscuring its absence. Perhaps he performs now the one and now the other of these functions.

Summing up, however, one is surely constrained to turn down the thumb on him. In English fiction what scientifically-minded critics have called the stereotype of the poor gentleman is always a good figure to bring forward when associations of honourable feeling, decent conduct, fair play, and the like, are to be canvassed. The narrator possesses these qualities, he is trusted and esteemed by such characters of unimpaired moral perception as he makes contact with, and we are therefore prepared to accept his verdicts and evaluations, even when he is rather obsessively insistent in proffering them. "I will only remark here," he says early on, "that this is not a story of the West of Europe"(25)—and, later, "this is a Russian story for Western ears."(163) Of Victor Haldin's crucial letter to his sister, which there is ground for supposing to have been open and generous, he notes "the flimsy blackened pages whose very hand-writing seemed cabalistic, incomprehensible to the experience of Western Europe"(133)—and, again, "vague they were to my Western mind and to my Western sentiment."(169) Miss Haldin herself stands in a sense beyond a chasm. "I was but a Westerner, and it was clear that Miss Haldin would not, could not listen to my wisdom."(141) At the end: "To my Western eyes she seemed to be getting farther and farther from me, quite beyond my reach now, but undiminished in the increasing distance."(374)

"Quite beyond my reach now." This has, of course, its significance. The narrator's final reference to himself is as "a mute witness of things Russian,"(381) and it is Russian passions, it is the committing and expiating of a Russian sin, that the novel, after all, judges it profitable to chronicle. The Russian soul offers a larger spiritual theatre than does the Western. Yet the Devil is abroad in it, and it is against the normative background of what the narrator calls "the old, settled Europe"(330) that his hideous ravages are observed. Time was not to deal kindly with this conception of Conrad's. There is a place in Virginia Woolf's early novel, *The Voyage Out*, in which the heroine, looking out over London at night, tells herself that "no darkness would ever settle upon those lamps." But it did, for several years, a quarter of a century later. Similarly, near the beginning of *Under Western Eyes*, we are bidden to consider "any young Englishman" imaginatively projected into Razumov's position:

The only safe surmise to make is that he would not think as Mr. Razumov thought at this crisis of his fate. He would not have an hereditary and personal knowledge of the means by which a historical autocracy represses ideas, guards its power, and defends its existence. By an act of mental extravagance he might imagine himself arbitrarily thrown into prison, but it would never occur to him unless he were delirious (and perhaps not even then) that he could be beaten with whips as a practical measure either of investigation or of punishment.(25)

We need not argue this, or spread stories that police-stations are not quite what they were. But we may certainly maintain that Conrad is building upon a fallacious estimate of the political maturity and stability of the Western world. Conrad has invented an Iron Curtain of his own, and thinks to cage "ferocity and imbecility" behind it. This is why *Under Western Eyes*, austere and powerful tragedy though it be, does not strike us, as *Nostromo* does, as possessing prophetic character. He foresaw much of Russia's future more clearly than most. Other destinies were dark to him.

But Russia was, in a special sense, dark to him, too, and in this lay its fascination. "The confused immensity of the Eastern borders"(346) represented one of those "dark places of the earth" which so often acted as a magnet to Conrad's imagination. For this passionate devotee of Latin logic and clarity extracted a singular satisfaction from the contemplation of the unaccountable. Ready to declaim against mysticism in all its forms, he seems seldom to have been compelled by phenomena which left under scrutiny no residuum of the mysterious. The Russian mind belonged here. "That propensity of lifting every problem from the plane of the understandable by means of some sort of mystic expression, is very Russian,"(104) we are told. It goes along with "Russian simplicity," which proves to be a sinister sort of thing: "a terrible corroding simplicity in which mystic phrases clothe a naïve and hopeless cynicism."(104) This is a constant thought. "Russian simplicity often marches innocently on the edge of cynicism for some lofty purpose."(125) The precise sense Conrad, here and elsewhere in the novel, attaches to the term "cynicism" is not easy to determine. "In its pride of numbers, in its strange pretentions of sanctity, and in the secret readiness to abase itself in suffering, the spirit of Russia is the spirit of cynicism."(67) And Razumov, accused by Peter Ivanovitch of aiming at stoicism, says:

"Stoicism! That's a pose of the Greeks and the Romans. Let's leave it to them. We are Russians, that is—children; that is—sincere; that is—cynical, if you like. But that's not a pose."(207)

If it is not a pose, it is at least a puzzle, and by the time we reach the end of the novel we have probably had enough of the unaccountable morphology of the Russian mind. But Conrad's predilection here goes a little further. If only in the sense that they grip and repel him, he may be said to have a taste for the senseless and—it is a favourite word—the "imbecile." And the emphasis he sets upon the operation of these in the political sphere tends to bear more hardly upon his revolutionists than upon his representatives of autocracy. Haldin's assassination of Mr. de P——, indeed, is purposeful and effective—so much so that we may be surprised that the perpetrator has to seek Razumov's help in the random way he does. But the revolutionists as a group, unlike their adversaries, have very little notion of what they are about: sporadic terrorism, or the inciting of some small-scale mutiny, appear to be the measure of what is planned even in their highest counsels. It is strange that Conrad, who saw so clearly that for Russia revolution lay ineluctably ahead, could present as its instruments no more than an assemblage of Conradian grotesques. As we listen to their vapourings, as we watch them going soft, there must sometimes hover in our consciousness the somewhat different figure of Vladimir Ilyitch Lenin.

Conrad certainly saw the problem presented to him by his total lack of sympathy with the enemies of tyranny, by his intellectual and emotional conviction that when successful they would turn tyrants themselves. It is a view that he places in the mouth of his narrator, effectively and soberly, in the course of a conversation with Miss Haldin:

In a real revolution—not a simple dynastic change or a mere reform of institutions—in a real revolution the best characters do not come to the front. A violent revolution falls into the hands of narrow-minded fanatics and of tyrannical hypocrites at first. Afterwards comes the turn of all the pretentious intellectual failures of the time. Such are the chiefs and the leaders. You will notice that I have left out the mere rogues. The scrupulous and the just, the noble, humane, and devoted natures; the unselfish and the intelligent may begin a movement—but it passes away from them. They are not the leaders of a revolution. They are its victims: the victims of disgust, of disenchantment—often of remorse. Hopes grotesquely betrayed, ideals caricatured—that is the definition of revolutionary success.(134-5)

In *Under Western Eyes* the "unselfish" are represented by Tekla, whose harrowing early experiences of social injustice have brought her into the revolutionary movement on the most altruistic grounds. She labours devotedly for her self-appointed leaders, Peter Ivanovitch and Madame de S——, whose treatment of her is so callous that she finally abandons their cause to devote herself to a pure work of mercy, the care of the shattered Razumov. In his correspondence with Garnett, Conrad pointed, justly enough, to his creation of Tekla as instancing the fact that he by no means lacked impartiality in contemplating his conspiratorial world. He pointed, too, to Sophia Antonovna, who is a fanatic indeed, but at the same time a woman of integrity and some humanity. With the further exception of an unnamed elderly man with "a mild, sad voice,"(367) who attempts to get Razumov away from Laspara's house before the outrage is perpetrated upon him, these are the only revolutionists who are not evil, debased, or contemptible.

The chief of them, Peter Ivanovitch, once a young officer in the Guards, is a portrait brilliantly achieved—this largely on the score of the vivid and horrible comedy of his escape across Russia, clutching his ball and chain, and already exploiting that power over women which he is later to extend beneath the cloak of a hypocritical feminism. The physical man, moreover, is brought vividly before us. Peter Ivanovitch has "one of those bearded Russian faces without shape."(120) It is a "soft enormous face,"(130) and along with it goes the "great effortless voice"(128) which can say "I never make a mistake in spiritual matters."(130) His corruption is perhaps altogether too pervasive. Recalling the total impression he makes, we are not very clear that Conrad has indeed "left out the mere rogues."

Certainly as the novel develops, we are likely to feel that Peter Ivanovitch becomes too much of an Aunt Sally. Moreover, should we come to it direct from *The Secret Agent*, and be experiencing a certain relief in the absence of that book's remorselessy pervasive ironic manner, we may be irritated by the return of the old periphrastic technique in relation to him. He is variously described as "the noble arch-priest of Revolution,"(210) "the 'Russian Mazzini,' "(214) "the 'heroic fugitive,' "(227) "the burly feminist,"(229) and even "the popular expounder of a feministic conception of social state."(219) He has published his autobiography (the great literary success of its year), and "other books written with the declared purpose of elevating humanity."(125) He is ceaselessly hunting up his compatriots and "conferring upon them the honour of his notice in public gardens when a suitable opening presented itself."(126) Sophia Antonovna somewhere tells Razumov that "women, children, and revolutionists hate irony,"(279) and it appears to be in this faith that Conrad pursues Peter Ivanovitch with the method. As he says in his Author's Note, the chief of his revolutionists—together with Madame de S——, "his painted Egeria"(230)—is "fair game."(ix)

Revolutionists are represented as living in a congenial dirt and squalor—in one instance symbolically rather than realistically so. Julius Laspara's three little rooms *en suite* are dark, with dusty windowpanes, a "litter of all sorts of sweepings all over the place" and "half-full glasses of tea forgotten on every table."(286) This seems appropriate to the man's condition and temperament. But the state of Madame de S——'s Château Borel (named by Conrad, one must suppose, after the most extravagant of French late Romantic writers) is less plausible. This "house of folly, of blindness, of villainy and crime"(248) appears to be virtually unfurnished and derelict, and only a quite pathological parsimony could account for a wealthy woman's living in it. Something of the kind is, in fact, posited—but, at the same time, one cannot miss the significance of the disgraced mansion. As a boy Conrad had known the life of great houses, and what they meant to him he was to express in a letter to Hugh Walpole in 1917, when the Russian Revolution seemed certain to bring to an end their already long-threatened existence:

And those houses where, under a soul-crushing oppression, so much noble idealism, chivalrous traditions, the sanity and the amenities of Western civilization were so valiantly preserved,— are they to vanish into smoke? *Cela aussi est très possible.* And at any rate moral destruction is unavoidable.[7]

The Château Borel had never been like one of these gallant outposts of aristocratic Latin culture. A retired Hamburg banker had built it. Nevertheless, stripped as it now is, and frequented by the imbecile and the recreant who are like "evil mushrooms in a dark cellar,"(206) it makes its symbolic statement clearly enough.

That Conrad saw revolution and incitement to revolution exclusively as so much sanguinary futility limits both the

reach of his imagination and the play of his sympathy. And
he faced another temperamental difficulty in addressing himself to the story of Razumov.

The subject which—he assured Garnett—he had simply
"picked up" from a number lying about was at the start a
straightforward story of betrayal. Razumov, Haldin, and
Councillor Mikulin were, he declared, the only characters of
whom he had a clear view. He began, that is to say, with a
central figure much in the position of the hero of *Lord Jim*.
Razumov is a self-absorbed young man who suddenly experiences very bad luck. "He was as lonely in the world as a man
swimming in the deep sea"(10)—or as Jim on the deck of the
Patna. He dreams of distinction, since "a man's real life is
that accorded to him in the thoughts of other men by reason
of respect or natural love."(14) Then, with the effect of a
sudden lurch felt by his whole being, Victor Haldin is before
him, shattering his "solitary and laborious existence"(82) by
claiming a confidence which Razumov, as he perfectly fairly
feels, has never provoked. Had Razumov at once ordered
Haldin from his room to take his chance with his true associates, no question of betrayal could have been involved.
Had he genuinely possessed political convictions taking him
straight to the police, his situation would have been abomin-
able, but again no question of betrayal in its full sense would
have arisen. But Razumov accepts the task of securing the
services of Ziemianitch with his sledge, has the further misfortune of finding the man drunk and incapable, and cracks
beneath this additional strain. He persuades himself that he
possesses philosophical beliefs which in fact he has been too
egotistical ever to think out, and he precipitates himself into
the presence of his aloof father, Prince K——. There can now
be no doubt about what has happened. Later in the story,
the unconscious Mrs. Haldin is to fear that her son "may

have been betrayed by some false friend or simply by some cowardly creature."(117) Both these suspicions are justified. Jim, we may say, has jumped.

Conrad's grand difficulty seems now to have been at all to discern what should follow upon this old situation in its new setting. As formidably as Razumov himself at the close of the first part of the novel, he was confronted by a simple "Where to?" That his first thought was wide of his eventual mark is on record in a letter to Galsworthy at the beginning of 1908:

Listen to the theme. The Student Razumov (a natural son of a Prince K.) gives up secretly to the police his fellow student, Haldin, who seeks refuge in his rooms after committing a political crime (supposed to be the murder of de Plehve). First movement in St. Petersburg. (Haldin is hanged of course.)

2d in Genève. The student Razumov meeting abroad the mother and sister of Haldin falls in love with that last, marries her and, after a time, confesses to her the part he played in the arrest of her brother.

The psychological developments leading to Razumov's betrayal of Haldin, to his confession of the fact to his wife and to the death of these people (brought about mainly by the resemblance of their child to the late Haldin), forms the real subject of the story.[8]

Jean-Aubry notes Conrad as writing "done" in the margin of the first of these paragraphs, and "to do" in the margin of the second.

"And perhaps no magazine will touch it," Conrad goes on, beginning one of his periodic outbursts of desperation and despair, and he adds "Foreignness, I suppose" as the reason for the ill-success of his novels compared with Hardy's ("tragic enough and gloomily written too"). This note is worth pausing upon again. His financial straits and his nervous constitution appear between them to have made his work a long misery. Thus he had made his decision about the development of *Under Western Eyes*, and driven the latter stages of the story far on their way, when he wrote to Normal Douglas: "The novel hangs on the last 12,000 words, but there's neither inspiration nor hope in my work. It's mere hard labour for life—with this difference, that the life of the convict is at any rate out of harm's way." [9] It is amid these pressures that we have to view him as confronting the question "Where to?" and we must be impressed by the artistic discretion of the answer he eventually gave himself. That Razumov, having become a police spy (and this is implicit in the whole Mikulin episode already completed at the date of the letter to Galsworthy), should then actually marry Miss Haldin and have a child by her would surely have led to situations of a psychosexual complexity totally outside Conrad's range. Only melodrama could have been the result. (Indeed, melodrama is not wholly avoided anyway, as we shall see.) He did well to bring forward Razumov's confession and expiation to a point before such a hazardously novelistic development could realize itself.

What is perhaps chiefly significant is that the changed conception involved a drastic contracting of his original design. In effect, the space unfilled by an inconceivable courtship, a marriage, and the early years of a childhood had to be occupied by something else. Conrad supplied this, largely in the form of extended dialogues, turning in the main upon Razumov's position among the revolutionists, in the second and third parts of the novel. These are excellent, indeed masterly, in themselves. But they are drawn out to a point at which their dramatic momentum falters. Something of this may appear in a brief examination of the book's structure.

It is a simple structure, following save at one point a

straightforward chronological course and adopting a scenic method. After a preliminary section in which the narrator gives some account of himself, of Razumov, and of Razumov's diary, we see the assassination, Haldin's turning up on Razumov, Razumov's encounters with Ziemianitch, Prince K——, General T——, Haldin again—and all as taking place within a few hours. A day passes; Razumov goes to the University, converses with an inquisitive student, and returns to find that the police have searched his room. A night passes, he has his encounter with the sympathetic and admiring "madcap" Kostia, receives a summons from the police, obeys it at once, and suffers his interview with Mikulin. We have arrived at "Where to?" and are a little more than a quarter of the way through the book. This long, direct movement has been tense and unfaltering.

Part Two opens upon Haldin's mother and sister in Geneva, and the manner of the narrator's making their acquaintance some six months before the assassination. In under twenty pages we have the news of this deed, the weeks during which the ladies receive no letters from Haldin, the arrival of the English newspaper with the fact or rumour of his arrest, the acknowledgment that he must be dead, and the beginning of Mrs. Haldin's obsessive wish to understand the circumstances in which he was caught. The narrator is absent from Geneva for a fortnight; on his return Peter Ivanovitch is on the scene, and we hear at length about his past history and his present involvement with Madame de S——. With no break in time, we hear of Haldin's former letter praising Razumov, of Razumov's being in Geneva in a confidential relationship with the revolutionists, and of Miss Haldin's consequent resolution to brave a visit to the disreputable Château Borel. Several days pass, and she gives the narrator an account of the visit: her long talk with Tekla,

her meeting with Razumov, his strange appearance of shock.
Razumov has been elusive since then, but now—as Miss
Haldin continues to talk to the narrator—he appears, and
the narrator converses with him, ponders his enigmatical
manner, and leaves him leaning over a bridge. This is the
end of Part Two.

Part Three opens without a break in time; Razumov is
still on the bridge. But we immediately learn of him as with-
drawing into seclusion "for a few days." Then, on the following page, the narrator tells us that "once or twice" he saw
Razumov and Miss Haldin strolling together, and he adds at
once: "They met every day for weeks." A short talk between
the narrator and Miss Haldin follows; she reports herself as
not yet understanding Razumov very well; she seems to be
expecting him to turn up, but he fails to do so. "Less than
an hour afterwards" the narrator sees him making for the
Château Borel. We are at once transported there ourselves,
and are present at a long interview between Razumov and
Peter Ivanovitch. We are now a little more than half-way
through the book, and have in fact arrived at the day upon
which its action is to conclude. Perhaps with this opening of
Part Three it is as with the plays of Shakespeare: there is no
point in inquiring into the "time scheme" if the imaginative
effect is right. But it is not going to appear quite right when
we look back, and we come to suspect that room has been
made for the implied developing relationship between Razumov and Miss Haldin only in a perfunctory fashion because
Conrad has not really faced up to it.

The interview with Peter Ivanovitch continues in the
presence of Madame de S——, and then further continues as a
dialogue once more. A conversation with Tekla follows, and
immediately after that a long conversation with Sophia
Antonovna is resumed. Upon leaving her, Razumov runs into

Julius Laspara, is asked to contribute something to his revolutionary journal, and under this prompting buys writing materials in a stationer's shop and settles down to produce his first report as a spy instead. He is still writing as Part Three ends. We have had just under a hundred pages in which the flow of time has been uninterrupted.

At the beginning of Part Four, however, comes a short chapter embodying the only time-shift in the book. We go back to "Where to?" and are given an account of Razumov's leaving Russia; this retrospect is balanced by a forward glance at the eventual disgrace of Mikulin. The narrative then picks up Razumov as he finishes writing his report. He posts it while under the observation of the narrator, who is emphatic about being suddenly shocked by the young man's expression. The narrator calls on the ladies that evening, and joins Miss Haldin in seeking out Razumov in order to bring him into the presence of her mother. The search takes them to a gathering of revolutionists, but is unsuccessful; they return to the Haldins' house and find that Razumov has arrived and is talking to Mrs. Haldin. He comes out, makes his confession to Miss Haldin, returns to his rooms and completes his diary, goes to Laspara's, and the catastrophe follows. The final chapter describes the narrator's last meeting with Miss Haldin a fortnight after "her mother's funeral," and a final meeting with Sophia Antonovna nearly two years later.

Under Western Eyes is the story of a man who commits a crime—the ultimate crime of a betrayal of human trust—and sees ever-deepening degradation before him as a consequence. He faces these facts, and achieves repentance and expiation. Viewed simply in this light, Razumov comes very near to being one of the greatest creations in English fiction. Again and again he strives to assume before the mirror of his own conscience the mask of a ruthless operator in the underworld that has engulfed him. He seeks relief in fencing with the revolutionists, in dark sayings and dangerous double meanings:

"Ah, Peter Ivanovitch, if you only knew the force which drew— no, which *drove* me towards you! The irresistible force. . . . I have been impelled, compelled, or rather sent—let us say sent— towards you for a work that no one but myself can do . . . some day you will remember these words, I hope."(228)

"Suppose I were to tell you that I am engaged in dangerous work?"(234)

"I am very much in earnest about my mission. I mean to succeed."(244)

"The late Haldin . . . was inclined to take sudden fancies to people, on—on—what shall I say—insufficient grounds."(274)

But an irony more cruel than this—an irony of simple ignorance and misconception—is constantly bearing the other way. Sometimes, in the classical fashion, it is at play only upon ourselves, as when Miss Haldin says to the narrator: "There is no guessing what he may have to tell us."(137) More commonly it thrusts at Razumov himself, and phrases almost casually dropped are often heavy with it. "Surely that needn't cost you a great effort."(196) "You no doubt know the whole truth."(186) "You looked as if one could trust you."(233)

The greatest concentration of effect here comes with the revelation of Miss Haldin's identity. "He positively reeled," she reports to the narrator. "He leaned against the wall of the terrace. Their friendship must have been the very brotherhood of souls!"(172) And she herself was much moved; was she not meeting the man described by her brother as among the "unstained, lofty, and solitary existences"?(135) There is really no need for Razumov to fall in love with Miss Haldin in order to deepen the horror of his position. Nor, we may feel, is he in a situation in which, outside the bounds of a novel, this is at all likely to happen. That the girl should idolize him, and that this should turn, in a scarcely conscious way, into a falling in love on her own part, is another matter. But it may be that Conrad, having already so judiciously tempered the romantic resonance of his story, might have done well to mute it still further.

Motivation in the final stages of the book, indeed, is not very clearly articulated. There is marked stress on what immediately succeeds upon Razumov's actually taking his first positive step in the new sort of treachery for which he has been sent to Geneva. His "shocking"(317) expression is also "extraordinary hallucined, anguished, and absent,"(320) "worse than if he had seen the dead."(325) Later, the narrator recalls it as "the look of a haunted somnambulist"(336) which is presently to take on (a prelude, this, to a revelation yet to come) "the shadow of something consciously evil."(337) And all this is a matter of quite new observation. It would seem to be the posting of the letter to his masters in Russia that brings Razumov, reasonably enough, to a naked realization of his past guilt and present ignominy, and that drives him into Mrs. Haldin's drawing-room. That his first duty, upon repentance, is to confess to Haldin's mother and sister may be taken as self-evident, whether there be any question of a love-relationship or not.

It is not certain what Razumov tells Mrs. Haldin, or even if her mental state any longer enables her to comprehend him. As he comes out and encounters her daughter, "the thought that he would have to repeat the story he had told already was intolerable to him."(339) But this is ambiguous, and what follows is a surprise. There is at first the suggestion of the birth—if the tragically abortive birth—of a simple and positive relationship:

> It was as though he were coming to himself in the awakened consciousness of that marvellous harmony of feature, of lines, of glances, of voice, which made of the girl before him a being so rare, outside, and, as it were, above the common notion of beauty. He looked at her so long that she coloured slightly. . . . To me, the silent spectator, they looked like two people becoming conscious of a spell which had been lying on them ever since they first set eyes on each other.(324-5)

None of this reads very well. Prepared for only by things like "They met every day for weeks," it comes to us as a rapid and belated working up of a *motif* that has been largely neglected hitherto. And Conrad appears to feel that something more forcible is needed. For suddenly we get novelty with a vengeance: a development utterly unprepared for except by that mention of a "shadow of something consciously evil" tipped in a few pages earlier. Razumov is confessing not only everything we know about; he is also confessing an "atrocious temptation"(354) immeasurably blacker still. "An hour after I saw you first I knew how it would be,"(354) he says—and almost immediately snatches up Miss Haldin's veil from the floor and dashes from the house. It is now that he returns to his rooms and completes his diary. This is eventually received by Miss Haldin, wrapped in the veil. Completing his confession in it, Razumov declares that, to revenge himself upon Haldin, he had determined to "steal his sister's soul from her."(359) "Natalia Victorovna, I was possessed! I returned to look at you every day, and drink in your presence the poison of my infamous intention. . . . I sat alone in my room, planning a life, the very thought of which makes me shudder now."(360)

We may turn back and search the novel in vain for any hint of the "atrocious temptation." What this strange aberration—for it can only be called that—suggests is the disastrousness of the story that Conrad succeeded in avoiding. He has returned—conceivably through fatigue and while incorporating matter from old notes—to the conventions of melodrama which his first plan would have enforced upon him. As it is, here almost at the end of the novel is its central character, hitherto deeply observed and subtly portrayed, constrained to talk fustian such as one might find in any Victorian novelette. It is a testimony to the immense vitality of *Under Western Eyes* that we are conscious of no essential damage to the integrity of the book. At the finish, as Razumov thinks "thus he saves me . . . he himself, the betrayed man"(362) and makes his way, redeemed, to his agony in Laspara's house, "the darkness returned with a single clap of thunder, like a gun fired for a warning of his escape from the prison of lies."(363) It is almost as if the "atrocious temptation" itself had been only part of that prison.

Under Western Eyes does not possess the economy and coherence, the triumphant artistic homogeneity, of *The Secret Agent*. It renders a slight effect of running down from an early climax instead of building up to a late one—and an effect, too, of its grip on character becoming less rather than more certain as we read. Nevertheless it is the deeper and bolder and larger book. The icy carapace of protective irony has been shed, and there are only sporadic retreats towards it; the increased vulnerability which the writer thus accepts invites us into a more genial relationship with his imagination and sensibility as they struggle with ungenial things. We are drawn into accepting our station among the ranks of a guilty humanity.

"You, at any rate, are one of *us*,"(208) Peter Ivanovitch

tells Razumov—and the queer appeal to patrician birth, perhaps because of its haunting echo from *Lord Jim*, seems like a momentary shaft driven deep into the strangeness of man's life in society. "Great men are horrible,"(232) the simpleminded Tekla says, and it is from within a context of experience which lends Dostoevskian authority to her words. "In this world of men"—Razumov reflects as he contemplates in Sophia Antonovna the true spirit of destructive revolution—"nothing can be changed, neither happiness nor misery. They can only be displaced at the cost of corrupted consciences and broken lives."(261) "You were appointed to undo the evil"—he says to Miss Haldin suddenly in that curiously uncertain final interview—"by making me betray myself back into truth and peace."(358) At the end of the book we learn that some of the revolutionists visit the broken Razumov from time to time—and it is the fanatical Sophia Antonovna who, revealing this, sums up his story:

"There are evil moments in every life. A false suggestion enters one's brain, and then fear is born—fear of oneself, fear for oneself. Or else a false courage—who knows? Well, call it what you like; but tell me, how many of them would deliver themselves up deliberately to perdition . . . ? He discovered that his bitterest railings, the worst wickedness, the devil work of his hate and pride, could never cover up the ignominy of the existence before him. There's character in such a discovery."(379-80)

"Character" is perhaps inadequate, since the term cannot quite be stretched to cover expiatory action taken in the light of an achieved self-knowledge. It is this which, in *Lord Jim*, we are left with no certainty of the hero's possessing. In *The Secret Agent* there is no question of anybody coming near it. But *Under Western Eyes* exhibits the spectacle of an authentic purification through suffering, and is a book in the great tragic tradition.

CHAPTER

Chance and *Victory*

Several critics have distinguished in *Chance* * the first
marked symptoms of Conrad's decline. This may be to some
extent a matter of reading back into it certain of the weaknesses that undeniably emerge in his writing later on. Had
it proved to be his last book, his career would certainly not
now appear to us as ending in any notable eclipse. And that
Chance chanced to be his first novel to achieve wide popular
success is not a circumstance by which our judgment should
be affected one way or the other.

The subtitle is *A Tale in Two Parts*—and on this one is
tempted to comment "a good one and a bad one." Here we

* Flora de Barral is the motherless only child of a dishonest financier. She
is almost sixteen when he is ruined and disgraced. The news is given to her
with revolting brutality by a corrupt and vengeful governess, and the shock
of this convinces her that she is wholly unloveable. Her father is sent to
prison for seven years. Her only relations are mean and vulgar people who
treat her with contempt and unkindness. She finds a measure of refuge and
support with former neighbours, the Fynes. Mr. Fyne is a well-meaning but
ineffective civil servant; his dominating wife is an implacable feminist who
believes that women must take every means, however unscrupulous, to assert
their independence. Flora's despair deepens. While meditating suicide by

are in contact with a major hazard of which most novelists
have had experience. A story—a single complete and significant action—glimmers into view; in no time its earlier phases
are making an urgent claim for embodiment and expression;
its people are beginning to move about and talk inside one's
head; pondering its later development at such leisure as this
allows, one is tempted to assure oneself (in James Joyce's
words) that "the good things will come," and that what is
merely schematic in one's mind so far will prove to be valid
and under one's command when its turn appears. "The
Rescuer," finally to be rescued after a fashion as *The Rescue,*
had been for Conrad a kind of cautionary tale here. Perhaps
he failed to heed it, or perhaps he could not afford to do so,
since simple economic necessity was always so urgent with
him. We know that he gave up *Chance* for a number of years,
and then resumed it again. It has been maintained that this
resumption was fatal to the rest of his career, that it implicated him disastrously in an area of experience which it
could never be his to control. The whole of the second part
of *Chance*—and it is nearly as long as the first—turns upon a
man and a woman involved in an obscure sexual situation
while more or less alone on a wide, wide sea. For Professor
Moser, the most skilled anatomist of Conrad's anti-climax,
this is "the uncongenial subject." [1] It is "love's tangled gar-
den" that Conrad is taking to sea, and the result cannot be
other than unsatisfactory. Sexual love—"the embrace," as

---

throwing herself over a precipice, she is observed by Mrs. Fyne's brother,
Roderick Anthony, captain and part-owner of a sailing-ship, the *Ferndale.*
Anthony, who is lonely and idealistic, is moved by her plight and then
quickly falls in love with her. Mrs. Fyne, determined to prevent what she
regards as an unsuitable match, insists that her husband show Anthony a
letter she has received from Flora: the girl, in great emotional confusion, has
adopted in it Mrs. Fyne's own theoretical attitudes, declaring that she does
not love Anthony but has no scruple in marrying him. Anthony still insists
that the marriage shall take place, if only that he may be in a position to
protect both Flora and her father, who is about to be released from gaol. All

Marlow calls it—made him uneasy; in his earliest writing it is associated with the alarming proliferations of the tropical jungle; he is unable to deal with it here.

There is much to be said for this criticism. A marriage could certainly be impeded—perhaps destroyed, or at least permanently impaired—by some such forces as Conrad is dealing with in his story. To this extent his intuition serves him well. But the actual situation he builds up is quite unreal. These people could not have continued to behave on the *Ferndale* as they are declared to have done. The point has been succinctly put by Mr. Douglas Hewitt:

> The effect can, perhaps, be summed up by saying that we are sure that at a number of points in the story the most natural remark (the most natural remark, that is, even of these two inhibited characters) would end the whole misunderstanding. We do not feel it to be "chance," and the previous histories of Conrad's personages which prolong the intolerably false position, but the guiding hand of the story-teller.[2]

There are other points in the novel at which this guiding hand may be felt as somewhat too palpably at work. What Henry James, in a celebrated discussion, called its "eccentricities of recital"[3] may be instanced. Consider the book's first sentence. It runs: "I believe he had seen us out of the window coming off to dine in the dinghy of a fourteen-ton yawl belonging to Marlow my host and skipper." The "he" here—Powell, formerly second officer of the *Ferndale*, and to

---

three at once set out on a five months' voyage on the *Ferndale*. The marriage remains unconsummated and the false situation continues: Anthony believes that Flora has accepted him out of mere desperation, and Flora believes that to Anthony she is nothing but an object of quixotic compassion. A second voyage is begun under the same circumstances of intolerable strain. Then de Barral, who has become insanely jealous of his daughter's husband, tries to poison him, is detected, swallows the poison himself, and dies. Flora, although she has not understood these events, is brought by the mounting tension of them into her husband's arms. The true marriage thus achieved endures happily until Anthony is drowned at sea some years later.

be revealed on the novel's last page as likely soon to marry Captain Anthony's widow—is going to tell a good part of the story to Marlow; Marlow is going to relate it to the "I"; and the "I" is going to relay it to us, with no more than a commenting word, mostly about Marlow, here and there. A number of other people are going to talk to Marlow, often at great length. But Marlow will always be between them and us (between them and "I," for that matter), sometimes offering a summary of their talk, but more often repeating it *verbatim*.

The most cursory inspection will reveal plenty of places in which this manner of narration is unverisimilar. Both Conrad and Marlow appear at times to be a little uneasy about it—to the surprise, perhaps, of the sophisticated reader, who experiences little trouble with the convention and is fascinated by its technical accomplishment. This aspect of *Chance*—its multiple points of view, its refraction of actual fact through report upon report, its effortless skill in time-shifts—is often commented upon as a load of virtuosity imposed upon a narrative pervasively inferior in quality and substance to Conrad's best work. However this may be, the handling, even in the markedly less satisfactory Part II, is masterly in itself. We may not be as ready as James to commend *Chance* for adopting "the way to do a thing that shall make it undergo most doing." [4] But at least we are unlikely to find in this aspect of the novel anything much to suggest that the guiding hand is in difficulty. It is rather in the characterization that uncertainty may be felt as beginning to appear.

It is a commonplace that the Marlow we meet in *Chance* is not really the Marlow we have met in "Heart of Darkness" and *Lord Jim*. It can be argued very effectively that these earlier works are, to a substantial degree, *about* Marlow.

This is plainly not true of *Chance*, where Marlow simply ferrets out a story and retails it—possibly, but not perceptibly, growing wiser as a result. A certain frivolity now marks the movement of his mind; he has "the habit of pursuing general ideas in a peculiar manner, between jest and earnest."(23) When he recounts his search, along with Fyne, at the foot of the quarry into which Flora de Barral may have thrown herself, he has "a whimsically retrospective air."(53) He is refusing to forget his opinion that the girl is a minx, and justifies himself:

> I have come across too many dead souls lying, so to speak, at the foot of high unscaleable places for a merely possible dead body at the bottom of a quarry to strike my sincerity dumb.(53)

Sometimes he appears cynical rather than sceptical. Indeed, in one important regard he is not sceptical at all, since he believes himself to be securely in possession of a great deal of truth about the nature of women. The interests we remember—betrayal, alienation and solitude, the duplicity of idealism—are still to be discerned. But his obsessive concern has become feminine psychology, and he has more to say about it than is at all likely to hold our attention. Much of his talk is misogynistic in tone. We may suspect that something in Conrad himself is here getting out of hand, but at the same time it is evident that artistic calculation is at work. We know Marlow to be intelligent and reflective; we acknowledge that much of what he has to say on this topic is shrewd and penetrating; we may be inclined, therefore, to accept other things he has to say about it as well. Into Marlow's "general ideas," in fact, are dropped from time to time confidently enunciated propositions serving to underpin, at points of maximum stress, the psychological plausibility of the chief female characters.

Of these there are three: Flora's governess, Mrs. Fyne, and

Flora herself. The governess is fairly plain sailing; she is required only to be so depraved that she keeps a worthless young man as a lover, and so abounding in repressed malignity that she cannot abandon Flora without inflicting upon her the most atrocious and gratuitous outrage. The governess, evil rather than merely wicked, exists very successfully in her own right, so that her big scene is one of the most horrifying things in Conrad. At the same time her character may be said to receive a certain amount of atmospheric support from the more sombre areas of Marlow's view of her sex.

Mrs. Fyne is not, like the governess, a *tour de force*. She is studied in some depth and with sublety. She is not, indeed, quite so good as her husband, and the reason for this is significant. Conrad has designs on Mrs. Fyne as he has not on Fyne himself. Mrs. Fyne as a piece of feminine psychology has to be manipulated so as to credibilize, at certain specific points, Flora de Barral as a piece of feminine psychology. Almost everything about Mrs. Fyne's feminism is totally convincing: her "girl-friends," for example, who so little detract from her being "a profoundly innocent person."(66) We accept the statement that she "did not want women to be women," and that "her theory was that they should turn themselves into unscrupulous sexless nuisances."(190) But "unscrupulous" here picks up and emphasizes something we have had elsewhere, and which does not similarly satisfy our sense of character. Marlow tells us confidently that Mrs. Fyne's doctrine extends to the view that pretty well any weapon is justified in a woman's hands. When we come to Flora's fatal letter to Mrs. Fyne (and—very characteristically—we get our first clear glimpse of it only in the three or four last pages of the book), we find that a great deal of weight has to be placed upon this precept. Here is a fragment of dialogue between Marlow and Flora, now for long the widow of Captain Anthony:

"Tell me what is it you said in that famous letter which so upset Mrs. Fyne, and caused little Fyne to interfere in this offensive manner?"

"It was simply crude," she said earnestly. "I was feeling reckless and I wrote recklessly. I knew she would disapprove and I wrote foolishly. It was the echo of her own stupid talk. I said that I did not love her brother but that I had no scruples whatever in marrying him."

She paused, hesitating, then with a shy half-laugh—

"I really believed I was selling myself, Mr. Marlow. And I was proud of it."(443)

This is unsatisfactory. We feel that merely mercenary marriage can scarcely have been a positive weapon in Mrs. Fyne's theoretical armoury, and that we have witnessed a kind of tinkering with her character in the interest of getting over an awkward patch in Flora's story.

From the moment that she meets Roderick Anthony, Flora de Barral's rôle is not an easy one to credibilize. Yet the trauma which she suffers at the time of her father's disgrace is so vividly evoked that we are disposed to allow a good deal to the "mystic wound"(118) it leaves upon her, and the effect of her domestication with her vulgar relatives—not directly described, but convincingly suggested through the brief appearances of the manufacturer of cardboard boxes, sublimely possessed of "all the civic virtues in their very meanest form"(130)—increases our sense of her desperate plight, of her being reduced to "washing about with slack limbs in the ugly surf of life with no opportunity to strike out for herself."(222) Yet, in all that she continues to experience and suffer, Flora has to be rather more passive than we may judge natural. But here Marlow on the female psyche is exploited again:

> Flora de Barral was not exceptionally intelligent but she was thoroughly feminine. She would be passive (and that does not mean inanimate) in the circumstances, where the mere fact of being a woman was enough to give her an occult and supreme significance. And she would be enduring, which is the essence of woman's visible, tangible power. Of that I was certain.(310)

These small manipulations in the interest of our acquiescence in the fable may, or may not, indicate some uncertainty of stance in Conrad. His handling of the character and destiny of Roderick Anthony is more significant. As the story stands, there seems no reason why the *Ferndale* should eventually be sunk and its captain drowned—or none except the purely formal one that Powell, who has recounted so much that happened long ago, does a little suggest himself as having to be bound into the action, in one way or another, at the end. One interpretation which has been offered here is that Conrad did not originally intend any sort of "happy" ending to Anthony's life, and that Anthony's early death constitutes a muted echo of some fully tragic close which had represented his creator's first conception. Something unresolved in the analysis of Anthony's character and motives may be judged to support this. It is not until near the end of Part I that we come upon a fairly full account of one of his first encounters with Flora in her dejected and desperate situation. And we read:

> What seemed most awful to her was the elated light in his eyes, the rapacious smile that would come and go on his lips as if he were gloating over her misery. But her misery was his opportunity and he rejoiced while the tenderest pity seemed to flood his whole being. . . . It was obvious the world had been

using her ill. And even as he spoke with indignation the very marks and stamp of this ill-usage of which he was so certain seemed to add to the inexplicable attraction he felt for her person. It was not pity alone, I take it. It was something more spontaneous, perverse and exciting. It gave him the feeling that if only he could get hold of her, no woman would belong to him so completely as this woman.(223-4)

Thus, again, Marlow—known to us as the historian of "dead souls at the foot of high unscaleable places." And on the *Ferndale* Marlow understands "the secret of the situation." Anthony was "intoxicated with the pity and tenderness of his part."(261) Did he, we are asked later, "wish to appear sublime in his own eyes"?(328) And then:

If Anthony's love had been as egoistic as love generally is, it would have been greater than the egoism of his vanity—or of his generosity, if you like—and all this could not have happened. He would not have hit upon that renunciation at which one does not know whether to grin or shudder. . . . At the same time I am forced to think that his vanity must have been enormous.(331)

It is his vanity—although we might ourselves call it a spiritual pride—which has constrained him "not only to face but to absolutely create a situation almost insane in its audacious generosity."(350)

But this intermittent anatomy of Anthony—certainly deeper than anything else in the book—need not be felt either as incompatible with his predominant moral nature nor as congruous only with a tragic close. He has been led into what Marlow calls, indeed, an utter falseness of aspiration. It has been a sort of illness, and we have been watching "the pain of his magnanimity which like all abnormal growths was gnawing at his healthy substance with cruel persistence."(416) The image is sufficiently sinister. But the disease has been a nervous one, after all; a temporary alienation from "the humble reality of things." That reality returns when, under the shock of inexplicable crisis, Flora is suddenly clinging round her husband's neck. "She looked as if she would let go and sink to the floor if the captain were to withhold his sustaining arm." But—we are told in a phrase itself so humble as to have attracted some critical censure— "the captain obviously had no such intention."(430)

There is thus very little reason to suppose that, during the course of its composition, *Chance* underwent any radical change of plan. But it may be the fact—and, if so, it is once more quite a humble one—that Conrad, when beginning Part II, had left himself with rather too many blank pages yet to fill. Moreover, by embarking on the ocean at this stage, he had hazardously cut himself off from one major source of strength in the earlier part of the book. The Fynes point this. "From that day I never set eyes on the Fynes," Marlow reports on page 252. They have been superb ironic comedy, with everything imaginatively right about them. "The Fyne dog was supposed to lead a Spartan existence on a diet of repulsive biscuits with an occasional dry, hygienic bone thrown in."(142) This, and more, about the dog plays its admirable part in defining the range of the Fynes' sympathies; their appalled encounters with de Barral's kinsman, the industrious manufacturer of cardboard boxes, are equally good; all in all, they exemplify a light and deftly cruel sketch of English upper-middle-class life reminding us of the novels of E. M. Forster. Less unexpected—because we have had something of it already in *The Secret Agent*—is the evocation of a London background almost Dickensian in its vitality.

When we board the *Ferndale*, all this is lost. Powell, the second officer, is no more than a nice and uncomprehending

young man, very "enthusiastic" about Mrs. Anthony.(407)
The first officer, sentimentally devoted to his captain, can
hardly strike us as other than an unfortunate creation—one
of those figures drifting in from magazine fiction which are
going to trouble Conrad's pages from now on. So we are left
with de Barral. He has the advantage of carrying round with
him Conrad's powerful imaginative comprehension of the
horror and degradation of imprisonment. "Resentful that
the child had turned into a young woman without waiting
for him to come out,"(356) pouring as a daily sinister mur-
muring into her ear his fixed idea that she must be saved
from the man who has possessed himself of her, a wreck with
"something fatuously venerable in his aspect,"(384) de Barral
is a skilfully evoked creation. Yet there is something not
altogether satisfactory about his final acts, the manner of
which seems to have been dictated by Conrad's coming to a
perception that he required a catastrophe sufficiently definitive while at the same time eluding the understanding of
Mrs. Anthony. We do not quite believe in the poison he is
mysteriously possessed of. Shortly before it is used, a carving
knife disappears from the mess-room of the *Ferndale*. We
scarcely need to recall Winnie Verloc's history to suppose
that it is going to turn up again later. But it never does, nor
is it again referred to. Painters call such surviving traces of
an abandoned intention *pentimenti*, or repentances.

Although the effect of Part I of *Chance* is quite different
from that of *The Secret Agent*, it nevertheless derives its
strength from the same source: an ability to fuse matter of
the most sombre contemplation with the tones of astringent
comedy. The emotional centre lies in Flora de Barral's sudden and dreadful experience as a girl, and in the long, deep
unhappiness of her young womanhood. But the impact of

this is very far from being diminished as a result of Marlow's viewing the whole action as what he calls a tragi-comical adventure. What Conrad appears to be feeling his way towards throughout Part I is a kind of fiction which, although pitched lower than the imaginative intensities of *Nostromo*, is yet richly resourceful in its command and exploitation of an English social scene, and capable of lending artistic coherence to that kind of intermingling of grave and gay which has always been prominent in the literature of his adoptive country. But Part II turns away from this, and accepts a more restricted theatre of human passion. And something like this more contracted spectacle is what Conrad carries on with in *Victory*, his next novel. It is the last in which he does anything like justice to his genius.

Victory * is sometimes approached as if it stood in the same relationship to *Chance* as does *Under Western Eyes* to *The Secret Agent*. There is again the continued pondering of an

---

* Baron Axel Heyst, the son of a Swedish philosopher, has accepted his father's doctrines of scepticism, non-attachment, and disillusion. He has for long drifted about the world of Borneo and the Malay Archipelago, anxious only to avoid involvement with other people—their passions and designs. But he is a man who cannot resist compassion. He comes to the aid of a certain Captain Morrison when in distress, and this leads him into a project for mining coal in the Tropics. The venture fails, and Heyst resolves to live a reclusive life on the island of Samburan. In Schomberg's hotel in Sourabaya, however, he comes upon an unfortunate English girl, a child of the people, who plays in a travelling orchestra and whom Schomberg is planning to seduce. He carries her off to his island. Schomberg, in revenge, persuades a ruffian called Jones that the island harbours treasure. Jones, with two accomplices, makes his way there, and soon both Heyst and the girl, whom he calls Lena, are in a nearly helpless situation. Eventually Lena, in order to secure a knife with which to arm Heyst, pretends to accept the advances of Ricardo, Jones's lieutenant. Jones has a pathological horror of women, and the sight of Ricardo at Lena's feet makes him at once attempt to shoot Ricardo dead. It is Lena who is killed. Jones a little later succeeds in killing Ricardo, and then himself perishes, along with his second accomplice. Heyst sets fire to his bungalow, and dies beside Lena's body.

almost identical theme, together perhaps with an attempt to
consider aspects of it more fully, at a deeper level, and with
a higher degree of generalized significance. *Victory* is the
story of a distressed girl, rescued and carried into near solitude by a compassionate man, with a resulting period of
strain and imperfect relationship which is only resolved—but
this time to a wholly tragic issue—by the irruption of villainy
and violence. There are other, if incidental, correspondences.
Both Roderick Anthony and Axel Heyst are the sons of
famous writers, and each is much influenced by his father's
memory. And there are similar confrontations with absolute
evil, with the actions of persons so lost to normal moral feeling as to seem to exist in an invulnerable world of their own.

But if *Victory* looks back to *Chance*, it looks farther back
as well. The hotel-keeper Schomberg, whose malignity towards Heyst stems in the first instance merely from Heyst's
failure to use his establishment, has already figured in
"Falk," a short story published in 1902, where the same
relationship to the central figure obtains. Before this, again,
Schomberg has appeared in *Lord Jim*. And *Victory* returns
us to *Lord Jim* in more than its setting in the Eastern Seas.
There is a close similarity of *dénouement*. Just as Jim and his
mistress Jewel, established in the withdrawn and lonely
Patusan, are assailed from the sea by the desperate Brown
and his gang, so in *Victory* Heyst and Lena, alone save for a
Chinaman and some elusive natives on the island of Samburan, are assailed from the sea by Mr. Jones and his two
followers—arriving, as the others do, in an extreme and dis-
arming state of physical privation. Moreover, Mr. Jones, like
Brown, is a disgraced gentleman, at an extreme of alienation
from the traditions of his class, and something is made of this
in the scene of his final confrontation with Heyst.

In none of these correspondences and parallels does the

advantage lie very evidently with *Victory*. Take the last of them. Heyst's character and history are not such that he can plausibly be represented as feeling himself to be in any special and significant relationship to Mr. Jones. Or at least, even if we agree with Mr. Hewitt that Heyst is aware of the "inhuman detachment" of Jones as akin to his own, we must conclude on the plain basis of the text that Conrad, working up his *dénouement*, does not consider the point sufficiently promising to reach out to. Nor is Jones in himself nearly so good as Brown. Throughout the book we have a lurking sense that Conrad has forgotten a good deal about the Archipelago; that it is not the "hallucination" it once was. And in particular we feel that he has forgotten about its desperadoes—with whom his contacts were certainly never very intimate, in any case. Jones is a thoroughly literary creation; if we grant him a certain power, as of a figure out of a Morality play, we must also allow him a more immediate ancestry among the society cracksmen and aristocratic re-mittance-men of popular fiction. Ricardo, his articulate follower, is worse; his wearisome insistence on the privilege of following a real gentleman like Mr. Jones suggests the first officer of the *Ferndale* trade-fallen and gone thoroughly to the bad. Nor are the contrasting sexual attitudes of these two impressive. Jones's horror of women, on which a good deal has to turn, is merely pathological; any recollection of Mr. Graham Greene's Pinkie in *Brighton Rock* is likely to prove damaging to our sense of Conrad's ability to deal with such a case. The lustfulness of Ricardo is equally shadowy, and his climactic "feral spring"(288) upon Lena behind the curtain has become celebrated for its comical ineptitude ("The self-restraint was at an end: his psychology must have its way"). As for the retired alligator-hunter, dog-like in his devotion to his brother's murderer, he is a mere schematic

addition to the camp of villainy, invented in order to constitute it an unholy trinity.

We are here looking, of course, at the simple side of
Victory. It is the longest side. The extended account of his
early adventures with Jones which Ricardo somewhat surprisingly offers to Schomberg is a fair measure of a good deal
of its course. *Victory*, somebody has said, is Conrad for use in
schools. This is not particularly true. Yet the narrative does
very substantially proceed at the level of an adventure story,
and is excellent in that kind; it thus looks forward to a good
deal in Conrad's last phase. It has the virtues, as well as some
of the weaknesses, of a novel produced without any large
degree of artistic consideration, yet with a perfected professional skill. Indeed, it would be reasonable to suppose that
Conrad, fresh from his first popular triumph with *Chance*,
was anxious to press on with something that should con-
solidate his new position.

The structure of the novel bears out this consideration.
Here we are worlds away from either *Chance* or *Lord Jim*,
and it is almost necessary to believe that Conrad started off
on it without thinking. There is an "I" in the second sentence—an "I" who is a good deal taken up with a "We."
There is being offered to us, in the first place, a view of Axel
Heyst as he casually appeared to the European community
in Sourabaya. Here and there we notice an element of omni-
science in the narrator's vision—it is hard to see how he can
have come by the detail of Heyst's confidential dealings with
the unlucky Captain Morrison—but on the whole he is just
picking up what he can: for example, Schomberg's malicious
gossip as he moves among his guests. Then Captain Davidson appears, and shows signs of settling into the same relationship to the narrator as Marlow bears to the narrator of
Chance. This takes us through Part I, the first sixty pages of

the novel. As he approached Part II, Conrad must have seen that he had no means of consistently deploying the method now so familiar to him. The story of Heyst and Lena was insusceptible of sustained presentation in narrative conceived as emanating from any character within the framework of the fable. In Part II, therefore, the point of view passes rapidly within the consciousness of Heyst, and thereafter shifts about, with a minimum of fuss, as convenience dictates. At the end of the novel Captain Davidson turns up again very abruptly, but there seems to be no particular reason why he should do so.

Through a large part of its outward action, then, *Victory*, although nearly always exciting and sharply visualized, would appear to be a work of secondary achievement and relaxed ambition, depending a good deal on the rehearsing of earlier themes. As soon as we move away from this to something else, we risk falsifying the total impression of the book. Nevertheless the novel's real interest is aside from anything we have considered so far. It lies in Conrad's bringing off, or very nearly bringing off, what (whether he recognized the fact or not) he had failed to bring off in *Chance*: a substantial, direct, and perceptive handling of Professor Moser's "uncongenial subject." When Heyst and Lena arrive on Samburan, the Round Island, and when to the girl, pausing before the verandah, Heyst says "This is the house,"(182) we have, in a sense, stepped on board the *Ferndale* once more. We have done so, however, to much greater effect than upon our first occasion.

For a start, Axel Heyst is a more finely observed figure than Roderick Anthony, and not in the same danger of appearing a romantic stereotype with dubious additions. Yet he is a creation more quintessentially romantic, in a way. His very name places him in the twilight of the romantic age.

Villiers de L'Isle-Adam's Axël held the title of Comte d'Auersperg, and Conrad originally thought to call Axel Heyst by the name of Augustus Berg. Axël's most celebrated pronouncement—to the effect that the mere business of living can be left to our servants—belongs to the class of precepts that Heyst has accepted from his father the philosopher, and which he sees no incongruity in passing on to his recently gained mistress: "I may say truly, too, that I never did care, I won't say for life—I had scorned what people call by that name from the first—but for being alive."(212) But Heyst, although he believes himself to be "a man of the last hour,"(359) does not subscribe merely to that modified withdrawal from the common traffic of the world in favour of life's finer vibrations which constituted the theory of fin-de-siècle aestheticism. There is a point at which he is credited with a portfolio of sketches, and it appears to be the visual beauty of the Archipelago that has held him spellbound and earned him the name of "Enchanted Heyst."(7) Moreover, it is the fineness of Lena's features and an indefinable beauty in her voice that constitute for him the basis of the girl's sensuous attraction. (There is to be no trouble about the "embrace" on Samburan. It is there from the first. The two lovers, with all their disparities of temperament and culture, must build on it as they can.) Yet Heyst is not an aesthete. The philosophy underlying his "unattached, floating existence"(18) is one of the most uncompromising disengagements from virtually all experience whatever. Action is out, for a start—as Captain Davidson learns, when he ventures (with some attempt at beneficent action himself, we may reflect) on his first visit to Heyst on his island. For Heyst says:

"I suppose I have done a certain amount of harm, since I allowed myself to be tempted into action. It seemed innocent enough, but all action is bound to be harmful. It is devilish.

That is why this world is evil upon the whole. But I have done with it!"(54)

Nor is thinking advisable. "If you begin to think you will be unhappy,"(193) he tells Lena. (The reply he receives—"I wasn't thinking of myself"—is the issue of a philosophy quite as profound as his own.) "Look on—make no sound,"(175) had been the elder Heyst's last words, and along with them his son has accepted an "inflexible negation of all effort"(173) and a complete absence of emotional ties. "Not a single soul belonging to him lived anywhere on earth."(66) "His most frequent visitors were shadows,"(4) we learn of him on Samburan. Even Wang the Chinaman is not much more than that.

Heyst is a Swedish nobleman who has become an English gentleman as well, and it is a commonplace in the criticism of *Victory* that its central figure is very close to Conrad himself—even closer, perhaps, than is Martin Decoud in *Nostromo*. Heyst's wanderings amid the rough life of the Islands are far from having induced him to veil his breeding. His bearing is invariably formal and courteous; he is incapable of outward cordiality; but he has evolved a delicately playful manner of address which, although evidently defensive, preserves him from seeming disagreeably aloof or contemptuous. The idiom which Conrad invents for him is exceedingly well conceived. In actual life, we may feel, it would quickly become intolerable, and it is very doubtful whether, in this particular at least, Conrad is noticeably indulging in self-portraiture. But as an imaginative correlative of facets of personality not readily to be caught in direct description it works admirably.

Conrad enjoys no such linguistic resource in the creating of Lena, the plebeian English girl in thrall to Zangiacomo's

Ladies' Orchestra, as it trails through Eastern cities, "murdering silence with a vulgar, ferocious energy."(68) He is no more capable of catching the speech of uneducated people than was his contemporary, Thomas Hardy, capable of catching that of the cultivated or the well-bred. (When this disability combines with another, Conrad's ineptitude can become grotesque. "You marvel, you miracle, you man's luck and joy—one in a million!"(398) is what the Priapic Ricardo finds to say in his rôle of would-be ravisher of Lena.) Yet—with the possible exception of Mrs. Gould—Lena ends as the most convincing of all Conrad's women. And she does this in face of a further disability. The melodramatic part of the story—which must again be stressed as much the larger part, so far as a count of pages goes—bears particularly hardly upon her. It is not easy to remain at all real when at grips with such a simulacrum of lust as Ricardo. Moreover, the mere mechanics of the suspense-story played out on Sumburan are not quite worthy of her. Basically, the motivation of her final actions is fine and true. But the point at which she first feels she has to conceal something from Heyst—the fact of her having encountered Ricardo—is clumsily fabricated.

These are matters of minor consideration. More significant is the quality of Lena's mind. Although extremely ignorant, she is not stupid, and Heyst is perfectly right in discerning in her face "the veiled glow of intelligence."(191) Heyst is almost comically unable to accommodate the nature of his conversation to her understanding, but the development of their relationship is based in part upon her flashes of comprehension and in part upon her perfectly unconscious penetration of his ironies by a clearer vision of her own. Thus Heyst tries to explain his father's philosophy:

"I suppose he began like other people; took fine words for good, ringing coin and noble ideals for valuable banknotes. He was a great master of both, himself, by the way. Later he discovered—how am I to explain it to you? Suppose the world were a factory and all mankind workmen in it. Well, he discovered that the wages were not good enough. That they were paid in counterfeit money."

"I see!" the girl said slowly.

"Do you?"(195-6)

We do not ourselves ask Heyst's question, for we believe that the girl sees. Later, when they are trapped, Heyst is regretting that he did not hail Davidson passing in his vessel some days before:

"No good, of course. We had no forebodings. This seemed to be an inexpugnable refuge, where we could live untroubled and learn to know each other."

"It's perhaps in trouble that people get to know each other," she suggested.

"Perhaps," he said indifferently.(352)

Wisdom passes this philosophic son of a philosopher by. So, in spite of all his fine considerateness, does the horror, for his mistress, of much that he has to say. Near the end, the teaching of her childhood prompts her suddenly to feel that perhaps Jones has been loosed upon them as a divine punishment for living in sin. Heyst makes fun of her—no doubt with what is elsewhere called "the well-known Heyst smile of playful courtesy."(221) And then he says seriously that he himself is not conscious of sin. Lena replies:

"You! You are different. Woman is the tempter. You took me up from pity. I threw myself at you."

"Oh, you exaggerate, you exaggerate. It was not so bad as that," he said playfully, keeping his voice steady with an effort.(354)

The effort has insufficient imagination to it. And what is a simple girl to make of a lover who murmurs to her that love itself may only be a counter in the lamentable or despicable game of life? All these failures of conduct are very well done. Yet the masterstroke here is the manner in which Captain Morrison's story suddenly advances for a time into the forefront of Heyst's and Lena's relationship.

The novel begins with Captain Morrison—honourable, simple-hearted, and (we are told) "one of us"—in trouble in the port of Delli, where he is unable to pay a small fine, with the result that the Portuguese authorities propose to auction his ship. He is observed by Heyst, who speaks to him, characteristically, "in the manner of a prince addressing another prince on a private occasion."(12) Heyst pays the fine, and it is his delicacy in face of Morrison's unbounded and continued gratitude that lands him in the whole ridiculous venture of the Tropical Belt Coal Company and his final proprietorship of its abandoned territory on Samburan. The malign Schomberg has spread the story that Morrison's subsequent death lies virtually at Heyst's door, and this calumny Lena has heard. When she divulges this Heyst is quick to misinterpret her attitude, for he is very constantly aware that there may be gulfs of moral feeling between himself and one who is virtually a child of the streets. But already he has done his best to explain to her how his having gone to the help of Morrison strikes him now:

"What captivated my fancy was that I, Axel Heyst, the most detached of creatures in this earthly captivity, the veriest tramp on this earth, an indifferent stroller going through the world's bustle—that I should have been there to step into the situation of an agent of Providence. *I*, a man of universal scorn and unbelief . . ."

"You are putting it on," she interrupted in her seductive voice, with a coaxing intonation. . . . "You saved a man for fun —is that what you mean? Just for fun?"

"Why this tone of suspicion?" remonstrated Heyst. "I suppose the sight of this particular distress was disagreeable to me. . . . Already his gratitude was simply frightful. Funny position, wasn't it? The boredom came later, when we lived together on board his ship. I had, in a moment of inadvertence, created for myself a tie. How to define it precisely I don't know. One gets attached in a way to people one has done something for. But is that friendship? I am not sure what it was. I only know that he who forms a tie is lost. The germ of corruption has entered into his soul."

Heyst's tone was light, with the flavour of playfulness which seasoned all his speeches and seemed to be of the very essence of his thoughts.(198-200)

Heyst, we are told a little later, when thinking about Lena, has a "physical and moral sense of the imperfections of their relations."(222) He might, perhaps, have put it to himself more strongly. Everything he has said about Morrison, rescued out of mere compassion from the Portuguese, might have been said—the girl must think—about herself, rescued from Schomberg and the Zangiacomos. To talk thus in a profound unconsciousness of what his words must convey speaks of a truth about himself which he is only to realize and express on the eve of his death:

"Ah, Davidson, woe to the man whose heart has not learned while young to hope, to love—and to put its trust in life!"(410)

But Lena, on her part, does not falter. "She felt in her innermost depths an irresistible desire to give herself up to him more completely, by some act of absolute sacrifice."(201) And this—"something rapturous and profound going beyond the mere embrace"(308)—is the victory she achieves.

The long scenes between Heyst and Lena, both in Schomberg's hotel and afterwards on the island, are far from being a uniform success. But they are much more successful than not. If we pause in the middle of them and think back to *Chance*, we realize that only in the earliest scenes between Anthony and Flora is a comparable advance upon difficult territory being made. Conrad, with the tenacity he knew himself to possess, has returned to a sexual theme and achieved his most serious study of it. He has done this even while building up an adventure story in which there is a premium on the achieving and maintaining of simple physical suspense. The chief indication in *Victory* of a mounting fatigue is perhaps our sense that disparate aims have markedly impaired the book's unity of interest.

CHAPTER

XI

"The Secret Sharer" and
The Shadow-Line

"The Secret Sharer" is a simple story, sparely told; yet both its quality and its meaning have been very variously pronounced upon by critics, and it is not easy even to sketch the action without feeling that one may be unfairly slanting the emphasis in such a way as to prejudge the issues. The narrator is a sea-captain, and what he has to tell succeeded immediately upon his taking over, at an early age, his first command. His new ship is anchored at the head of the Gulf of Siam, "at the starting point of a long journey." (*Twixt Land and Sea Tales*, 92) There is no suggestion that it is a journey involving special hazards, and the young man already feels able to lean on his "ship's rail as if on the shoulder of a trusted friend."(92) But he has other feelings as well:

What I felt most was my being a stranger to the ship; and if all the truth must be told, I was somewhat of a stranger to myself. The youngest man on board (barring the second mate), and untried as yet by a position of the fullest responsibility, I

232

was willing to take the adequacy of the others for granted. They had simply to be equal to their tasks; but I wondered how far I should turn out faithful to that ideal conception of one's own personality every man sets up for himself secretly.(93-4)

It is a familiar Conradian situation and speculation.[1] Indeed, one of the difficulties about "The Secret Sharer" is the insistence, as it were, of other works of Conrad's on prowling round its fringes as we read.

The captain's "strangeness" makes him sleepless, and he decides—very unconventionally—to set no anchor watch, and himself to remain on deck during the earlier part of the night. One result is that a rope-ladder is left hanging over the side of the ship. When the captain himself goes to pull this up, he finds a naked man clinging to it. As soon as the stranger knows he is speaking to the captain, he identifies himself:

"My name's Leggatt."
The voice was calm and resolute. A good voice. The self-possession of that man had somehow induced a corresponding state in myself. It was very quietly that I remarked:
"You must be a good swimmer."
"Yes. I've been in the water practically since nine o'clock. The question for me now is whether I am to let go this ladder and go on swimming till I sink from exhaustion, or—to come on board here."

I felt this was no mere formula of desperate speech, but a real alternative in the view of a strong soul. I should have gathered from this that he was young; indeed, it is only the young who are ever confronted by such clear issues. But at the time it was pure intuition on my part. A mysterious communication was established already between us two—in the face of that silent, darkened tropical sea. I was young, too; young enough to make no comment. The man in the water began suddenly to climb up the ladder, and I hastened away from the rail to fetch some clothes. . . . In a moment he had concealed his damp body in a sleeping-suit of the same grey-stripe pattern as the one I was wearing and followed me like my double on the poop.(99-100)

It is thus that the secret sharing begins—the "mysterious communication" being established before the captain learns anything of Leggatt's circumstances. Even that sense of identity with Leggatt which is to be insisted upon with a sort of obsessed reiteration throughout the narrative establishes itself initially in face of the same ignorance. Nevertheless, Leggatt's story is soon told. He has swum from the *Sephora*, a ship at anchor some two miles away. He has been first mate on board her, and during the crisis of a terrible storm he has seized and strangled an incompetent and disobedient member of the crew. Now he has made a bid to escape the law.

The captain accepts at once, and without an indication of internal debate, that it is his duty to harbour Leggatt, and the greater part of "The Secret Sharer" is taken up with an account of the various stratagems he has to employ. If he is resourceful, he is not unperturbed. On the contrary, the dangers of the situation, and in particular a degree of identification with Leggatt extending to an insane sense of being in two places at once, make it almost impossible for him to preserve a rational demeanour before his officers and crew. Leggatt remains completely self-controlled. "Whoever was being driven distracted, it was not he."(131) But the captain knows what he must do; he must steer sufficiently near the land in the night to give the fugitive a fair chance of a swim to safety. In this he succeeds—although he is impelled, when the critical moment comes, to drive so close to the shore beneath "the black mass of Koh-ring"(142) that his ship is in terrible danger, and all those on board her are amazed and appalled. Leggatt departs, and it is all over—the ship saved by a hat which the captain has given him as protection against the sun, and which in fact serves at a crucial moment to show when the vessel has gathered sternway:

Already the ship was drawing ahead. And I was alone with her. Nothing! no one in the world should stand now between us, throwing a shadow on the way of silent knowledge and mute affection, the perfect communion of a seaman with his first command.

Walking to the taffrail, I was in time to make out, on the very edge of a darkness thrown by a towering black mass like the very gateway of Erebus—yes, I was in time to catch an evanescent glimpse of my white hat left behind to mark the spot where the secret sharer of my cabin and of my thoughts, as though he were my second self, had lowered himself into the water to take his punishment: a free man, a proud swimmer striking out for a new destiny.(143)

We are likely to feel some affinity between Leggatt and Lord Jim. Both are ship's officers who commit an act which makes outcasts of them. Both have extremely bad luck—or, to put it differently, may be credited with a good deal in the way of extenuating circumstances. And the story of the mate on the *Sephora*, like the story of the mate on the *Patna*, turns out to be founded on fact. Curiously enough, these several facts were more or less chronologically coincident. The same issue of the *Straits Times* that reported the arrival of A. P. Williams, chief officer of the *Jeddah*, in Singapore reported "another painful story from the sea." [2] This was the news that a certain Sydney Smith, chief officer of the *Cutty Sark*, had killed a Negro seaman and subsequently fled from justice. It became known subsequently that the *Cutty Sark*'s captain had aided Smith's escape and committed suicide a few days later. When we recall the suicide of Captain Brierly in *Lord Jim*, we see that these two concurrent sensations had some power to interweave themselves in Conrad's imagination.

His manipulation of the *Cutty Sark* story is interesting but not remarkable. According to the evidence given against Smith when he was eventually caught and brought to trial, a Negro had first disobeyed his order and then come at him with a capstan bar—which Smith seized and brought down on the man's head so hard that he died a few days later. This might have been called self-defence. But Smith (although given a good character by his employer) had a reputation for rough methods, and he had already had a stand-up fight with the Negro. He suffered the severe penalty of seven years' imprisonment, but eventually rehabilitated himself. Conrad makes Leggatt a different type. Like Jim, he is a Conway boy and—although the phrase is not actually applied to him— plainly "one of us." There is a suggestion that, like Jim, he has got himself on the wrong sort of ship. And although he has no title to claim that he acted to defend himself against attack, he had intended nothing but decisive action against an insolent disregard of orders in the very moment that—his captain having panicked—he was taking resolute measures which in fact saved the ship. These circumstances may be of some relevance if we consider it useful to inquire into Conrad's conscious intentions in "The Secret Sharer."

There is a theory that certain Elizabethan plays were thought of as "nocturnals," and performed in indoor theatres, in which any amount of darkness could be turned on at will. It is arguable that Conrad has his "nocturnals," and that "The Secret Sharer" is one of them. This is the view of Mr. Guerard, whose analysis of the story is acute, persuasive, and deserving of close attention. His notion of "nocturnals" (he does not, of course, use the term) is more sophisticated than the theatrical historian's, although it might apply to *Macbeth*. What is in question is stories which "are unmistakably journeys within, and journeys through a darkness." The conception stems from the psychology of Jung, in the light of which this archetypal myth may be seen as an introspective process involving "a risky descent into the preconscious or even unconscious . . . a restorative return to the primitive sources of being and an advance through temporary regression." [3] In Mr. Guerard's opinion "The Secret Sharer" represents this kind of "night journey" undertaken in a rather more than commonly conscious fashion.[4] It would thus be in a symbolic sense, as well as in actual fact, that the captain first appears "at the starting-point of a long journey," and a similar deliberate symbolism attends such elements in the story as the rising up out of a dark sea of a mysterious *alter ego*, the sleeping suits which suggest a world of dream, the need to take the ship to the very brink of disaster. Even the incident of the captain's hat, although it has what may be called a perfectly simple adventure-story function at the crisis of the tale, has such a significance, since hats are said to be symbols of personality.* Leggatt, according to this manner of interpretation, represents the captain's personality at a repressed and hitherto unacknowledged level—what in himself must be kept hidden from the world, but at the same time reckoned with and done justice to if some psychic integration is to be achieved.

---

* There are other places in Conrad—notably *Lord Jim*—in which hats come and go with symbolic effect, whether consciously or unconsciously achieved. Men's hats were more important in Conrad's time than they are now. On his hall-table at Rye, Henry James kept a large selection, each individual hat being regarded as peculiarly appropriate to some specific one among his rural occasions. There was a kind of symbolism in this, it may be maintained.

How are we to estimate this interpretation of "The Secret Sharer"? Early in the story, the captain, a little unsure of himself in his first command, and meditating upon fidelity to an "ideal conception of one's own personality,"(94) takes comfort from what actually lies ahead:

And suddenly I rejoiced in the great security of the sea as compared with the unrest of the land, in my choice of that untempted life presenting no disquieting problems, invested with an elementary moral beauty by the absolute straightforwardness of its appeal and by the singleness of its purpose.(96)

We guess at once that this is a stiff—even heavy—dramatic irony; and its tone does soon turn out to be congruous with all that is explicit and emphatic in the story. But, in fact, there is no *temptation* ahead. There is an ordeal and a test; but nothing suggesting feelings of guilt, or imaginative identification with moral failure in another, seems to be in question. The relationship of the captain to Leggatt is markedly different from that so clearly intimated as existing between Marlow and either Kurtz or Jim. It is much closer to that between Razumov and Victor Haldin. The nautical setting of the story has perhaps served to obscure this.

Leggatt has no sooner confessed his crime—if it be a crime—to the captain than he murmurs, "A pretty thing to have to own up to for a *Conway* boy."(101) The unverisimilar character of this remark has not escaped the notice of criticism. It is as if he were saying, "A pretty pickle for an Etonian," or "A nice position for a Balliol man." Englishmen do not offer such observations about themselves. It may, of course, be maintained that Jim, implicitly and by way of appeal, says the same thing to Marlow. But Jim is a boy and Marlow is a mature man, whereas here we are immediately told that the captain had left the *Conway* only very shortly before Leggatt joined. They are young men together, just as Razumov and Haldin are young men together. And now there is little suggestion that the captain—initially, at least—feels any moral problem whatever. Here is a man who might be himself, and who has had the most damnable bad luck when putting his ship first in a moment of terrible danger—which is what "a *Conway* boy" will without question do. Moreover, Leggatt remains in his sudden misfortune very much the master of his fate and the captain of his soul. His rescuer simply knows that he must stand by Leggatt and match him in resolution and nerve. The story concerns his struggle to do so. The captain must be a Razumov who does not fail his Haldin. Nor does he—with the result that Leggatt, as we have seen, departs "a free man, a proud swimmer striking out for a new destiny." But it is not Leggat alone who has obtained his freedom. The captain has passed his test, and his ship is his own.

There *has*, of course, been a moral issue. It comes in, overwhelmingly, at the end of the story. But, implicitly, it begins earlier. The captain, as soon as he has taken the fugitive into his cabin, has set a personal loyalty—instantly recognized—above a public duty. Instinctively and spontaneously, he has made, we may say, Antigone's choice. But it is a grave choice, and so must not be an easy one. In the end he risks his career, his ship, and the lives of all under his command by steering to the very brink of destruction in order that Leggatt's chance of surviving may be even marginally improved.

We may perhaps conclude that the relationship of "The Secret Sharer" to that important aspect of both *Lord Jim* and "Heart of Darkness" which Mr. Guerard calls "The Journey Within" is more apparent than real. It is significant that "The Secret Sharer" is not a Marlow story, and even more significant that its narrator's voice and manner of interrogating experience do not suggest Marlow either. Conrad, as we have seen, broke off *Lord Jim* to write "Heart of Darkness"; and clearly he did so out of an impulse to isolate and explore with a high concentration what had revealed itself as a commanding interest while he was writing his novel. There is an equally notable *chronological* relationship between "The Secret Sharer" and *Under Western Eyes.* The story was written when the novel was nearing completion—and when Conrad was in that state of desperation to which he was commonly reduced by the strain of a long imaginative task. "There's neither inspiration nor hope in my work," we have seen him write to Norman Douglas about the novel in December 1909. "The Secret Sharer" was written in the previous month. With whatever degree of conscious intention, he had found relief from the theme of betrayal by turning aside to the story of a man who, appealed to in a dreadful crisis by one of his own kind, acknowledges an obligation and discharges it at great risk. It is no doubt true that the story as we have it incorporates undesigned elements which have percolated from that reservoir of obscure anxieties which seems to have occupied so large an area in Conrad's psyche. Indeed, the captain's sense of Leggatt as *Doppelgänger* is so insistently expressed that it is hard not to suppose it the reflection of some neurotic crisis of identity in the writer. We must conclude, nevertheless, that whereas "Heart of Darkness" represents a deeper exploration of certain problems urgent in *Lord Jim,* "The Secret Sharer" provides a simplified solution of the issue central to *Under Western Eyes.* These contrasting relationships may be a pointer to the approaching decline of Conrad's art.

The Shadow-Line, written five years later, is the last of Conrad's writings in which any of his highest powers are manifested. Even so, this holds true only of the later course of the narrative. Rather more than the first third of it must be described as disastrously bad.

It is again a story of a first command. And again certain sources are known to us. This time, they are from within Conrad's personal experience; indeed, the sub-title is "A Confession," and to his literary agent he wrote that the piece was "not a story really but exact autobiography." [5] The researches of Dr. Sherry have shown—what is not surprising—that this claim may be accepted only with some reserve.[6] Conrad is heightening and elaborating actual facts. At the beginning of January 1888, while at Singapore, he threw up his berth as first mate on the *Vidar*, seemingly for no very specific reason. Within a fortnight he was offered the command of the *Otago*, whose captain had died at sea. He joined the ship at Bangkok, and after various delays in port set sail for Sydney. The voyage down the Gulf of Siam was long and difficult; there was a good deal of fever on board; the vessel eventually put in at Singapore for medical advice and medical supplies. Those members of the crew who were seriously ill were replaced, and the voyage continued.

These are the main authentic circumstances built into the story, and in addition to them much of the detail appears to be drawn directly from memory. The opening recalls that of *Chance*. There, at what seems disproportionate length, we learn how the freshly-qualified ship's officer, Powell, comes to find a berth on the *Ferndale*. Here, with Singapore and not London as a setting, there is an even more extended description of the narrator's manner of obtaining command of the unnamed vessel waiting in Bangkok. This is so little related to what is to come that we may suspect it of having been designed, in the first place, as the beginning of a piece of autobiography proper. It is written in the relaxed prose that Conrad elsewhere employs for such a purpose, and with intermittent recourse to that sort of rhapsodizing about a man and his ship to which he was prone in his more facile sketchings of a sailor's life:

A ship! My ship! She was mine, more absolutely mine for possession and care than anything in the world: an object of responsibility and devotion. . . . Her call had come to me as if from the clouds. . . .(40)

That feeling of life-emptiness which had made me so restless for the last few months lost its bitter plausibility, its evil influence, dissolved in a flow of joyous emotion. . . . Nothing could equal the fullness of that moment, the ideal completeness of that emotional experience. . . . In all the parts of the world washed by navigable waters our relation to each other would be the same—and more intimate than there are words to express in the language.(49-50)

Authentically in the line of Conrad's autobiographical writing, too, is the narrator's initial insistence on the unaccountability of his giving up his berth as first officer on a good ship. Conrad was fond of emphasizing something mysteriously involuntary in the fateful decisions of his life; his account of how he began to write *Almayer's Folly* is a notable example. Yet here the narrator—at least as he looks back upon his younger self—has some notion of the forces at work. He had come near the "shadow-line," when the region of early youth must be left behind:

I left it in that, to us, inconsequential manner in which a bird flies away from a comfortable branch. It was as though all unknowing I had heard a whisper or seen something. . . . The green sickness of late youth descended on me and carried me off. Carried me off that ship, I mean.(5)

The young man is obscurely aware, in fact, that he must extend himself—and he is fortunate in meeting what he courts. For *The Shadow-Line* is another story of the test, the ordeal. And, as in "The Secret Sharer," the young captain comes through. At the end (a shade smugly or priggishly, we may feel) he is to speak of the whole little epic of many men's endurance in the Gulf of Siam as "that episode which had been maturing and tempering my character—though I did not know it."(129)

It is perhaps with some intention of suggesting nervous malaise that the character of the narrator—at least while still unmatured and untempered—is represented as distinctly disagreeable. He is irritable, impatient and "malicious"(42) with the benevolent Captain Giles; his attitude to the pitiful steward of the Officers' Home, who feebly intrigues to secure the new appointment for a burdensome guest, is ungenerous; and—later on—there is something unsympathetic in his statement that he treated the crazed and tiresome mate, Mr. Burns, "to my invariable kindness."(69) We are even inclined, to feel that the hostile and unmannerly behaviour of the captain of the steamer taking him to Bangkok may have been provoked or exacerbated by something in the demeanour of the young man himself. It is possible that in all this, as in other small indications of the narrator's personality and bearing, the autobiographical pressure is greater than Conrad realized, and that it brings us closer than we get elsewhere to the nervous irritability which, as a young man, the future writer all too probably bore around with him.

With the arrival of the new captain on board his ship fiction takes over—greatly to the story's advantage. The narrator finds the first officer Mr. Burns, if still in his right mind, yet a good deal disturbed by the extent to which the late captain had ended his life decidedly out of his. We never learn this unfortunate man's name (there is a great deal of namelessness in Conrad, requiring some minor virtuosity to maintain) but we do hear much about his more recent behaviour. He had sailed his ship in an unaccountably and potentially disastrous manner; spent most of his time playing the fiddle (dreadfully loudly) in the saloon; and died uttering the atrocious wish that neither the ship nor any on board her should ever reach port. The narrator, although he has no wish to be particularly impressed by this grotesque narrative, has to admit to himself the horror of its climax. Disregarding the plain fact that his predecessor must have been insane, he judges that "the end of his life was a complete act of treason, the betrayal of a tradition which seemed to me as imperative as any guide on earth could be. . . . It appeared that even at sea a man could become the victim of evil spirits. I felt on my face the breath of unknown powers that shape our destinies."(62) Incidentally, the dead captain is buried straight ahead of the course the ship must now take. Mr. Burns is convinced that he is "ambushed down there under the sea with some evil intention."(74) Later, when nearly the whole crew is down with fever and a deadly calm has immobilized the ship, the narrator is to feel "the inexpugnable strength of common sense being insidiously menaced by this gruesome, by this insanse delusion."(82)

Here, at the heart of the story, we are, of course, very close to "The Secret Sharer." (Koh-ring, "lying upon the glassy water like a triton amongst minnows,"(84) floats remotely here, even as it towers menacingly in the earlier tale.) Each of these young men has the same view of a first command. It is less like gaining promotion than coming to a throne; and the burden and the challenge are experienced not as an aggravation of strains already known, but as new in kind. In each case the resulting test is made stiffer by the hovering presence of something preternatural: in "The Secret Sharer" the uncanny sense of identification with Leggatt; in *The Shadow-Line* the unnerving superstition of Mr. Burns and the malign mystery of the quinine-bottles that prove to contain only a worthless powder. But there are marked differences, too. In "The Secret Sharer" the captain's resolve to hide Leggatt associates him, suddenly and staggeringly, with a man cast out from society for an impulsive act such as he might himself have committed; at the same time he is utterly severed from everyone else on his ship; even if he does not feel guilty, his behaviour has become that of a guilty man. In *The Shadow-Line* the captain actually feels guilt; but this is because he has not himself checked the medical stores—and as he believed a doctor to have done so in port his actual fault is venial, and we are not made to feel that he will be deeply marked by it. He has nothing to conceal. (He tells the crew at once about the missing quinine.) He is in no sense isolated—except to the extent that a captain is necessarily isolated. Mr. Burns, although he has been disappointed of the command, is a loyal and efficient officer, despite the obsession which the fever intensifies in him. The second officer is an unimpressive youth, but in no way troublesome. The crew—so stricken that they can only totter or crawl about the deck—are loyal and courageous to a man: worthy, we are told, of the captain's "undying regard." [7] Among these brave men the cook, Ransome, is pre-eminent. No longer an able seaman, since severe physical exertion might be fatal to his weak heart, he risks death day after day with selfless devotion. And he loves life—for when the ship has gained Singapore he insists on being paid off:

"But, Ransome," I said, "I hate the idea of parting with you."
"I must go," he broke in. "I have a right!" He gasped and a

look of almost savage determination passed over his face. For an instant he was another being. And I saw under the worth and the comeliness of the man the humble reality of things. Life was a boon to him—this precarious hard life—and he was thoroughly alarmed about himself.(129)

But with this we may compare the introduction of Ransome early in the story:

Even at a distance his well-proportioned figure, something thoroughly sailor-like in his poise, made him noticeable. On nearer view the intelligent, quiet eyes, a well-bred face, the disciplined independence of his manner made up an attractive personality.(67-8)

From Conrad, there must strike us as something exhausted about language of this sort. And it is, indeed, only at the crisis of the narrative that the writing is other than rather flat.

That crisis is simply the story of the ship becalmed, the crew sick to death about her decks, impenetrable blackness bearing "an effect of inconceivable terror and of inexpressible mystery,"(108) the coming of torrential rain and alarming wind, the dire and triumphant struggle into port. Conrad has returned to celebrating *les valeurs idéales*: brave men fighting against odds, and an inflexibly preserved resoluteness in command. Communing with his diary, indeed, the captain can speak of "that strange sense of insecurity" in his past, and suspects he may be "no good" because he is conscious of a "shrinking" when he has to go on deck during the worst hours of the ship's ordeal.(107) It even takes a quiet word from Ransome to get him there. But we have ourselves no more fear that he will fail than if he were the familiar hero of a series of Westerns. In *The Shadow-Line* the accent of romance has begun to predominate; the Conradian overworld is indeed present, and deftly interwoven with it; but the tension which produced Conrad's greatest writing has somewhere been resolved.

Epilogue

If we seek to account for the marked inferiority of Conrad's last books we shall not find much help in anything he himself has to say. Consider the following:

> I am glad you think I've done something. It's but 50,000 words of rubbishy twaddle,—and it's far from enough. Very far. I am sinking deeper and deeper. The state of worry in which I am living,—and writing,—is simply indescribable. It's a constant breaking strain. And you know that materials subjected to breaking strain lose all their elasticity in the end,—part with all their "virtue" on account of profound molecular changes. The molecular changes in my brain are very pronounced. It seems to me I have a lump of mud, of slack mud, in my head.[1]

This was not written in 1918 or 1919, when he was struggling with *The Arrow of Gold* or *The Rescue*; it is from a letter to Galsworthy dated 6 May 1907, six months after he had finished *The Secret Agent*, six months before he began *Under Western Eyes*. And in Jean-Aubry's book it follows immediately upon a letter to his agent, J. B. Pinker, in which he declares that his "health shows signs of general improvement," and that he is in consequence looking forward to "a fresh lease of mental life again." [2] During his final years of imaginative impoverishment his letters to his intimates are no more, and no less, despairing than this much earlier one to Galsworthy; correspondingly, his letters to mere acquaintances, and anything touching his work which might affect it publication or reception, are contrived—as Mr. Moser justly says—to "convey a sense of culmination and fulfillment." [3] Conrad is not a reliable witness.

It is not even easy to determine the extent to which he was himself conscious of the inferiority of his work in this phase. For one thing, none of it is, in fact, wholly bad. It nowhere comes near a state of pathological degeneration such as is evident—to take a random example—in the last canvases of Utrillo. The best discussions—and notably that by Mr. Guerard—find something, if not perhaps much, to commend in all the products of Conrad's anti-climax. But the salient fact remains: Conrad is very much a writer who enjoyed a "major phase." *Almayer's Folly* and (to a lesser extent) *An Outcast of the Islands* have evident originality and power; nevertheless Conrad's great period does not begin until *The Nigger of the "Narcissus,"* published in 1897, when he was forty. *Chance* (1913) and *Victory* (1915) are variously impressive and remain full of interest; yet *Under Western Eyes*, which was completed by the beginning of 1910, is the last of his unchallengeable masterpieces. It was within a span of thirteen years, that is to say, that this expatriate Polish gentleman turned ship's officer established himself abundantly as one of the greatest English novelists. The achievement is beyond wonder—so that it seems idle to waste even a moment in surprise that exhaustion should have been the aftermath of such a harvest.

The Arrow of Gold, The Rescue, The Rover, and *Suspense* are likely to disappoint the mature reader. (*The Rover* is a good adventure story for boys.) But for criticism they have their substantial interest, if only because they make possible a comparison between Conrad and the Conradesque. The author of *Lord Jim* is at work for us, but with a difference. And this difference seems not wholly a matter of things sufficiently obvious: extreme physical and nervous fatigue, and that dearth of fresh subject matter which sometimes leads a writer to the rehearsing of old themes, characters, and relationships to an extent escaping his awareness. These aspects of the books have been fully documented by scholars: for example, Mr. Moser has shown in detail how *The Arrow of Gold* harks back not merely to the unfinished *The Sisters* of twenty years before, but also to people and situations in *The Sisters* which had received full and successful expression in *Nostromo.* Conrad professed, and no doubt believed, that he had been waiting through his active career as a writer for the ripe moment in which he was to draw for a novel upon certain experiences of his youth in Marseilles; but in fact he had embodied these in a work of the highest imaginative pressure long before. The same holds of *The Rover.* When, at its climax, we find "three strangely assorted men in a small boat on a dangerous mission of political intrigue," we must agree with Mr. Moser that the situation "is rather an old one." [4] It goes back to autobiographical material already given quasi-imaginative expression in *The Mirror of the Sea,* where Conrad describes his voyage on board the *Tremolino* along with Dominic Cervoni and Cervoni's treacherous cousin. It also goes back to something much more striking, and again in *Nostromo:* the Capataz de Cargadores, Martin Decoud, and the craven Hirsch on board the lighter amid the darkness of the Placid Gulf.

But all this is far from explaining the difference between Conrad and the Conradesque. Something quite radical is missing from the final books, and it is not easy to define. But we must surely feel that, if fully successful in their kind, they would have been superb romances, and nothing more. They convey an effect of great labour—it is like a swimmer's at his last gasp—but of little travail. Some tension of the spirit has departed.

It is perhaps not entirely irrelevant here to glance at Dr. Gustav Morf's theory of Conrad's literary career, propounded in his book *The Polish Heritage of Joseph Conrad*. Dr. Morf may be said to subscribe to the notion, once enunciated by D. H. Lawrence, that "we shed our sicknesses in books." Conrad's sickness is a powerful and enduring sense of guilt at having deserted Poland. "His 'guilt-complex' . . . expresses itself in all his books," [5] and hence the poignancy of their dominant themes of exile and betrayal. But *The Rover* is a special case. It is the story of a French seaman, Peyrol, who after long expatriation comes home in the end, and there gives his life for his country:

Conrad has fixed a vision which had been the great vision of his boyhood: that of a free Rover going out into the world in search of adventure and glory, fighting his way all over the seas, and finally coming home again, white-haired but still strong, admired but modest, and with a bag of money. For this figure, symbolizing his youthful enthusiasms and aspirations, the old Conrad finds a significant and befitting end. A better fate awaits the Rover at home than the usual well-deserved rest and freedom from material cares—it is given him to die for his country. [6]

The Rover, in fact, is the *successful* sickness-shedding book. Here is a compensatory fantasy in which Conrad has at last wiped his own slate clean. Significantly, *The Rover* is "the last novel which he could finish." [7]

Dr. Morf's is the kind of work—naïve in literary judgment, singly concerned to urge an interpretation of its subject's personality—that rarely fares well at the hands of professional critics. And it does, indeed, tell us very little about the character of Conrad's genius. But its main contention is not without at least some persuasiveness, although we may be inclined to read the evidence of *The Rover* in a slightly different sense from Dr. Morf's. If Conrad was really troubled about Poland, then Peyrol's story may well be viewed as some sort of compensatory fantasy. But it is certainly no more than that, and it would be absurd to hint that it held any healing power for Conrad's spirit. Received as an allegory of his own situation, the fable takes on a facile quality which merely speaks once more of the decline of his imagination. Yet the link with Poland has its valid suggestiveness. Poland, that is to say, may be a significant term in the problem we are considering.

As a boy Conrad read the romances of Captain Marryat, but the greater part of his reading was certainly in his own language. At the start of the present study we noted Mr. Zdzisław Najder as writing illuminatingly about this. "Honour, duty, fidelity, friendship" are the cardinal conceptions in Polish romantic literature of the later nineteenth century, and they clearly provide Conrad with his earliest conception of *les valeurs idéales*. Of these simple values, romantic and chivalric, his first mature work, *The Nigger of the "Narcissus,"* is already an almost final celebration. From that book, so splendid in itself, Conrad goes on to look far more deeply into human experience than do, we may believe, the writers of his youth. By a kind of bitter paradox he becomes the peer, not of Mickiewicz and Slowacki, but almost of Dostoevski and Tolstoy. Razumov's expiation in *Under Western Eyes* is the crown of his achievement here—and what follows *Under Western Eyes* is *Chance*, in which the conventions of romance begin to close in on him. Is this, conceivably, the sense in which Conrad returns to Poland in his premature old age? There can at least be no doubt of that prematurity, and it is well known that senescence tends in many matters to bring us back where we began. *The Rover* is not quite like Captain Marryat. And almost certainly *The Arrow of Gold* and *Suspense* bear no striking resemblance to any of the Polish books surrounding Conrad as a boy. But at least it is clear that in his final phase as a writer—however it may have been with him as a man—Conrad has ceased to sustain that unflinching gaze into a heart of darkness; has come to move, rather stiffly and painfully, in the light which most of us can alone support—the light of common day, a little softened by the veil of romantic sentiment.

Notes

References to Conrad's fiction, as given within parentheses in the text, are to the collected edition published in Great Britain by Dent. The collected edition published in America by Doubleday follows the same pagination. Works referred to below only by author's name may be identified in the bibliography.

CHAPTER 1

1. Baines, p. 372.
2. Najder, p. 15.
3. Ibid., p. 16.
4. Ibid., pp. 37 & 41.
5. Ibid., p. 177.
6. *A Personal Record*, pp. 113–20, gives a vivid account of Conrad's obtaining his certificate as a British master mariner.
7. Najder, p. 54. Mrs. Hay, pp. 34–6, considers that Bobrowski's perturbation at his nephew's conduct stemmed in part from its approximation to that of an uncle of his own, Seweryn Pilchowski, who appears to have enjoyed the status of Bobrowski family skeleton. Mrs. Hay even suggests that Conrad himself, when in Marseilles, may have been burdened by a sense of treading in the path of this unworthy relative. But Najder, p. 18, implies that Conrad may have known nothing about Seweryn Pilchowski. His knowledge of his family background was largely confined to what Bobrowski chose to

tell him. And we know Bobrowski to have been very close about his black sheep of an uncle.

8. Najder, p. 64.
9. Baines, p. 123, and Najder, p. 148.
10. Najder, p. 215.
11. Garnett, p. xxii.
12. Baines, p. 140.
13. Baines, pp. 156–7.
14. Jessie Conrad, p. 14.
15. *A Personal Record,* p. 101.
16. *Typhoon and Other Stories,* p. 113.
17. Ibid., p. 125.
18. Garnett, p. xix.
19. *Last Essays,* p. 166.
20. Russell, p. 81.
21. Jean-Aubry, vol. I, p. 241.
22. *A Personal Record,* p. 68.
23. Blackburn, pp. 26–7.
24. Wells, vol. II, p. 617.
25. *The Transatlantic Review,* vol. I, No. 1, p. 99, Jan. 1924.
26. MacShane, p. 50.
27. Baines, p. 180.
28. Conrad's own sense of the significance of *The Nigger of the "Narcissus,"* both for his career and as "a landmark in literature," is well documented by Gordan, pp. 235–40, who also prints a passage cancelled from the Preface.
29. Najder, p. 113.
30. Woolf, p. 27.
31. Jean-Aubry, vol. I, p. 234.
32. Baines, p. 178.
33. Blackburn, p. 29.
34. Najder, p. 22.
35. *A Personal Record,* p. 121.
36. *Last Essays,* p. 36.

CHAPTER 2

1. Baines, p. 146.
2. Jean-Aubry, vol. II, p. 206.
3. Baines, p. 147.
4. *A Personal Record,* p. 5.
5. Ibid., pp. 74–89.
6. Ibid., p. 87.
7. Moser, p. 57.

8. Baines, p. 191.
9. Moser, p. 61.

CHAPTER 3

1. Gurko, pp. 81–93.
2. Guerard, p. 112.
3. *Accent*, XII (Spring 1952), pp. 67–81. Gurko believes that the captain, first mate, and second mate are named Allistoun, Baker, and Creighton because they "suggest God and his loyal angelic entourage; their initials, A. B. C., point to the beginning of things." This is to bring to bear on *The Nigger of the "Narcissus"* the kind of exegesis currently held to illuminate *Finnegans Wake*.
4. *Last Essays*, p. 94.
5. Gordan, pp. 132–50, gives a very full account of the book's composition.
6. Crankshaw laments (p. 217) that Conrad lacks "style"—a "je ne sais quoi" which Ford Madox Ford commands. Conrad's bold magniloquence has often failed to please his critics.
7. Jean-Aubry, vol. I, p. 270.
8. "Wistful regret, reminiscent tenderness," Conrad says, p. xi, is *not* the note of the succeeding story, "Heart of Darkness."

CHAPTER 4

1. The "unspeakable rites" are the subject of conjecture by Stephen A. Reid in *Modern Fiction Studies*, IX, No. 4 (Winter 1963–4), pp. 347–56. He concludes that Kurtz had become a cannibal.
2. Leavis, p. 180.
3. Guerard, p. 39.
4. Baines, pp. 278–9. William Blackwood may be described as having been doggedly appreciative of Conrad's "stuff" to the end. "As far as it goes at present," he wrote warningly of the first instalment of "The End of the Tether," "one can hardly say one has got into the story yet." But, three months later, he managed: "The interest seems to me to steadily increase, and the story has now reached a stage which holds the attention of the reader." (Blackburn, pp. 148, 164.)

CHAPTER 5

1. Leavis, p. 190.
2. Sherry, p. 299.
3. Ibid., p. 300.
4. Ibid., pp. 302–5.

5. The photograph is reproduced by Sherry (Plate 3).
6. *The Rescue*, p. 4.
7. Sherry, p. 135.
8. Ibid., p. 137–8.
9. Van Ghent, pp. 229–44, although noting Marlow's attitude, finds Jim "an extraordinarily simplified *type*" and compares him with the Orestes of Aeschylus and the Oedipus of Sophocles. This is one of the most interesting esoteric discussions of the novel.
10. *The Shadow-Line*, p. 129.
11. Hough, after remarking of Conrad, p. 213, that "his is largely a male world," adds that he "has a largely male public too." The explanation is that "the characteristic concerns and occupations of the woman's world play such a very small part in Conrad's work." This is true. Yet educated women sometimes have "concerns" outside their "occupations"—or so one imagines—and do in fact often read Conrad.

CHAPTER 6

1. Guerard, p. 204.
2. Ibid., p. 202.
3. Jean-Aubry, vol. I, p. 314.
4. Ibid., vol. I, p. 315.
5. *Review of English Studies* (February, 1959), pp. 45–52.
6. *The Mirror of the Sea*, p. 164.
7. Najder, p. 218n.
8. Ibid., p. 26.
9. Jean-Aubry, vol. I, p. 311.
10. Ibid., vol. I, p. 317.
11. Ibid., vol. I, p. 335.
12. Conrad's neurasthenia is fully documented by Baines. See his index under *Personal Characteristics*.
13. *A Personal Record*, pp. 98–9.
14. Wells, vol. II, pp. 615–22.
15. *The Nigger of the "Narcissus,"* p. x.

CHAPTER 7

1. That Nostromo himself remains the "center of attention and center of gravity" of the entire novel is, however, argued by Friedman, pp. 83ff.
2. The "manoeuvering" is largely in the interest of plunging Decoud into solitude. The deeper theme here, the "crisis of moral isolation"

so frequently treated by Conrad, is well discussed by Zabel.

3. Guerard, p. 204.

4. Rothenstein, vol. II, p. 61. "I don't suppose it'll damage me," Conrad tells Rothenstein; and adds, "It is something—but not *the* thing I tried for."

5. Jean-Aubry, vol. I, p. 301.

6. Ibid., vol. I, p. 222.

7. The phrase is from Robert Penn Warren's introduction to *Nostromo*, one of the best discussions of the novel.

CHAPTER 8

1. Leavis, p. 214.

2. E. M. W. Tillyard, in a paper which compares *The Secret Agent* with *Much Ado about Nothing* (*Essays in Criticism*, XI, No. 3 (July 1961), 309–18), sees no reason why Ossipon should continue nervously out of sorts.

3. Mann, pp. 234–5.

4. The "seriousness" of *The Secret Agent* is far from incompatible with its aspect as comedy. Hay, pp. 235–6, writes persuasively of the book as "almost a parody of Dostoevsky." But in point of technique, too, here as elsewhere in Conrad's work, there is a good deal that suggests masters he was far from eager to acknowledge. On his "Russian method of elaboration, a delving deeply enough into attendant and antecedent circumstances to produce the effect of power, not speed," see Follett, p. 95.

5. Jean-Aubry, vol. II, p. 37.

6. Ibid., vol. II, p. 37.

7. Ibid., vol. II, p. 38.

8. Leavis, p. 210.

CHAPTER 9

1. Baines, p. 360. André Gide records of Conrad that "le seul nom de Dostoïewsky le faisait fremir." (*La Nouvelle Revue française*, Nouvelle série, cxxv (December 1, 1924, p. 661.) According to Thomas Mann (*op. cit.*, p. 234), Gide "had learned English in order to read Conrad in the original." Gide's most interesting remarks on Conrad (and notably on *Under Western Eyes*) will be found in his journal under 23 February 1930 (*Journals*, trans. J. O'Brien (1949), vol. III, pp. 92–3).

2. Gurko, p. 204.

3. Ibid., p. 205.

4. *Notes on Life and Letters*, p. 89.

5. Ibid., pp. 102–3.
6. Najder, p. 25.
7. Jean-Aubry, vol. II, p. 194.
8. Ibid., vol. II, pp. 64–5.
9. Ibid., vol. II, p. 105.

CHAPTER 10

1. Moser, Chap. II.
2. Hewitt, p. 95.
3. Henry James, *The Art of Fiction*, ed. M. Roberts (1948), p. 205.
4. Ibid., pp. 202–3.

CHAPTER 11

1. "The risk of personal collapse before a hostile world" is Miss Brad-brook's formulation (p. 26) of the theme of "The Secret Sharer." It is, clearly enough, the chief fear Conrad carried through life with him.
2. Sherry, p. 255.
3. Guerard, p. 15.
4. The "conscious" element is also stressed by Said, who finds (pp. 127ff.) "The Secret Sharer" to be "an intellectual story of qualified emotional force."
5. Jean-Aubry, vol. II, p. 181.
6. Sherry, pp. 211–7.
7. "Worthy of my undying regard." Conrad uses these words from the text as epigraph on the title-page. All his major works have epigraphs, and he gave much care to choosing them.

EPILOGUE

1. Jean-Aubry, vol. II, p. 47.
2. Ibid., vol. II, p. 46.
3. Moser, p. 179.
4. Ibid., p. 199.
5. Morf, p. 222.
6. Ibid., p. 180.
7. Morf's whole interpretation may be described as being on Freudian lines, and he provides the following footnote (166n):

> In the *Nouvelle Revue Française*, December, 1924, M. Lenormand relates how he started once to speak to Conrad of Freud, but Conrad changed the conversation at once. M. Lenormand at-

tributes this very rightly to the fact that Conrad did not want to know the objective truth about his own work.

In fact, Conrad "changed the conversation at once" not when Lenormand began to speak specifically of Freud, but when (a shade impertinently towards a mere hotel acquaintance) he addressed himself to the theme of a submerged incestuous element in *Almayer's Folly* (*La Nouvelle Revue française*, Nouvelle série, cxxv, 1er Décembre 1924, p. 669). Then, some days later, Conrad spoke of Freud "avec une ironie méprisante" (Ibid., p. 670). Lenormand's essay is interesting as giving a vivid picture of Conrad in decline.

Conrad's Works in Order of Publication

Almayer's Folly. 1895.
An Outcast of the Islands. 1896.
The Nigger of the "Narcissus." 1897.
Tales of Unrest. ("Karain," "The Idiots," "An Outpost of Progress," "The Return," "The Lagoon"). 1898.
Lord Jim. 1900.
The Inheritors. (In collaboration with F. M. Hueffer.) 1901.
Youth. (*Youth,* "Heart of Darkness," "The End of the Tether.") 1902.
Typhoon. (*Typhoon,* "Amy Foster," "Falk," "To-morrow.") 1903.
Romance. (In collaboration with F. M. Hueffer.) 1903.
Nostromo. 1904.
The Mirror of the Sea. 1906.
The Secret Agent. 1907.
A Set of Six. ("Gaspar Ruiz," "The Informer," "The Brute," "An Anarchist," "The Duel," "Il Conde.") 1908.
Under Western Eyes. 1911.
Some Reminiscences. (Reissued as *A Personal Record.*) 1912.
'Twixt Land and Sea Tales. ("A Smile of Fortune," "The Secret Sharer," "Freya of the Seven Isles.") 1912.
Chance. 1913.
Victory. 1915.
Within the Tides. ("The Planter of Malata," "The Partner," "The Inn of the Two Witches," "Because of the Dollars.") 1915.
The Shadow-Line. 1917.
The Arrow of Gold. 1919.
The Rescue. 1920.

Notes on Life and Letters. 1921.

The Rover. 1923.

The Secret Agent: A Drama. 1923.

Laughing Anne and *One Day More.* (Dramatic versions of "Because of the Dollars" and "To-morrow.") 1924.

Suspense. 1925.

Tales of Hearsay. ("The Warrior's Soul," "Prince Roman," "The Tale," "The Black Mate.") 1925.

Last Essays. 1926.

Conrad's Principal Works in Order of Completion *

Almayer's Folly.	1894	May
An Outcast of the Islands.	1895	September
The Sisters (fragment).	1896	March
"An Outpost of Progress."	1896	July
The Nigger of the "Narcissus."	1897	February
Youth.	1898	June
The Rescuer (*The Rescue* Parts I-III).	1898	December
"Heart of Darkness."	1899	February
Lord Jim.	1900	July
Typhoon.	1901	January
"Amy Foster."	1901	June
"The End of the Tether."	1902	October
Nostromo.	1904	August
The Mirror of the Sea.	1905	October
The Secret Agent.	1906	September
A Personal Record.	1909	Spring?
"The Secret Sharer."	1909	November
Under Western Eyes.	1910	January
Chance.	1912	March
Victory.	1914	June
The Shadow-Line	1915	March
The Arrow of Gold.	1918	June
The Rescue	1919	May
The Rover.	1922	July

* Drawn from similar lists in Hewitt, in Moser, and in Stallman.

Bibliography

Allen, J. *The Sea Years of Joseph Conrad*. New York, 1965.

Baines, J. *Joseph Conrad: A Critical Biography*. London, 1960.

Blackburn, W. (ed.). *Joseph Conrad: Letters to William Blackwood and David S. Meldrum*. Durham, North Carolina, 1958.

Bradbrook, M. C. *Joseph Conrad: Poland's English Genius*. Cambridge, 1942.

Conrad, Jessie. *Joseph Conrad as I Knew Him*. London, 1926.

Crankshaw, E. *Joseph Conrad: Some Aspects of the Art of the Novel*. London, 1936.

Curle, R. *The Last Twelve Years of Joseph Conrad*. London, 1928.

Follett, W. *Joseph Conrad: A Short Study of his Intellectual and Emotional Attitude toward his Work and of the Chief Characteristics of his Novels*. New York, 1915; reissued 1966.

Ford, F. M. *Joseph Conrad: A Personal Remembrance*. London, 1924.
—— *Mightier than the Sword*. London, 1938.

Friedman, A. *The Turn of the Novel*. New York, 1966.

Garnett, E. (ed.). *Letters from Conrad, 1895 to 1924*. London, 1928.

Gordan, J. D. *Joseph Conrad: The Making of a Novelist*. Cambridge, Mass., 1940.

Guerard, A. J. *Conrad the Novelist*. Cambridge, Mass., 1958.

Gurko, L. *Joseph Conrad: Giant in Exile*. London, 1965.

Harkness, B. (ed.). *Conrad's "Heart of Darkness" and the Critics*. San Francisco, 1960.

Hart-Davis, R. *Hugh Walpole*. London, 1952.

Hay, E. K. *The Political Novels of Joseph Conrad*. Chicago, 1963.

Hewitt, D. *Conrad: A Reassessment*. Cambridge, 1952.

Hough, G. *Image and Experience*. London, 1960.

James, H. *Notes on Novelists*. London, 1914.

Jean-Aubry, G. *Joseph Conrad: Life and Letters*. 2 vols. London, 1927.

Leavis, F. R. *The Great Tradition*. London, 1948.

MacShane, F. *The Life and Work of Ford Madox Ford*. London, 1965.

Mann, T. (trans. H. T. Lowe-Porter). *Past Masters and Other Papers*. London, 1933.

Morf, G. *The Polish Heritage of Joseph Conrad*. London, 1950.

Moser, T. *Joseph Conrad: Achievement and Decline*. Connecticut, 1966.

Mudrick, M. (ed.). *Conrad: A Collection of Critical Essays*. Englewood Cliffs, New Jersey, 1966.

Najder, Z. *Conrad's Polish Background*. London, 1964.

Rothenstein, W. *Men and Memories*. 2 vols. London, 1931-2.

Russell, B. *Portraits from Memory*. London, 1956.

Said, E. W. *Joseph Conrad and the Fiction of Autobiography*. Cambridge, Mass., 1966.

Sherry, N. *Conrad's Eastern World*. London, 1966.

Stallman, R. W. (ed.). *The Art of Joseph Conrad: A Critical Symposium*. Michigan, 1960.

Van Ghent, D. *The English Novel: Form and Function*. New York, 1953.

Warner, O. *Joseph Conrad*. London, 1951.

Warren, R. Penn. *Introduction to* Nostromo *(The Modern Library)*. New York, 1951.

Wells, H. G. *Experiment in Autobiography*. 2 vols. London, 1934.

Woolf, V. *A Writer's Diary*. London, 1953.

Zabel, M. D. *Craft and Character in Modern Fiction*. New York, 1957.

Index